跟任何人都可以用英语聊聊天

蔡莱蒙德 著

北京理工大学出版社
BEIJING INSTITUTE OF TECHNOLOGY PRESS

使用说明
User's Guide

Point 1
30个日常生活主题

作者根据自身在海外生活的经验，归纳出日常生活中最常遇到的30个生活情境主题，根据主题精选出老外最常使用的单词以及句子。一天学一个主题，以规律的步调学习英语，循序渐进，30天后英语想不进步都难！

Point 2
生活便利贴

作者长期在海外生活，熟悉海外一些不为人知的小秘密！这本书通通都会告诉你！学习语言要能灵活运用到生活以外，本书连文化常识也一并兼顾到了！

Point 3
在国外都用这些词

乏味的单词书总是能列出数以千计的单词，但是生活中会用到的单词其实真的只有几百个！作者精选出的情境主题单词绝对让你每个都用得到，不浪费你一分一毫的脑容量！

词性说明
- n 名词
- a 形容词
- v 动词
- ph 短语
- ad 副词

Point 4
在国外都说这几句

每单元收录超过80句常用会话，完整模拟国外地道生活情境，随机补充短语，更有语法小补充，让你的英语不只学得精，更学得巧。

apples.
这个传统的手工果酱是用新鲜的草莓跟苹果制成的。
★ 短语 be made with... 由 / 用…制作的

- It's very nice to meet you. My name is Kyle.
很高兴见到你。我叫凯尔。
★ 短语 nice to meet you 很高兴认识你 / 很高兴见到你

- I cannot live without coffee.
我不能没有咖啡。
★ 短语 cannot live without ... 没有…就活不下去（不能没有…）

- Personally, I prefer tea to coffee.
就我个人来说，比起咖啡，我更喜欢茶。

常识补给站
大部分咖啡厅所售卖的咖啡都是以意式浓缩黑咖啡为基底，进而调配出拿铁、卡布奇诺以及玛奇朵……而一杯由意式咖啡机所萃取出来的完美黑咖啡基底，所花费的时间应该在 25~30 秒，容量为 30 毫升，这样，咖啡的口感及风味最佳。

Point 5 常识补给站

美国知名女性主义作家丽塔·梅·布朗（Rita Mae Brown）曾说过："语言是文化的地图。它告诉人们从哪里来，又要到何处去。"学习语言就要深知当地的文化，作者精心设计的常识补给站，让你的英语学习更有趣！

Point 6 外籍老师亲录 MP3

由外籍老师亲自录制单词以及句子，让你边听边学，不只发音变好，听力也更上一层楼！

★本书附赠音频为MP3格式★

Point 7 30 天学习进度表

自己的进度自己就能轻松掌握，按进度表学习，循序渐进，一天读一课，只要 30 天，英语就能不一样！

003

（请在完成的 Unit 前打上钩吧！）

| Day13 ~ Day18 | Day19 ~ Day24 | Day25 ~ Day30 |

继续加油

- ☐ Unit 13
- ☐ Unit 14
- ☐ Unit 15
- ☐ Unit 16
- ☐ Unit 17
- ☐ Unit 18

继续加油

- ☐ Unit 19
- ☐ Unit 20
- ☐ Unit 21
- ☐ Unit 22
- ☐ Unit 23
- ☐ Unit 24

太棒了！

- ☐ Unit 25
- ☐ Unit 26
- ☐ Unit 27
- ☐ Unit 28
- ☐ Unit 29
- ☐ Unit 30

Don't Give Up!!

YEAH!!

目录 Contents

Chapter 1 饮食与健康 Diet & Health

- Unit 1 ｜ 在咖啡厅悠闲过一天／002
- Unit 2 ｜ 享受阳光的美好／012
- Unit 3 ｜ 让人浑身不舒服的感冒／022
- Unit 4 ｜ 预防胜于治疗／032

Chapter 2 娱乐与休闲 Leisure Time & Recreation Activities

- Unit 5 ｜ 适度的购物是对自己的犒赏／044
- Unit 6 ｜ 令人小鹿乱撞的约会／054
- Unit 7 ｜ 友谊是人生的调味品／064
- Unit 8 ｜ 家是永远的避风港／074
- Unit 9 ｜ 大自然就是我的家／084

Chapter 3 让身心放松的出国旅游 Going Abroad

- Unit 10 ｜ 没有它，你就出不了国／096
- Unit 11 ｜ 完美的旅行计划／106
- Unit 12 ｜ 准备飞向云端／116

目录 Contents

- Unit 13 ｜ 过了海关就能到另一个国家 ／ 126
- Unit 14 ｜ 关于饭店与迷路 ／ 136
- Unit 15 ｜ 旅行是梦想的实践 ／ 146
- Unit 16 ｜ 优雅地处理突发状况 ／ 156

Chapter 4 求学与就职 School & Work

- Unit 17 ｜ 留学生活的点点滴滴 ／ 168
- Unit 18 ｜ 校园与房屋租赁 ／ 178
- Unit 19 ｜ 面试就像是一台舞台剧 ／ 188
- Unit 20 ｜ 做个有活力的职场人 ／ 198
- Unit 21 ｜ 职场就像社会的缩影 ／ 208
- Unit 22 ｜ 沟通是最好的桥梁 ／ 218
- Unit 23 ｜ 增长见识的贸易博览会 ／ 228
- Unit 24 ｜ 接待礼仪很重要 ／ 238
- Unit 25 ｜ 没有一个辞职是真的说再见 ／ 248

Chapter 5 特殊节庆与活动 Holidays & Special Occasions

- Unit 26 ｜ 浪漫的约会 ／ 260
- Unit 27 ｜ 女孩一生最重要的时刻 ／ 270

Unit 28 | 浪漫的圣诞节 / 280

Unit 29 | 一年一次的大日子 / 290

Unit 30 | 中国人最重视的新年 / 300

Chapter 1

饮食与健康
Diet & Health

Unit 1 | 在咖啡厅悠闲过一天
Unit 2 | 享受阳光的美好
Unit 3 | 让人浑身不舒服的感冒
Unit 4 | 预防胜于治疗

跟任何人都可以用英语聊聊天

Unit 1 在咖啡厅悠闲过一天

[生活便利贴]

咖啡在现代人的生活中，已经成为一项不可或缺的精神补给，现代人总是借助咖啡来提神醒脑，还有少部分的人会利用黑咖啡来燃烧脂肪、消除水肿！在国外，咖啡更像是"维生素"，可以让人补充体力。这个单元，我们就来学学和咖啡有关的单词与会话吧！

Vocabulary 在国外都用这些词

MP3 01-01

coffee ['kɒfɪ]
n 咖啡

decaf ['diːkæf]
a 低咖啡因

traditional [trəˈdɪʃənl]
a 传统的

latte ['lɑːteɪ]
n 拿铁

espresso [eˈspresəʊ]
n 意式浓缩黑咖啡

research [rɪˈsɜːtʃ]
n 研究

large [lɑːdʒ]
a 大（份）的

starving ['stɑːvɪŋ]
a 饥饿的

Alzheimer's ['æltshaɪməz]
n 阿尔茨海默症

popular [ˈpɒpʊlə]
a 受欢迎的

spaghetti [spəˈgetɪ]
n 意大利面

Parkinson's ['pɑːkɪnsənz]
n 帕金森病

homemade [ˈhəʊmˈmeɪd]
a 手工的

vegetarian [ˌvedʒəˈteərɪən]
n/a 素食者；素食的

European [jʊərəˈpɪən]
n/a 欧洲人；欧洲的

medium [ˈmiːdɪəm]
a 中杯的

caviar [ˈkævɪɑː]
n 鱼子酱

grind [graɪnd]
v 研磨

Dialogue 在国外都说这几句

- I have a cup of coffee every morning.
  我每天早上都要喝一杯咖啡。
  ★ 语法 "coffee"这个单词是不可数名词，因此当我们要计算咖啡的数量时，一定要记得使用与介词搭配的量词：a cup of（一杯，通常指马克杯）。

- Excuse me, can I have a large latte, please?
  不好意思，我可以点一杯大杯的拿铁吗？
  ★ 语法 中文点菜时，我们常会说"我想点～"，但若将中文直译成英语的"I want to order…"，则会显得不够地道，最正确的说法应该使用"Can I (please) have + 想买的物品"。

- What is the most popular coffee here?
  这里最受欢迎的咖啡是哪一种？

- I'm going to have a piece of cake with coffee.
  我要点一块蛋糕来搭配我的咖啡。
  ★ 语法 咖啡店卖的蛋糕都是切好一块一块的，因此若要形容一块蛋糕，可以说"a piece of cake"。

- I enjoy having these fresh homemade cookies a lot.
  我真的很喜欢这些新鲜的手工饼干。
  ★ 语法 "enjoy"若后面要接动词，要使用动名词"v-ing"的形式。

- What size of coffee would you like? We have small, medium and large.
  你的咖啡要多大杯的？我们有小杯、中杯和大杯。

- I'd like to have a medium iced latte with no sugar, please.
  我想点一杯中杯冰拿铁，不加糖。
  ★ 语法 "I'd like (to have)…"也是美国人点餐时十分常用的句型。例如：I'd like to have a smoked chicken sandwich.（我想点一份熏鸡三明治。）

Yes, we went on a date last night.

Did he ask you out?

在国外都说这几句

- I'd rather have some juice because caffeine would keep me awake at night.
  我宁可喝一些果汁，因为咖啡因会让我晚上睡不着。
  ★ 短语 would rather 宁愿、宁可

- Why don't you try our decaf coffee?
  何不试试我们的低咖啡因咖啡呢？
  ★ 语法 "why don't"和"why doesn't"为建议用法，通常不是真的想问他人原因，而是"建议他人做某事"时常用的句型。

- Are you interested in trying today's special (coffee)?
  你有兴趣试试我们今天的招牌咖啡吗？
  ★ 短语 be interested in 对～有兴趣

- Excuse me. Is this seat taken?
  抱歉打扰，这个位置有人坐了吗？
  ★ 语法 "be taken"表示"某物已经有人使用"。

- No, it's not, feel free to sit here if you want to.
  这个位子没有人坐，你可以坐在这里。
  ★ 语法 在这里的"if"中文的对应意思是"假如、如果"，当你不确定某人的想法时，就可以用"if"试探性地询问。

- Wow! What are you having? Your coffee smells better than mine.
  哇！你点了什么？你的咖啡闻起来比我的香。
  ★ 短语 better than 比～好

- You look so familiar. Have we met somewhere else before?
  你看起来好面熟。我们是不是在哪里见过面？
  ★ 语法 当要形容某个人看起来"很～"的时候，可以使用"人 + look + a."。

- I love that black dress that you are wearing. It suits you.
  我喜欢你现在穿的这件黑色连衣裙。它很适合你。

- I prefer to sit by myself if that's okay with you.
  如果你不介意的话，我宁愿自己一个人坐。

- The eye shadow really brings out the color in your eyes.
  你涂的眼影真的很能衬托你眼睛的颜色。
  ★ 短语 bring out 使～出现、阐明，在此衍生为"衬托"。

Dialogue 在国外都说这几句

- **Would you like to have another espresso? It's on me.**
  你想再喝一杯意式浓缩咖啡吗？我请客。
  ★ 短语 "It's on me." 的意思是 "我请客"。

- **I do not recommend you try their caramel macchiato. It's too sweet.**
  我不推荐你喝他们的焦糖玛奇朵。它太甜了。
  ★ 短语 "A recommend B ..." 的意思是 "A 推荐 B ～"。

- **The freshly brewed coffee tastes amazing. You have to give it a try.**
  现煮的咖啡美味极了。你一定要试试。
  ★ 短语 give... a try 一定要试试～、一定要给～一个机会

- **It is time for lunch. I'm starving.**
  吃午饭的时间到了。我饿极了。
  ★ 语法 "it is (about / high) time for + n." 的意思是 "是时候要～了、～的时候到了"

- **Hmm, I have no idea. What do you have in mind?**
  嗯，我不知道。你想要吃什么？

- **This café is famous for its smoked chicken hamburger. Would you like to try it?**
  这家咖啡厅的熏鸡汉堡很有名，你要不要试试看？
  ★ 短语 be famous for 以～闻名、以～出名

- **How about French toast? It looks delicious and only costs 35 dollars.**
  何不试试法式吐司？它看起来很好吃而且只要 35 美元。
  ★ 语法 "how about" 表示推荐或建议别人某样东西或是某样物品。要记得，"how about" 后面可加名词或动词，但在加动词时，要改成动名词 v-ing 的形式。

- **Today's lunch special is spaghetti with meatballs. It comes with a medium soft drink.**
  今日午餐特餐是肉丸意大利面，并附上一杯中杯饮料。
  ★ 短语 come with 附上

常识补给站

咖啡豆一般分为两种，分别为阿拉比卡豆（Arabica）以及罗伯斯特豆（Robusta）。通常坊间咖啡厅使用的意式浓缩咖啡机大多都是使用阿拉比卡咖啡豆，而罗伯斯特咖啡豆则比较常用于超市卖的即溶咖啡粉。

Dialogue 在国外都说这几句

- The strawberry pancake sundae is available for a limited time only.
  草莓松饼圣代为限时销售商品。
  ★ 短语 be available for　可供～利用

- Our new menu with light meal choices will satisfy all kinds of customers.
  我们新推出的轻食菜单将可满足各式各样的顾客。
  ★ 短语 all kinds of...　各式各样的～

- Our lunch combo includes a sandwich of your choice and a soft drink.
  我们的午餐套餐包含一个口味任选的三明治和一杯饮料。
  ★ 短语 ...of your choice　可供你任选的～

- As you can see, we also offer vegetarian dishes on the menu.
  如你所见，我们的菜单也提供素食餐点。

- This is one of the most family friendly coffee shops in Beijing.
  这家咖啡厅是北京众多适合全家聚餐的咖啡厅之一。
  ★ 短语 "family friendly" 照字面上翻译为"对家庭友善的"，引申为"适合家庭的"。

- The coffee shop offers the best afternoon tea desserts in town.
  这家咖啡店提供镇上最棒的下午茶甜点。
  ★ 语法 best 是 good（好的）的最高级，代表"最好的"。

- It has been a very busy week; a trip to the café for High Tea will be beneficial for us.
  经过了忙碌的一个星期，去咖啡厅喝个下午茶对我们是有益处的。
  ★ 短语 be beneficial for...　对～有益处的

- I am not sure if I can afford the caviar for afternoon tea.
  我不确定我能否负担得起鱼子酱当下午茶。
  ★ 语法 afford 后面可接名词，代表"买得起～、负担得起～"。

- This store is famous for the crispy scones and creamy butter.
  这家店以香脆的英式松饼和绵密的奶油闻名。

- You will be served coffee or tea at your table, accompanied by an assortment of tasty finger sandwiches and cakes.
  我们会为您送上咖啡或茶，并佐以各式各样的美味又小巧的三明治以及蛋糕。
  ★ 短语 finger 一般来讲是"手指"的意思。在此指的则是不需使用刀叉，只需用"手指"则可轻易拿起食用的小三明治。

在国外都说这几句

- Our freshly baked chocolate chip cookies are definitely worth a try. You will not regret it.
  我们的新鲜现烤巧克力碎片饼干很值得一试。你一定不会后悔的。
  ★ 短语 ...is worth a try　～值得一试

- This classic brownie is a treat no matter how old you are. Enjoy it with a glass of milk.
  不论年龄，经典的布朗尼都是一大享受。搭配一杯鲜奶吧。
  ★ 短语 no matter　不论

- Would you like some room for milk in your coffee?
  你的咖啡需要留一些加牛奶的空间吗？
  ★ 语法 在国外点咖啡时，店员常常都会问咖啡需不需要留一些加牛奶的空间，如果不需要的话，店员通常会将咖啡装满一点。

- Lots of guests are queuing up to try the famous English High Tea.
  许多客人排队等候要试试有名的英式下午茶。
  ★ 短语 queue up　排队

- This traditional homemade jam is made with fresh strawberries and apples.
  这个传统的手工果酱是用新鲜的草莓跟苹果制成的。
  ★ 短语 be made with...　由／用～制作的

- It's very nice to meet you. My name is Kyle.
  很高兴见到你。我叫凯尔。
  ★ 语法 nice to meet you　很高兴认识你／很高兴见到你

- I cannot live without coffee.
  我不能没有咖啡。
  ★ 短语 cannot live without ...　没有～就活不下去（不能没有～）

- Personally, I prefer tea to coffee.
  就我个人来说，比起咖啡，我更喜欢茶。

> **常识补给站**
>
> 大部分咖啡厅所售卖的咖啡都是以意式浓缩黑咖啡为基底，进而调配出拿铁、卡布奇诺以及玛奇朵……而一杯由意式咖啡机所萃取出来的完美黑咖啡基底，所花费的时间应该在25~30秒、容量为30毫升，这样，咖啡的口感及风味最佳。

在国外都说这几句

- To be honest, I do not like this coffee. It is too acidic.
  事实上，我不喜欢这杯咖啡。它太酸了。
  ★ 短语 ▶ to be honest　事实上，说实话

- I need more sugar and milk in my coffee. It is too bitter to drink.
  我的咖啡需要加更多糖跟牛奶。它太苦了，我没办法喝下去。
  ★ 短语 ▶ too a. to v.　太～以至于不能～

- Most coffee shops also offer fresh juice as a healthier option.
  大部分的咖啡店也提供新鲜果汁作为更健康的选择。

- The coffee is very hot. Don't forget to request a coffee sleeve.
  咖啡非常烫，别忘了要一个咖啡杯套。
  ★ 语法 ▶ forget 这个词有两个用法，"forget + to v." 意思是"忘记要去做～"，"forget + v-ing" 的意思则是"忘记已经做过～"。

- Can you please grab a latte for me on your way to the office?
  你来公司的时候，可以请你顺路帮我买杯拿铁吗？
  ★ 语法 ▶ "one's way (to the) + 地方" 意思是"某人在去～的路上"。

- My coffee is not hot enough. Is it possible to make a new one for me?
  我的咖啡不够烫，可以帮我重新做一杯吗？
  ★ 短语 ▶ Is it possible...　是否有可能/可以～吗

- There is a growing body of research to suggest that green tea is probably way better for the human body than coffee.
  越来越多的研究报告指出，绿茶对人体的益处比咖啡大多了。
  ★ 语法 ▶ 此处的 growing 是动名词当形容词使用，修饰 body，表示绿茶比咖啡更好的研究报告有逐渐增多的趋势。

- You can benefit from drinking coffee; it protects people against many diseases.
  喝咖啡对你有益处，它可以保护你免除许多疾病。
  ★ 短语 ▶ protect A against B　保护 A 免受 B 的伤害

- Would you like some cream and sugar in your coffee?
  您想要在咖啡里加些奶油和糖吗？

在国外都说这几句

- There is a great deal of research that shows having a few cups of coffee a day can actually improve your health condition.
  大量的研究报告指出，一天喝几杯咖啡可以改善人的健康状况。
  ★ 短语 "a great deal of + 不可数名词"意思是"大量的，许多的"。

- Drinking coffee not only protects people from diseases such as Alzheimer's and Parkinson's, but also brings a lot of joy into people's life.
  喝咖啡不仅可以保护人们免受某些疾病的侵害，比如阿尔茨海默症以及帕金森，也可以给人们的生活带来很多乐趣。
  ★ 短语 not only... but (also)... 不仅～，而且～。在此的 also 也可以省略。

- I've had enough coffee for today. I'd like to try some hot chocolate tonight.
  我今天咖啡喝得够多了。晚上我想试试热巧克力。

- Jessica is addicted to coffee. She drinks more coffee than any other liquid.
  杰西卡对咖啡上瘾了。她喝咖啡比喝其他饮料都多。
  ★ 短语 be addicted to 对～上瘾

- The caffeine could actually help me concentrate on things.
  咖啡因真的可以帮我集中注意力。
  ★ 语法 help 这个单词当动词使用时，表示"帮助，帮忙"的意思，后面接不定式的 to 可以省略。

- When I don't want to get too hyper, I will have a cup of decaffeinated coffee.
  当我不想太过亢奋时，我会喝一杯低咖啡因的咖啡。

- Drinking coffee in the morning is a great way to start my lovely day.
  每天早上喝杯咖啡来迎接美好的一天是个好方法。
  ★ 短语 "A is a great way to..." 意思是"A 是～的好方法"。

- However, some people might find the taste of coffee unbearable.
  然而，有些人可能觉得咖啡的味道令人无法忍受。
  ★ 语法 find 在这里是及物动词，指后面接的宾语"the taste of coffee"令人无法忍受。

- Most Europeans do not prefer to have iced coffee.
  大部分欧洲人不喜欢喝冰咖啡。

在国外都说这几句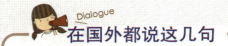

- **It is too late to have coffee now.**
  现在太晚了,我不能喝咖啡。
  ★ 语法 "too... to..." 对许多英语初学者来说,是个较容易犯错的句型,因为其中没有否定的词,因此要特别注意。它的中文意思是"太~以至于不能够~"。

- **The espresso is too strong for me to drink.**
  这杯浓缩咖啡对我来说太浓了,我无法下咽。

- **The weather is so cold that I do not want to have iced latte.**
  天气太冷了,我不想喝冰拿铁。
  ★ 语法 so... that... 如此~以至于~

- **All I need is a cup of coffee to keep me awake.**
  我只需要一杯咖啡来让我保持清醒。
  ★ 短语 all I need 我只需要~

- **Do you know how to enjoy coffee to the fullest?**
  你知道要如何充分地享受咖啡吗?
  ★ 短语 "to the full(est)" 的意思是"完全地,达到尽可能大的程度,充分地"。

- **If you wish to find the perfect coffee, you might want to pay a visit to Italy.**
  如果你想要找到完美的咖啡,那么就去一趟意大利吧!
  ★ 短语 pay a visit 拜访,参观

- **When I traveled to Italy last year, I was lucky to taste the richest coffee in the world.**
  我去年去意大利玩的时候,很幸运地尝到了最浓郁的咖啡。
  ★ 短语 travel to... 到~旅游

- **Coffee remains one of the most popular beverages for these times.**
  多年来,咖啡一直是最受人们欢迎的饮料之一。
  ★ 短语 for these times 一直以来

- **I would never buy any coffee from this café again because they have the worst customer service.**
  我以后绝对不会再到这家咖啡店消费,因为他们的顾客服务非常差。

- **I gave up coffee years ago because it made me too jittery.**
  咖啡让我感到神经紧张,所以我几年前戒了。
  ★ 短语 give up 放弃

Dialogue 在国外都说这几句

- Can I have a long black and a muffin to go?
  我可以外带一杯黑咖啡和一份松饼吗？
  ★ 短语 to go 外带，（指餐厅或商店出售的熟食）外卖的

- One of my favorite things about tea is that no two taste the same.
  我最喜欢茶的原因之一是因为没有茶喝起来是一模一样的。
  ★ 短语 the same 相同的，一样的

- With any purchase of a new mug, a medium sized coffee will be given for free.
  只要购买任何新款的马克杯，就免费送一杯中杯咖啡。
  ★ 短语 medium sized 中杯

- The history of coffee can be traced back to more than a thousand years ago.
  咖啡的历史可以追溯到一千多年前。
  ★ 短语 be traced back to （时间）追溯到

- In fact, over 50% of people in America drink coffee every day.
  事实上，在美国，超过50%的人每天都喝咖啡。
  ★ 短语 in fact 事实上，实际上

- When ordering coffee at a shop, what size do you usually have?
  在咖啡厅点咖啡的时候，你通常都点多大杯的？
  ★ 语法 "at + 地方" 时，通常是表示在 "地方" 的空间及其附近地方。

- My co-worker says he is less productive on the job without a cup of coffee.
  我的同事告诉我，若不喝杯咖啡，他的工作效率会变差。
  ★ 短语 on the job 工作当中，正做着一件事时

- As a coffee addict, Claire decided to buy an espresso machine.
  作为咖啡上瘾的人，克莱尔决定买一台意式浓缩咖啡机。
  ★ 语法 "as" 在此表示 "作为～"，后面可接名词。

- Now that you have an espresso machine, you also need a grinder to grind the coffee beans.
  现在有了意式咖啡机，你还需要一台研磨机来研磨咖啡豆。
  ★ 短语 now that 既然，因为

- In general, coffee is the best when the beans are ground by hand.
  一般来说，手工研磨的咖啡品质最好。
  ★ 短语 by hand 手工，以手工方式

跟任何人都可以用英语聊聊天

Unit 2 享受**阳光**的美好

[生活便利贴]

趁着艳阳高照，何不放下手中的电子产品，到户外进行运动。运动不但可以加速身体的代谢，有益健康，而且还可以增进亲子以及朋友间的情感交流。不过长时间曝晒在阳光下，对人体也会造成一定的影响，所以到户外运动时，千万不要忘记涂防晒霜。这个单元就让我们一起学习如何进行健康的户外活动吧！

Vocabulary 在国外都用这些词

MP3 01-11

concrete jungle
ph 都市丛林

picnic
['pɪknɪk]
n 野餐

rock climbing
ph 攀岩

horseback riding
ph 骑马

landscape
['lændskeɪp]
n 风景

map
[mæp]
n 地图

cyclist
['saɪklɪst]
n 自行车手

cocktail party
ph 鸡尾酒派对

sunbathing
['sʌnbeɪðɪŋ]
n 日光浴

camping
['kæmpɪŋ]
n 露营

swimming
['swɪmɪŋ]
n 游泳

vegetable
['vedʒtəbl]
n 蔬菜

fishing
['fɪʃɪŋ]
n 钓鱼

multi-cultural
a 多元文化的

cruise
[kruːz]
n 邮轮

honeymoon
['hʌnɪmuːn]
n 蜜月

snow skiing
n 滑雪

park
[pɑːk]
v 停车

在国外都说这几句

- You may think Beijing is a concrete jungle, but you'll be surprised by how many options you have for outdoor activities.
  你可能觉得北京是都市丛林，但如果你知道这里也有许多户外活动的选择，你可能会很惊讶。
  ★ 短语 "concrete jungle"是指"（都市中充满建筑物的）水泥丛林"。

- If you're an outdoor enthusiast, the state park will definitely take you there.
  如果你热衷户外活动，那么这座州立公园一定能够满足你。
  ★ 短语 "take A there"的原意是指"带 A 到哪里"，引申为"达到 A 的需求，满足 A"。

- The city and its beautiful surroundings are perfect for such outdoor activities as biking and mountain climbing.
  这座城市和美丽的环境使得户外活动，比如骑自行车和登山成为完美之选。
  ★ 短语 be perfect for... 对～来说很完美

- You can experience nature by doing some outdoor exercises.
  你可以通过户外活动来亲近大自然。

- A bonfire gives you a chance to socialize with people.
  篝火晚会是让人们互相交流的好机会。
  ★ 短语 give A a chance to... 给 A 一个～的机会

- The parks in the city offer you great places to take a rest from your busy life.
  都市里的公园是一个让你可以在忙碌的生活中稍作休息的地方。
  ★ 短语 take a rest 休息

- Teenagers are proud of being part of a summer camp.
  青少年对于可以成为夏令营的一分子而感到骄傲。
  ★ 短语 be proud of... 以～自豪，为～感到自豪

- The park allows people to have various activities, such as concerts, weddings and picnics.
  这座公园提供场地让人们可以进行不同种类的活动，比如演唱会、婚礼以及野餐。
  ★ 短语 such as 举例，比如

- For most people, rock climbing is the activity they have to be really careful when doing.
  对大部分的人来说，攀岩是一项需要非常小心的活动。

013

Dialogue 在国外都说这几句

- Have you ever tried horseback riding? If so, would you recommend it to other people?
  你骑过马吗？如果骑过的话，你会推荐其他人从事这项活动吗？
  ★ 短语 ▶ horseback riding 骑马

- Do you think hosting a party in the central park would be a good idea?
  你觉得在中央公园举办派对是个好主意吗？
  ★ 短语 ▶ "host a party" 的意思是"主持一个派对"。

- Is there any area where we can fly our kites?
  这里有地方可以让我们放风筝吗？
  ★ 短语 ▶ 要形容"某地方有什么人 / 东西"，就要使用"there is + 单数名词"以及"there are + 复数名词"。

- There are a range of activities for all seasons in this small town.
  这个小镇一年四季都有一系列不同种类的活动。
  ★ 短语 ▶ a range of... 许多的～，一系列的～

- You can enjoy sandwiches by the lake, but please do not throw the crusts to the birds.
  你们可以在湖边享用三明治，但请不要丢面包屑喂食任何鸟类。
  ★ 短语 ▶ throw... to A 把～扔向 A，把～丢给 A

- Some of the amusement parks and zoos offer discount from time to time.
  有些游乐场和动物园会不时提供折扣。
  ★ 短语 ▶ from time to time 有时，偶尔，不时

- The national park is renowned for the diversity of its wild animals and magnificent landscapes.
  这座国家公园以多元的野生动物以及令人叹为观止的环境景观而享有盛誉。
  ★ 短语 ▶ be renowned for... 以～闻名，以～享有盛誉

- Crossing the bridge on foot is a walk you will never forget.
  步行跨越大桥绝对是让你难忘的散步经验。
  ★ 短语 ▶ on foot 步行

- The Golden Gate Bridge in San Francisco is one of the longest suspension bridges on earth.
  旧金山的金门大桥是世界上最长的吊桥之一。
  ★ 短语 ▶ on earth 全世界，地球上

Dialogue 在国外都说这几句

- We should take advantage of the free musical festival throughout the summer.
  我们应该把握机会享受夏季的免费音乐节。
  ★ 短语 take advantage of... 善用～，占～的便宜

- Let's check out the information center of the park and pick up some maps.
  我们去一趟公园的游客中心了解情况，并拿几本公园地图。
  ★ 短语 pick up... 拾起～，收拾～

- When you go biking, make sure you wear a helmet as it will prevent you from getting hurt.
  去骑自行车时，要记得戴头盔，因为它可以避免你受到伤害。
  ★ 短语 "prevent 人 from..." 的意思是"防止人～，阻止人～"。

- Look! That little boy almost got run over by a bike.
  看！那个小男孩差点被自行车撞到。
  ★ 短语 "get / be run over by..." 的意思是"被～撞到"。

- Visitors will find this guide with useful information about restaurants and sites.
  游客会觉得这本印有餐厅和景点的指南十分好用。
  ★ 短语 information about... 关于～的信息

- My father and I used to enjoy shooting hoops in the driveway.
  我爸爸和我曾经喜欢在车道上打篮球。
  ★ 短语 shoot hoops 打篮球（口语）

- Plenty of cyclists still got injured by cars even though they wore helmets.
  就算戴头盔，许多自行车手还是被车撞伤。
  ★ 短语 "be / get injured" 的意思是"受伤"。

- I'd like to have a cocktail party on the cruise.
  我想要在邮轮上举办一场鸡尾酒派对。
  ★ 短语 on the cruise 在游艇上

- Before going swimming, it's important to go through these water safety instructions with children.
  游泳前，与小朋友们讲解这些水上安全指南是很重要的。
  ★ 短语 go through 讲解

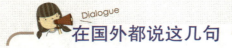

在国外都说这几句

- **No matter where you live, there are always plenty of activities that you can do outside.**
  不管你住哪里，都会有许多户外活动可以做。
  ★ 语法 "no matter"表示"不论，不顾"，引导让步状语从句，后面必须与how, what, when, where, whether, which, who 等词连用。

- **When sunbathing on the beach, please do not forget to put on sunscreen.**
  在沙滩做日光浴的时候，请不要忘记擦防晒乳。

- **When playing golf, be careful not to get hit by a golf ball.**
  打高尔夫球时，要小心别被高尔夫球砸到。
  ★ 短语 be careful not to... 小心别被～

- **Setting up safety instructions on the beach can come in handy as summer approaches.**
  当夏天临近，在海滩上设置安全指南是很有用的。
  ★ 短语 "...come in handy"的意思是"～迟早有用，～会很便利"。

- **When you decide to go for a picnic, choose dishes that require little preparation.**
  当你决定要去野餐时，要选择几乎不需准备工作的食物。
  ★ 短语 decide to... 决定～

- **You should read the pamphlet before going camping with your family.**
  在与家人露营前，你应该先阅读这本小册子。
  ★ 短语 go camping 去露营

- **Outdoor activities don't necessarily need to be limited to the daytime.**
  户外活动并不非得限于白天。
  ★ 短语 limit to... 限制～，限定～

- **No visit to Hong Kong is complete without a cup of famous local bubble tea.**
  若没有喝一杯当地有名的珍珠奶茶，就不算去过香港。
  ★ 语法 "without"是介词，意思为"没有，假如没有"。

- **The kids are having fun jumping on the bouncy bed.**
  小朋友们在蹦床上玩得很开心。
  ★ 短语 "have fun + v."的意思是"～玩得很开心"。

在国外都说这几句

- My family and I are crazy about bird watching.
  我的家人和我非常热衷于赏鸟。
  ★ 短语 "be crazy about..." 的意思是 "对～感到热衷/疯狂"。

- The rules of playing sports don't really matter as long as you are having fun and no one gets hurt.
  只要你在运动时开心，并且没有人在过程中受伤，那么运动规就没有那么重要。
  ★ 短语 "as long as" 的意思是 "只要"，在此是用来引导条件状语从句。

- All you need is a hook, a line and a can of worms, and then you are all set to go fishing.
  你只需要一根钓竿、一条线和一罐小虫，就可开始你的钓鱼之旅了。
  ★ 短语 go fishing 去钓鱼

- Playing badminton can be fun and educational at the same time.
  打羽毛球既有趣，同时又具有教育意义。
  ★ 短语 at the same time 同时

- Fresh fruit, vegetables and meats are all on sale at the farmer's market.
  在农夫市场中，新鲜水果、蔬菜和肉类全都有折扣。
  ★ 短语 "farmer's market" 的意思是 "（农民自己将农产品拿到集中地贩卖的）农夫市场"。

- The park is available for everyone to use and a popular place to relax.
  这座公园对所有人开放，而且是个让人放松的好地方。
  ★ 短语 "...be available for A" 的意思是 "对A来说，～是可以使用的"。

- The state park holds a multi-cultural festival every year.
  这座州立公园每年都会举办多元文化节。
  ★ 短语 "multi-cultural" 的意思是 "多元文化的"。

- Do you want to see a movie under the sky for free in the park tonight?
  今晚你想去公园看场户外的免费电影吗？
  ★ 短语 for free 免费的，不须花钱的

- My parents promised to take me on a cruise for my birthday.
  我父母答应在我生日的时候带我去搭邮轮。
  ★ 短语 promise to... 答应会～

在国外都说这几句

- Dad wants to create more memories as a family by escaping into the wilderness.
  爸爸想要借郊外野游之机，创造更多与家人在一起的记忆。
  ★ 短语 escape into...　逃遁到～，逃离到～

- The cabins are the best way to enjoy a carefree vacation.
  度假小屋是享受无忧无虑假期的最好方法。
  ★ 短语 "...is / are the best way(s)" 的意思是 "～是最好的方法"。

- The couple is looking for a romantic honeymoon package.
  这对情侣正在找浪漫的蜜月套装行程。
  ★ 短语 look for...　寻找～（表示还没找到）

- The hotel offers suites with ocean views and a jacuzzi.
  这家饭店提供附有海景以及按摩浴缸的套房。
  ★ 短语 ocean view　海景

- The family had a wonderful time together by the riverside and would like to come back again in the future.
  这家人在河边玩得很开心，并且打算以后再来这边玩。
  ★ 短语 by the riverside　在河边，在河畔

- What does it feel like to camp out in the forest?
  在森林里露营感觉怎么样？
  ★ 短语 "feel like" 在此的意思是 "感觉如何"；"camp out" 指 "在（野）外露营"。

- If you want to give hiking a try, the local ranger service actually offers all kinds of equipment.
  如果你想尝试远足，当地的管理服务处就提供各种各样的设备。
  ★ 短语 "give... a try" 的意思是 "试试～，给～一次机会"。

- Beach parties often involve a series of outdoor activities, such as volleyball and surfing.
  沙滩派对通常都包含一系列的户外活动，例如排球、冲浪。

- The fishermen usually depart from the bay and fish on the open sea for tuna and salmon.
  渔夫通常从这个海湾出发到开放海域捕鲔鱼和鲑鱼。
  ★ 短语 depart from...　从～启程，从～出发

在国外都说这几句 (Dialogue)

- A hotspot for snow skiing is very close to the resort.
  滑雪胜地与这个度假村距离很近。
  ★ 短语 be close to... 离～很近

- The best part of this skiing resort is the cheap entrance fee; it's affordable for everyone.
  这个滑雪场最棒的地方就是入场费便宜，每个人都负担得起。
  ★ 短语 be affordable for... 对～来说负担得起

- Let's sign up for the skiing lessons.
  我们去报名滑雪训练课程吧。
  ★ 短语 sign up for... 报名～，注册～

- Last Friday night, my boyfriend and I got off work and went straight to the National Park for some adventures.
  上星期五晚上，我男友和我下班后直接开车到国家公园来了一场冒险之旅。
  ★ 短语 get off work 下班

- Come on, let's park our car and set up the tent.
  来吧，我们把车停好，来搭帐篷。
  ★ 短语 "park + 车辆"的意思是"停车"。

- I feel really insecure when I am in the middle of nowhere.
  在杳无人烟的地方，我觉得很没有安全感。
  ★ 短语 in the middle of... 在～的当中，在～中途

- If you want to keep in good shape, the best way is to work out.
  如果想保持好身材，最好的方法就是健身。
  ★ 短语 keep in good shape 保持良好的体态

- Most men would need to spend long hours lifting weights in the gym in order to have a six-pack.
  大多数男生会花很多时间在健身房举重，只为了塑造出六块腹肌。
  ★ 短语 lift weight 举重

常识补给站

根据研究发现，持续性的运动可以使人分泌脑内啡 (endorphin)，脑内啡是一种类吗啡激素，可以使人产生愉快、轻松的效果。不过，脑内啡不是来自体外的物质，而是由人体自然分泌，所以不会有成瘾的问题。

在国外都说这几句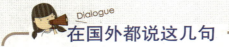

- **According to** the experts, it's better to do higher intensity exercise for a shorter amount of time.
  据专家称,在较短时间内从事较高强度的健身运动是比较好的。
  ★ 短语 according to... 根据~,依据~

- If you're just starting to exercise, it's best to **take it easy**.
  如果你是刚开始运动,最好慢慢来。
  ★ 短语 take it easy 不着急,慢慢来

- After 15 minutes on the treadmill, I am already **out of breath**.
  在跑步机上15分钟,我已经喘不过气来。
  ★ 短语 out of breath 喘不过气,上气不接下气

- You should **pay attention to** the protein you take in if you wish to build your muscles.
  如果你想要练肌肉的话,那就要多注意你的蛋白质摄取量。
  ★ 短语 pay attention to... 关心~,注意~

- Drink water **on a regular basis** throughout the day.
  每天要保持经常喝水的习惯。
  ★ 短语 on a regular basis 固定,经常

- I **hop on** the exercise bike and start working out every night.
  每天晚上,我会跳上健身自行车运动。
  ★ 短语 hop on... 跳上~,跳上(车辆)

- **Give me a break**. I'm too tired to even move my fingers today.
  饶了我吧。我今天累到连手指都不能动了。
  ★ 短语 "give A a break" 常用在口语,意思是"让A休息一下,饶了A吧"。

- Exercising **causes** the brain **to** produce endorphins, the chemical that can help a person feel calmer.
  运动会让人产生脑内啡,脑内啡是一种会让人感到更平静的化学物质。
  ★ 短语 cause to... 导致~,使~发生

- Exercising always makes me feel **a sense of achievement**.
  运动总是让我觉得很有成就感。
  ★ 短语 a sense of achievement 成就感

- People who exercise **burn** more **calories** and that is why they look fitter.
  运动的人燃烧更多热量,这也就是为什么他们看起来更健美。
  ★ 短语 burn calorie(s) 燃烧热量

在国外都说这几句

- Trust me! Doing exercise is the healthiest way to lose weight.
  相信我！运动是最健康的减肥方式。
  ★ 短语 lose weight　减肥，减重

- My father has started to work out regularly because he wants to lower his risk of heart disease.
  我爸爸因为想降低得心脏病的风险，所以开始有规律地运动。
  ★ 短语 lower the risk of...　降低～的风险

- How many sit-ups and push-ups can you do in 60 seconds?
  你一分钟内可以做多少下仰卧起坐和俯卧撑？

- Which are the best facilities to operate on to burn fat at the gym?
  健身房中最能够燃烧脂肪的器材是哪些？
  ★ 短语 burn fat　燃烧脂肪

- I'm new to Yoga. Is there any program for beginners?
  我是第一次学习瑜伽，有哪些课程是适合初学者的呢？
  ★ 短语 new to...　～的新手，对～是第一次接触

- The girl is on a healthy diet and tries to avoid junk food because she doesn't want to ruin her figure.
  这个女孩正在采取健康的饮食并且试着避免吃垃圾食物，因为她不想毁掉自己目前的身材。
  ★ 短语 on a healthy diet　健康的饮食

- No matter how tired you are, schedule at least 3 compulsory days a week to work out in the gym.
  不管你有多累，每周至少规划3天到健身房运动。
  ★ 短语 "数字 + day(s) a week" 的意思是 "一星期～天"。

- In general, the key to losing weight is to burn more calories than the amount you take in.
  一般来说，减肥的诀窍就是你所燃烧的热量要比摄取的多。
  ★ 短语 in general　一般而言，一般来说

- It's better to exercise 3 times a week.
  最好一星期运动3次。

跟任何人都可以用英语聊聊天

Unit 3 让人浑身不舒服的感冒

[生活便利贴]

　　季节交替时，是感冒的高发期，所以这段时间要穿着保暖的衣物，平时也要饮食均衡、增加自己的抵抗力来预防感冒；若真的感冒了，要记得多补充维生素C，并且多喝水来帮助身体的新陈代谢，将感冒病毒更快速地排出体外。这个单元就让我们来看看有什么英语单词和句子是跟感冒有关系的！

Vocabulary 在国外都用这些词

MP3 01-21

examine
[ɪgˈzæmɪn]
v 检查，诊察

symptom
[ˈsɪmptəm]
n 症状

vaccination
[ˌvæksɪˈneɪʃn]
n 疫苗

hospital
[ˈhɒspɪtl]
n 医院

crowd
[kraʊd]
n 人群

hay fever
ph 花粉症

cough
[kɒf]
v / n 咳嗽

runny nose
ph 流鼻涕

stuffed nose
ph 鼻塞

pharmacy
[ˈfɑːməsɪ]
n 药店

medicine
[ˈmedsɪ]
n 药品

infect
[ɪnˈfekt]
v 感染

treatment
[ˈtriːtmənt]
n 治疗，疗程

appetite
[ˈæpɪtaɪt]
n 胃口

tonsil
[ˈtɒnsl]
n 扁桃体

temperature
[ˈtemprətʃə]
n 体温

blood pressure
ph 血压

antibiotics
[ˌæntɪbaɪˈɒtɪk]
n 抗生素

在国外都说这几句

- Influenza, also known as the flu, is a highly contagious disease.
  流行性感冒，又称为流感，是一种易传染的疾病。
  ★ 短语 "also known as..." 的意思是"亦称为～，又叫做～，别名为～"可简写为"a.k.a."。

- Anyone, even someone who is strong and healthy, can get the flu from time to time.
  任何人，即使是身体强壮及健康的人，也有可能不时得流感。
  ★ 语法 同位语，就是在一个名词之后的名词，后一个名词用来说明并解释前一个名词，通常会用逗号分开，但其实两个名词描述的是同一件事。

- I have a fever and my body feels achy at the same time.
  我发烧了，同时还觉得全身酸痛。
  ★ 短语 at the same time 同时

- Almost everyone in class has a runny nose, so the teacher requests them to wear masks.
  这个班上几乎所有人都在流鼻涕，所以老师要求他们戴口罩。
  ★ 短语 runny nose 流鼻涕

- Are you having difficulty swallowing?
  你吞咽的时候有困难吗？
  ★ 语法 "have difficulty + v-ing" 的意思是"～有困难，无法～"。

- Actually, serious complications from influenza can happen to people at any age.
  事实上，由流感引发的严重并发症有可能发生在任何年纪的人身上。
  ★ 短语 at any age 任何年龄

- My cold began with a stuffy nose and a sore throat and now I have a headache.
  我感冒一开始的症状是鼻塞和喉咙痛，现在连头都痛了。
  ★ 短语 stuffy nose 鼻塞

- My son caught a cold from one of his classmates.
  我儿子被他班上的一个同学传染感冒了。
  ★ 短语 catch a cold 感冒

- The common cold usually occurs in the fall and winter months, when the temperature is not stable.
  普通感冒通常发生在气温不稳定的秋天和冬天。
  ★ 短语 occur in... ～（何时）发生

在国外都说这几句

- Flu is unpredictable and it can be spread through many different medias.
  流感无法被预料，而且可以通过许多不同的媒介传播。
  ★ 短语 be spread through 经由～传染／传开

- If you have a severe cough and cannot stop sneezing, chances are (that) you have a cold.
  如果你咳嗽严重，而且不停打喷嚏，你有可能是感冒了。
  ★ 短语 chances are (that)... （有）可能～

- The doctor is examining him thoroughly and trying to find out what his symptoms are.
  医生很详细地帮他做检查，并且试着找出他的症状。
  ★ 短语 find out... 找出～，发现～，查明～（真相）

- Usually, winter is the time for flu. So you need to be careful and always keep yourself warm during this time.
  通常，冬天是流感高峰期。所以这段时间要特别小心并且要注意保暖。
  ★ 短语 ...is the time for 是～的时间

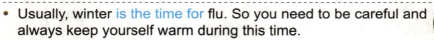

- Flu often comes with different symptoms, which include having a fever, cough, sore throat, runny nose, nose congestion, body aches, headache, etc.
  流感一般会伴随许多不同症状，像发烧、咳嗽、喉咙痛、流鼻涕、鼻塞、全身酸痛以及头痛等。
  ★ 语法 "include + v-ing" 的意思是 "包括～，包含～"。

- Staying on healthy diet can help you recover from the flu.
  保持健康的饮食有助于流感痊愈。
  ★ 短语 recover from... 从（疾病）～中恢复

- Do you know that flu vaccinations are provided at hospitals to the public to effectively lower the risk of catching the flu?
  你知道医院向一般民众提供流感疫苗，可以有效降低得流感的风险吗？
  ★ 短语 "A + be provided to" 的意思是 "把A提供给～"。

- A serious flu outbreak happened last week. You should avoid going to public places with huge crowds.
  上个星期严重的流感大暴发。你应该避免出入人流密集的地方。
  ★ 语法 "avoid + v-ing" 指 "避免～"。

在国外都说这几句

- **The flu is a contagious respiratory illness caused by viruses.**
  流感是由病毒所引发的传染性呼吸疾病。
  ★ 短语 be caused by... 由～引起，由～引发

- **How is the flu different from a common cold?**
  流感和一般感冒有什么不同吗？
  ★ 短语 be different from... 与～不同

- **When I get sick, I become grumpy and feel reluctant to interact with people.**
  当我生病时，我变得易怒，而且不想跟人互动。
  ★ 短语 "interact with A"的意思是"与A互动"。

- **My daughter is ill. Her condition has deteriorated in a matter of hours.**
  我女儿生病了。她的状况在几小时内就恶化了。
  ★ 短语 in a matter of... （时间）～之内

- **Ted's symptoms got worse and caused complications as a result of the flu.**
  泰德的症状变得更糟且引发了流感并发症。
  ★ 短语 "as a result of..."的意思是"由于～"，后面接"原因"。

- **Most people are confused about the difference between the flu and the common cold.**
  大部分的人常常无法分辨流感跟一般感冒。
  ★ 短语 "be confused about"的意思是"对～感到疑惑"。

- **The patient is not able to take in any solid food.**
  这个病人无法摄入任何固体食物。
  ★ 短语 take in... 让～进入，接受～

- **Sometimes flu symptoms happen very quickly and often catch you off-guard.**
  有时候流感的症状发生得很快，让你措手不及。
  ★ 短语 "catch A off-guard"的意思是"让A措手不及，事情在A还没有准备好的时候就发生了"。

- **Most students in school have been injected with the flu vaccinations.**
  学校大部分学生都已接种了流感疫苗。
  ★ 短语 be injected with... 接种～

- **When the flu gets worse and without proper treatment, at times it can lead to death.**
  当流感恶化而且没有适当的治疗，有时候会导致死亡。
  ★ 短语 at times 有时，偶尔，不时

在国外都说这几句

- According to doctors, flu symptoms are usually more severe than the typical sneezing and coughing that are associated with a cold.
  根据医生的说法，流感症状通常会比典型感冒出现更加严重的打喷嚏及咳嗽现象。
  ★ 短语 associate with... 与～联系在一起

- My flu symptoms improved a bit at the very beginning but then returned with a fever and body aches.
  我的流感症状刚开始有一点改善，但之后又开始发烧及全身酸痛。
  ★ 短语 return with... 又发生～，重新发生～

- I cannot tell the difference between a cold and hay fever. Sometimes the symptoms are so similar.
  我无法分辨感冒和花粉症的不同，有时候它们的症状非常相似。
  ★ 短语 difference between... ～之间的不同，～之间的差异

- The elderly should take the time to get a flu vaccination.
  老年人都应该找时间去接种流感疫苗。
  ★ 短语 take the time to... 找时间～，需要时间～

- In order to protect everyone against flu viruses, I recommend that everyone should eat properly and exercise regularly.
  为了保护所有人不受流感病毒攻击，我建议每个人都要饮食均衡并且养成定期运动的习惯。
  ★ 语法 "in order to..."的意思是"为了～，以便～"，后面接原形动词，可放在句首或句尾。

- We should all get a flu vaccination as soon as it's available.
  一旦疫苗投放市场了，每个人都该尽快接种流感疫苗。
  ★ 语法 "as soon as..."的意思是"一～就～，刚～就～"，可放置在句首或句中引导时间状语从句。

- Pregnant women are at high risk of serious flu complications which might lead to miscarriage.
  怀孕妇女是得流感并发症的高危群体，很有可能因此导致流产。
  ★ 短语 at high risk of... ～的高危群体

- In order to stop spreading germs, we should sanitize our hands now and then.
  为了阻止细菌传播，我们应该时不时给双手消毒。

在国外都说这几句

- **Cover your nose and mouth with a tissue** or your arm when you cough or sneeze, especially on public transportation.
  在公共交通工具上咳嗽或打喷嚏时，要用纸巾或是手臂遮住鼻子和嘴巴。
  ★ 短语 "cover A with..."的意思是"用～把A遮住，用～遮盖A的表面"。

- **Throw the tissue in** the rubbish bin after you use it.
  把你用过的纸巾丢到垃圾筒中。
  ★ 短语 "throw A in..."的意思是"把A丢到～中"。

- The doctor told me not to have **close contact** with people who are sick.
  医生告诉我要避免与生病的人近距离接触。
  ★ 短语 close contact 近距离接触

- **Wash your hands frequently with soap and water.** If not available, use an alcohol-based sanitizer.
  经常用肥皂和清水洗手。如果没有肥皂，就用含有酒精的洗手液。
  ★ 短语 "wash A with B"是指"用B洗A"。

- If your symptoms get worse, **seek professional treatment from your doctor** within the first 48 hours and do not take random medicine without a prescription.
  如果你的症状恶化，48小时内找医生寻求治疗，且没有处方别胡乱吃药。
  ★ 短语 "seek...from A"的意思是"向A寻求～"。

- If you are diagnosed with a flu with fever, the doctor usually recommends that you stay at home for **at least** 24 hours after the fever is gone.
  若你被诊断为流感加发烧，医生通常会建议你退烧后24小时内最好待在家。
  ★ 短语 at least 至少，起码

- You should **keep an eye** out for the critical symptoms, if no improvement, visit the doctor as soon as possible.
  你应该密切注意这些关键的症状，如果都没有好转的话，要尽快去看医生。
  ★ 短语 "keep an eye"字面上的意思是"睁一只眼睛"，引申为"照看～，留心～"。

- You should **watch out** because the flu can sometimes cause serious damage to your body.
  你应该小心，因为流感有时候会对人体造成很大的伤害。
  ★ 短语 "watch out"是指"注意～，小心～"，可以用作祈使句。

在国外都说这几句

- I'm going to the pharmacy to get some medicine for my fever and cough.
  我要去药店买一些治疗发烧和咳嗽的药。
  ★ 短语 be going to... 即将～，打算～

- The doctor suggested that I drink plenty of water at the first sign of the flu. It can help the flu virus to get out of my system quickly.
  医生建议我一旦出现流感征兆，就大量喝水。这样可以帮助身体将流感病毒迅速排出体外。
  ★ 短语 at the first sight of... 一看到～

- If you are too weak to get up, use a straw to drink from a cup. But don't choke yourself.
  如果你太虚弱没办法起床，那就用吸管从杯中喝水。但小心不要被呛到。
  ★ 短语 drink from... 从～喝（饮料）

- People who are suffering from the flu are usually told to drink a lot of fluids to keep from getting dehydrated.
  患流感的人通常被告知要大量喝水，以免脱水。
  ★ 短语 keep from... 避免～，阻止～

- I think you will recover from the flu in one or two weeks.
  我想你的流感再过一两个星期就会痊愈了。

- If you must leave the house while you are still sick, make sure you wear a facemask.
  生病时如果一定要出门的话，确保一定要戴口罩。
  ★ 语法 "must"为情态动词，意思与"have to"相近，意思是"必须"。

- Drink plenty of water and other clear liquids to prevent fluid loss.
  喝大量的水，或是其他清流食，避免水分流失。
  ★ 短语 plenty of... 很多～，大量～

- Once you notice that you have flu-like symptoms, you should keep distance from others as much as possible.
  一旦你发现自己有类似流感的症状，你就应该与其他人尽量保持距离。
  ★ 短语 keep distance from... 与～保持距离

- The sick schoolboy was told to take a day off and stay at home to keep other students from getting infected.
  生病的男学生被告知要在家休息一天，以免传染给其他同学。
  ★ 短语 take a day off 休息一天

Dialogue 在国外都说这几句

- When you are sick, do not have any soft drinks; there are other healthier options, such as water, chicken soup or sports drinks.
  生病的时候不要喝软饮料。可以选择其他较健康的饮品，像水、鸡汤或者运动饮料。
  ★ 短语 sports drink(s) 运动饮料

- Please do not drink alcohol or drinks with caffeine, such as tea and coffee, when taking medicine.
  吃药的时候，请不要喝酒或喝含有咖啡因的饮料，如茶和咖啡。
  ★ 短语 "such as"的意思是"像是～，例如～"，在此可以等于"like"。

- Please inform the doctor if you are allergic to anything.
  若你有过敏史，请告知医生。
  ★ 短语 be / get allergic to... 对～过敏

- I think I've caught a cold. I might call in sick and go to a doctor tomorrow.
  我想我感冒了。我明天可能要请假去看医生。
  ★ 短语 call in sick 因病请假

- I would like to make an appointment with Dr. Smith. Could you please tell me when he is available?
  我想要预约史密斯医生，你可以告诉我他何时有空吗？
  ★ 短语 be available 有空的；可供使用的

- I have scheduled an appointment with Dr. Johnson at 3 o'clock today.
  我已经预约今天3点强森医生的看诊时间。
  ★ 短语 schedule an appointment 安排会面，预定时间

- How can I be sure if I have the flu or just a common cold?
  我如何确定自己得的是流感还是一般感冒？

- Excuse me, I need to make an appointment with the doctor at once.
  不好意思，我需要立即与医生预约看诊时间。
  ★ 短语 at once 立刻，马上

- Under the circumstances, I am afraid giving you a shot is inevitable.
  照现在的情况来看，恐怕必须给你打一针。
  ★ 短语 give a shot 打一针，注射

在国外都说这几句

- Please **lie down** over here so that the doctor can examine you.
  请在这里躺下，医生才可以帮你检查。
  ★ 短语 ▶ lie down　躺下，平躺下来，稍作休息

- The doctor asked me to open my mouth to **have a look at** my tonsils.
  医生要我张开嘴巴，他要检查我的扁桃体。
  ★ 短语 ▶ have a look at　检查，看一看

- It is possible that your illness **arose from** not resting properly.
  你的病状有可能是因为没有好好休息而产生。
  ★ 短语 ▶ arise from...　由～引起，由～产生

- What side effects should I expect when taking these medicines?
  这些药物会有哪些副作用是我要注意的？

- Are there any foods or drinks that I should avoid while I **go through** the entire treatment?
  整个疗程中有哪些食物或饮料是我该避免的吗？
  ★ 短语 ▶ go through...　经过～，通（穿）过～

- After the treatment, how long do I have to wait until I can **go back to** work?
  疗程过后，要等多久我才能回去上班呢？
  ★ 短语 ▶ go back to...　回去做～

- I **lost** my **appetite** and felt like vomiting most of the time.
  我没有胃口，而且大多数时间都有想吐的感觉。
  ★ 短语 ▶ lose appetite　没有胃口，丧失食欲

- If you need to get **a copy of** your prescription, please report to the front desk.
  如果需要就诊的处方单，请告知前台人员。
  ★ 短语 ▶ a copy of...　～的副本，～的影本

- I wonder if these pills are going to **make me drowsy**.
  我想知道这些药物会不会让我犯困。
  ★ 短语 ▶ "make A drowsy" 的意思是"让～想睡觉"。

- Are the appointments running **on time** at the moment, or do I have to wait a bit longer?
  目前看诊时间是准时的，还是我要再等一段时间？
  ★ 短语 ▶ on time　准时

Dialogue 在国外都说这几句

- Are there any kinds of flu tests that can effectively tell me if it's flu or not?
  有没有什么流感测试能很精准地告诉我，我是不是得了流感？

- As your doctor, I will keep on tracks of your symptoms and treatments, and make adjustment accordingly.
  作为你的医生，我会持续追踪你的症状和治疗方法，并且依情况来做适当的调整。
  ★ 短语 keep on tracks...　追踪～，纪录～，了解～的情况

- Have you been on any sort of medication in the last 24 hours?
  你在过去24小时之内服用了任何药物吗？
  ★ 短语 on medication　正在服用药物，正在（某种）药物治疗

- I have flu symptoms and I am worried about passing them on to my family. What should I do?
  我有流感的症状，很担心会传染给我的家人。我该怎么办？
  ★ 短语 be worried about...　担心～，烦恼～

- Do I need to go to the emergency room if the pain in my chest doesn't go away?
  如果我的胸口疼痛没有好转，我需要去看急诊吗？
  ★ 短语 "emergency room" 是指"急诊室"，可简称"ER"。

- The emergency room should not be abused by people who are not in need of immediate medical care.
  不需紧急医疗看护的人不应该浪费急诊室的医疗资源。
  ★ 短语 in need of...　需要～

- These are the medicines that I will prescribe for treating your flu. The instructions are on the front of the package.
  这些是我为你开的处方药，用来治疗你的流感。请依照包装上的指示用药。
  ★ 短语 prescribe for...　为～开药方

- I'm going to take your temperature and blood pressure, so try to relax; otherwise the figures won't be correct.
  我要量你的体温和血压，所以请放轻松，不然出来的数据会不准确。
  ★ 短语 "take A's temperature / blood pressure" 的意思是"量A的体温／血压"。

- You only have a mild illness. There is no need to make a big fuss over it and ask your doctor for antibiotics.
  你的疾病很轻微。不需要小题大做地跟医生要抗生素来吃。
  ★ 短语 make a big fuss over it　小题大做

跟任何人都可以用英语聊聊天

Unit 4 预防胜于治疗

[生活便利贴]

现代人常常三餐不固定、常吃外卖且偏爱精致食物，导致摄取过多高热量食物，没有足够的纤维素，再加上欠缺运动，造成许多现代文明病（高血压、糖尿病等），让健康亮起红灯。所以定期做健康检查非常重要，很多疾病初期可能没有症状，若能早期发现，早期治疗效果很好。让我们来看看生活中哪些单词和会话可以应用在健康检查上。

在国外都用这些词

 MP3 01-31

health check-up
ph 健康检查

organic food
ph 有机食品

abnormal
[æb'nɔːml]
a 不正常的

hypertension
[ˌhaɪpə'tenʃn]
n 高血压

question
['kwestʃən]
n 问题，疑问

insurance
[ɪn'ʃʊərəns]
n 保险

alcohol
['ælkəhɒl]
n 酒精；酒类饮料

underwear
['ʌndəweə]
n 内衣；内裤

courage
['kʌrɪdʒ]
n 勇气

sponsor
['spɒnsə]
v / n 赞助；赞助者

accessory
[ək'sesərɪ]
n 饰品

calm
[kɑːm]
a 冷静的，平静的

prayer
[preə]
n 祈祷

thoughtful
['θɔːtfl]
a 体贴的

pain
[peɪn]
n 痛苦

brave
[breɪv]
a 勇敢的

quit smoking
ph 戒烟

blood pressure
ph 血压

Dialogue
在国外都说这几句

- The best way to evaluate your health condition is to have a medical check-up.
  健康检查是评估你自身健康状况的最佳方式。

- The doctor recommends that it's best for everyone to get an annual health examination.
  医生建议每个人每年最好都要做一次健康检查。
  ★ 语法 ▸ it's best (for A) to... 对（A 来）说～是最好的

- The exams and screenings that you need depend on your age, health condition and medical history.
  你需要哪种检验和筛检取决于你的年纪、健康状况和个人病史。
  ★ 短语 ▸ "depend on..." 的意思是 "视～而定，取决于～"。

- The purpose of the periodic health examination is to have a clear understanding of your health status.
  定期健康检查的目的就是要了解自己的健康状况。
  ★ 短语 ▸ the purpose of...   ～的目的

- My grandmother went to the clinic to screen for signs of any heart disease.
  我奶奶去诊所做心脏疾病的筛查。
  ★ 短语 ▸ screen for...   筛查～，全面检查～

- During the screening process, my doctor ran through different types of tests on me to make sure everything was fine.
  进行筛检时，我的医生对我进行了各种不同的检测以确保身体各方面都没有问题。
  ★ 短语 ▸ different types of...   不同的～

- To make the most of your next check-up, you can only drink water after 7 p.m. the night before.
  为了让你下次健康检查达到最佳功效，在健康检查前一天的晚上 7 点之后你就只能喝水。
  ★ 短语 ▸ make the most of...   充分利用～，做最有效的利用

- My grandmother was told to have more organic food because it is more beneficial for the human body.
  我奶奶被告知要多摄取有机食品，因为有机食品对人体好处较多。
  ★ 短语 ▸ organic food   有机食品

在国外都说这几句

- **Based on** my grandmother's recent examination, the doctor has informed her not to have too many sweets.
  根据我奶奶最近一次的健康检查,医生告知她不要吃太多甜食。
  ★ 短语 based on... 根据～

- Knowing what to expect during a health exam can **ease the anxiety**.
  知道健康检查时会碰上哪些状况,可以减轻焦虑感。
  ★ 短语 ease the anxiety 减轻焦虑

- You should make **a list of** concerns and questions and take it with you when you have the appointment with your doctor.
  你应该将你担心的事情以及任何问题写在纸上,看诊的时候带在身上。
  ★ 短语 a list of... ～的清单

- It is important to **be honest with** your family doctor about your condition.
  将你的情况如实告知家庭医师是非常重要的。
  ★ 短语 be honest with... 对～诚实,对～说实话

- The doctor has requested you to **take** your previous chest X-ray films **to** your next appointment.
  医生交代你下次去看诊的时候要把之前的胸部 X 光片一起带去。
  ★ 短语 take to... 带到～,带去～

- I would like to **make an appointment for** a health examination next week.
  我想要预约下星期做身体检查。
  ★ 短语 make an appointment for... 预约～的会面,做～约定

> **常识补给站**
>
> 　　成人正常的收缩压(高压)应小于120mmHg,舒张压(低压)小于80mmHg。如果成人收缩压大于或等于140mmHg,舒张压大于或等于90mmHg 为高血压。

在国外都说这几句

- Our family doctor provides free counseling service for people who are over 65 years old.
  我们的家庭医生给 65 岁以上的人提供免费的健康咨询服务。
  ★ 短语 family doctor　家庭医师

- How much is the cost of having a physical health examination?
  健康检查的费用是多少？
  ★ 短语 the cost of...　～的费用，～的花费

- The cost for the physical examination is $5,000 payable in cash only.
  健康检查的费用是 5000 美元，只收现金。
  ★ 短语 in cash　付现金

- Is it possible to pay the examination fee by credit card?
  可以用信用卡支付检查费用吗？
  ★ 短语 by credit card　以信用卡付款

- Every now and then, there may be additional charges if the doctor recommends additional testing.
  若医生建议额外检查项目，有时候会有附加收费。
  ★ 短语 every now and then　有时候

- The purpose of screening and evaluation is to make sure the existing disease doesn't get worse.
  筛查和评估的主要目标就是确认现有疾病没有恶化。
  ★ 短语 the purpose of...　～的目标，目的就是～

- Before the examination, my grandmother felt so nervous that she couldn't remember the questions she was about to ask.
  检查前，我的奶奶觉得非常紧张，以至于她忘了她本来要问的问题。
  ★ 语法 "be about to..." 后接动词原形，表示"正要～，即将要～"，用来说明即将发生的事，此种用法是完全客观的描述。

- If you have any doubts or questions, write them down before going to your appointment.
  如果你有任何疑问或问题，在看诊之前，把问题先写下来。
  ★ 语法 "before" 是表示时间的连词，用来表示句中两个动作发生的时间先后顺序，意思是"～之前"。

- I suggested my grandmother contact the clinic prior to her appointment to confirm the time.
  我建议奶奶在去就诊之前，先与诊所联系确认看诊时间。
  ★ 短语 prior to...　在～之前

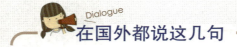

在国外都说这几句

- My grandfather called and enquired about the examination fees and payment method in advance.
  我爷爷事先打电话询问了有关检查的费用及付款方式。
  ★ 短语 in advance   在前面，预先，事先

- My doctor took my grandmother's blood pressure to make sure nothing is abnormal.
  我的医生测量我奶奶的血压以确定没有任何不正常的状况。
  ★ 短语 take A's blood pressure   量 A 的血压

- If you want to have an extensive health check-up, you should go to the state hospital.
  如果你想要做进一步的健康检查，那你就应该去州立医院。

- It is for your own good to take the examination to make sure you are fit and healthy.
  为了你自己着想，你应该做健康检查，以确保自己身体健康强壮。

- Measurement of blood pressure is intended to screen for hypertension.
  测量血压的目的是要查出是否有高血压。
  ★ 短语 be intended to...   想要～，打算～

- The doctor asked me to keep track of my blood pressure measurements at home.
  医生要求我将所有在家量血压的数据记下来。
  ★ 短语 keep track of...   将～记录下来

- The cost of health examinations varies based on your insurance coverage.
  健康检查的费用会因为你的保险项目不同而有所不同。
  ★ 短语 base on   根据

- If a woman is suffering from any pain or an irregular period, she should arrange an appointment to have thorough check-up as soon as possible.
  若女性发觉经期疼痛或是月经不规律，应该尽快进行全身检查。
  ★ 短语 arrange an appointment   安排会面 / 预约

在国外都说这几句

- My brother **is** a bit **worried about** the health exam tomorrow; even though the doctor has told him there is no need to panic.
  我哥哥对于明天的健康检查有点紧张；即使医生告诉他没有什么好害怕的。
  ★ 短语 be worried about... 对～感到担心，紧张～

- Every patient **is responsible for** taking care of himself/herself; therefore, it is important to follow the doctors' instructions.
  每个病患都要为自己的健康负责，因此遵照医生的指示非常重要。
  ★ 短语 be responsible for... 对～负责；是～的原因

- Do not schedule any physical exam if you are currently **under other treatment**.
  如果你目前正在接受其他治疗的话，先不要预约做健康检查。
  ★ 短语 under... treatment 接受～治疗

- You should **take a deep breath** and try to relax if you are feeling nervous.
  如果你觉得紧张的话，先深呼吸，然后试着放松。
  ★ 短语 take a deep breath 深呼吸

- One of a doctor's duties is to **educate** patients **about** the risks for future diseases.
  医生的一项责任就是要教育病患有关疾病的风险。
  ★ 短语 educate about... 教育有关～

- Regular gynecological examinations are **a** crucial **part of** any woman's health care.
  常规妇科检查对每位妇女来说都是健康管理重要的一部分。
  ★ 短语 a part of... ～的一部分

常识补给站

由于个人的体型、骨架不同，为了同时顾及身高和体重的配合，采用的指标是身体质量指数（Body Mass Index，缩写为 BMI），其计算公式如下：BMI = 体重 (kg) / 身高的平方 (m^2)；最有利于健康与寿命的理想值为 22，上下浮动 10% 都是理想的范围，通常年轻者适用较低的 BMI 值，年长者适用较高的 BMI 值。

Dialogue 在国外都说这几句

- **Counseling about** smoking cessation is free as it's a government sponsored service.
  戒烟咨询是由政府赞助的免费服务。
  ★ 短语 counsel about... 关于～的咨询

- You must **stay away from** alcohol for at least 24 hours prior to your exam.
  体检开始前 24 小时，你绝对不可以喝酒。
  ★ 短语 stay away from... 远离～，与～保持距离

- What **ought to** be included in a routine check-up and how long will it take?
  例行健康检查应该包含哪些（项目），需要花多久时间完成？
  ★ 短语 ought to... 应该～、应当～，等于 should

- **Is** the health examination **beneficial for** everyone?
  健康检查对每个人来说都是有益的吗？
  ★ 短语 be beneficial for... 对～有益的，对～有帮助的

- Don't worry, Grandpa. It's just a routine check-up. The doctor **won't bite**.
  别担心，爷爷。这只是个例行的健康检查，医生不会伤害你的。
  ★ 短语 ...won't bite 字面上的意思是"不会咬人"，在此引申为"不会伤害你"。

- It should be mandatory for women to have women's health exams **by age 21**.
  年满 21 周岁后，所有女人都应该做妇女健康检查。
  ★ 短语 "by age + 数字"是指"年满……岁后，满……岁时"。

- In order to **avoid causing** any harm, clinicians should selectively choose screening tests according to a patient's condition.
  为了避免伤害，临床医生应该依照病人的情况，有选择性地进行筛检测试。
  ★ 语法 avoid + v-ing 避免～，防止～

- Please take off your shirt and lie down on your stomach on the bed. The doctor will start a brief physical inspection of your heart, lungs, neck and abdomen.
  请将上衣脱掉平躺在床上，医生将会开始简单的身体检查，比如对心脏、肺、脖子和下腹部检查。

在国外都说这几句

- **Immunization plays an important role.** It defends our body from viruses attacking.
  免疫系统扮演着重要角色，它帮助我们抵抗病毒的侵袭。
  ★ 短语 ...play an important role ～扮演重要角色

- All women are advised to have health exams when they are sexually active.
  建议所有女性在开始有性行为后，就要做健康检查。
  ★ 短语 be advised to... 被劝告～，被建议～

- On the whole, a basic physical exam should include measurement of weight and blood pressure.
  一般来说，基本的身体检查包括测量体重和血压。
  ★ 短语 on the whole 一般说来，就整体而言

- Counseling with a doctor during the health examination is essential as well.
  在做健康检查时，询问医生的专业意见和咨询也很重要。
  ★ 短语 as well 也，同样地

- When the exam is over, you can get dressed and consult with your clinician.
  检查结束后，你可以穿上衣服，并向临床医师咨询。
  ★ 短语 get dressed 穿衣服，着衣

- The nurses instructed us to fill out a medical history form.
  护士请我们填写病历表格。
  ★ 短语 fill out... 填写～（表格、申请书）

- I would prefer to have a female doctor do the breast exam on me.
  我希望帮我做胸部检查的是位女医生。
  ★ 短语 do an exam on A 对A做检查，对A做检验

- The nurse first showed her to the dressing room and asked her to put on the robe for examination.
  护士先带她去更衣室，并要她换上长袍以便做检查。
  ★ 短语 show A to... 展示（地方）～给A，带领A到～

在国外都说这几句

- Take all your clothes and accessories off for examination but feel free to keep your underwear on.
  做检查的时候要把你所有衣服和饰品拿下来，但是你的内衣可以不用脱。
  ★ 短语 keep on... 继续～，继续拥有～

- The doctor was kind and reviewed my medical history with me.
  医生人很好，并跟我一起检阅了我的病历。
  ★ 短语 review... with A 与 A 一起检阅～

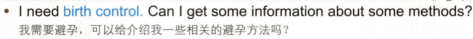

- I have a couple of questions that I would like to ask my doctor.
  我有一些问题想要问我的医生。
  ★ 短语 a couple of... 一对～，两个～；几个～

- I need birth control. Can I get some information about some methods?
  我需要避孕，可以给介绍我一些相关的避孕方法吗？
  ★ 短语 "birth control" 是指"避孕，生育控制"。

- Patients with abnormal results will be notified by phone and be requested to set up an appointment immediately.
  若有不正常的结果，会以电话通知病患，并且立即确认下一次就诊时间。
  ★ 短语 by phone 用电话，以电话（通知）

- Can I choose to receive my laboratory results via e-mail or telephone?
  我可以选择用电子邮件或电话获得检验结果吗？
  ★ 短语 via... 经由～，凭借～，通过～

- If the results are normal or as expected, we will notify you through text message.
  如果你的结果正常或是如预期的结果一样，我们会以短信的方式通知你。
  ★ 短语 as expected 与预期的（结果、状况、情况）一样

- I visited my grandma in the hospital yesterday. She looked very calm but still a bit weak.
  我昨天去医院探视奶奶。她看起来很平静，但还是有一点虚弱。
  ★ 语法 "look"是"感官动词"，这类的动词后面都接形容词，不管是原级、比较级或最高级形容词都可以。常见的感官动词有：become（变成）、feel（感觉起来）、look（看起来）、smell（闻起来）、sound（听起来）、taste（尝起来）。

- When I walked into the door, my grandmother welcomed me with a smile, which means she is feeling better now.
  当我走进门的时候，奶奶用微笑迎接我，这表示奶奶的状况又好转了一些。
  ★ 短语 welcome A with... 用～欢迎 A，用～迎接 A

在国外都说这几句

- My grandmother laughed as I told her a funny joke I **heard from** school.

  我跟奶奶讲了一个我在学校听到的笑话，她听了之后笑得很开心。

  ★ 短语 hear from... 从～听到

- I asked the nurse to keep her voice down as she walked **in and out** of the room.

  当护士进出病房的时候，我请她尽量降低音量。

  ★ 短语 in and out 进进出出

- My sister always knows how to **cheer** my grandmother **up**.

  我妹妹总是知道要怎么做才能让奶奶开心。

  ★ 短语 cheer A up 使A高兴起来，帮A打气

- I could **say a** little **prayer for you** to give you some emotional support.

  我可以为你祈祷，在情绪上支持你。

  ★ 短语 say a prayer (for A) （为A）祈祷

- I just brought my grandmother a **BLT** sandwich and some hot soup.

  我为奶奶带了一个培根生菜番茄三明治和热汤。

  ★ 短语 "BLT"是指"Bacon, Lettuce and Tomato"。

- I admire your courage in whatever you're **suffering through**.

  我很钦佩你挺过病痛的勇气。

  ★ 短语 suffer through... 挨过～，遭受～

- Thank you for bringing me these flowers. They **made my day**.

  谢谢你带这些花给我。它们让我很开心。

  ★ 短语 make my day 让我今天很开心

- Do you want to listen to some music or watch TV to **keep you occupied** in bed?

  你想在床上听音乐或看电视让自己找点事做吗？

  ★ 短语 keep A occupied 让A保持忙碌，让A有事做

- My granddaughter is funny and thoughtful. **Having her around** me makes me feel so much better.

  我孙女很幽默又体贴。有她在身边，我就觉得好多了。

  ★ 短语 have...around 在～身旁，围绕在～

Dialogue 在国外都说这几句

- Thank you for taking care of me in the hospital and making me laugh.
  谢谢你来医院照顾我并逗我笑。
  ★ 短语 take care of A　照顾A，关怀A

- A get-well card, a call from a friend and some fresh flowers brought me happiness.
  一张早日康复卡，朋友打来的一通电话或是一些新鲜的花就让我觉得很幸福。
  ★ 短语 "get-well card"　是指祝人早日康复的卡片。

- When I am in pain, I will call my best friend and try to distract myself from it.
  当我感到痛苦时，我会打电话给我的好朋友，来转移我的注意力。
  ★ 短语 in pain　感到痛苦

- You are so brave. How do you deal with all of this?
  你好勇敢。你是怎么处理这些事的？
  ★ 短语 deal with...　处理～，应付～

- Is there anything I can do to make you more at home?
  我能做些什么事，让你觉得比较舒服吗？
  ★ 短语 at home　自在的；在家的

- You need to be careful with what you eat at home, no more junk food.
  你在家要注意饮食均衡，不可以再吃垃圾食品了。

- If you have no idea what to say, then just stand by quietly.
  如果你不知道要说什么，只要安静地给予支持就行了。
  ★ 短语 stand by...　站在～旁边；支持～

- I totally understand what you are going through.
  我完全了解你正在经历的事情。
  ★ 短语 go through...　经历～；通过～

- In order to stay healthy, it's time to quit smoking.
  为了保持健康，该戒烟了。
  ★ 短语 quit + v.-ing　停止～；戒掉～

Chapter 2 娱乐与休闲
Leisure Time & Recreation Activities

Unit 5 | 适度的购物是对自己的犒赏
Unit 6 | 令人小鹿乱撞的约会
Unit 7 | 友谊是人生的调味品
Unit 8 | 家是永远的避风港
Unit 9 | 大自然就是我的家

跟任何人都可以用英语聊聊天

Unit 5 适度的购物是对自己的犒赏

[生活便利贴]

逛街、买衣服，人人都爱！由于网络的发达，只要坐在家中，想要购买的东西只要点点鼠标就有专人送货到家，有些甚至在24小时以内就可以收到。不过，不管是在实体商店消费、还是在网上购物，结账前都要先确认尺寸和退款方式，以及店家是否提供商品退货期，以避免不必要的纷争。这个单元就让我们来看看，购物时有什么英语单词是需要注意的。

Vocabulary 在国外都用这些词

MP3 02-01

accessory
[ək'sesərɪ]
n 配件；首饰

budget
['bʌdʒɪt]
n 预算

shopping spree
ph 疯狂的购物

world
[wɜːld]
n 世界

spring
[sprɪŋ]
n 春天

designer brand
ph 名牌、设计师款

guilty
['gɪltɪ]
a 愧疚的

charity party
ph 慈善舞会

ball gown
ph 长礼服

cheongsam
[tʃɒŋ'sæm]
n 旗袍

colour
['kʌlə]
n 颜色

malfunction
[ˌmæl'fʌŋkʃn]
n 故障

warranty
['wɒrəntɪ]
n（产品的）保证书

valid
['vælɪd]
a 合法的，有效的

discount
['dɪskaʊnt]
n 折扣

bargain
['bɑːgən]
v 讨价还价

employee
[ɪm'plɔɪiː]
n 员工

promotion
[prə'məʊʃn]
n 促销

在国外都说这几句

- The department store has the newest fashion brands on women's and men's clothing and accessories.

  这家百货公司提供最新的男女服装及配饰时尚品牌。

  ★ 语法 department store 是指"百货公司",通常指楼层较多的购物场所。而英语的 mall 是指"购物中心",占地广大,通常只有一到二层,不一定是在室内。outlet 则是指"折扣／打折中心",通常是在开放的空间,各品牌树立在独栋空间,专门贩卖过季商品,时常提供大幅折扣。

- Our best friend's birthday is coming. We have to buy her something nice and throw her a surprise party.

  我们最好的朋友生日快到了。我们必须要买礼物送她并且为她举办惊喜派对。

  ★ 短语 have / has to 必须

- That dress looks amazing on you. You should totally wear it for your date tonight.

  这件礼服穿在你身上很好看,你今天晚上去约会的时候应该穿它。

  ★ 语法 "某物 + look(s) + a. + on + 某人"的意思是"某人穿（戴）某物看起来很～"。

- I spent too much money this month, so I can only do window-shopping today.

  我这个月花钱太多了,所以今天只逛不买。

  ★ 短语 window-shopping 只浏览,不花钱购物

- Look at all the discounts the mall offers. It's going to save me a lot of money.

  看看购物中心提供的这些折扣,这样我可以省下不少钱。

  ★ 短语 look at 看,检查,考虑,研究

- The shoes are on sale. You are not going to get another chance like this, so don't miss it.

  这些鞋子在打折。你之后不会再看到这样的折扣,所以千万不要错过。

  ★ 短语 on sale 拍卖中,打折,削价出售

- If you are available tonight, how about going to the shopping mall with me? We can go on a shopping spree.

  如果你今晚有空,要不要跟我一起去购物中心？我们可以大买特买。

  ★ 语法 "how about"通常有"建议"的意味,后面可接名词或动词,若接动词,要改成 v-ing 的形式。

- You can buy anything you want as long as you have the budget.

  只要你的预算够,你想买什么都可以。

  ★ 短语 as long as 只要,既然

在国外都说这几句

- The dress looks stunning. However, I don't think I will be able to afford it.
  这件连衣裙好美。但是我想我可能买不起它。
  ★ 短语 be able to... 能够做~

- Shopping is one of the most exciting things in the world. It always makes me happy.
  购物是世上最令人兴奋的事之一了，它总是能够让我开心。
  ★ 短语 in the world 全世界，世界上

- There is nothing like shopping to make me feel happy.
  没有比逛街血拼可以让我更开心的事了。
  ★ 短语 there is nothing like... 没有比~更棒、更好的了

- These brands are very difficult to pronounce; I don't think I can say them right.
  这些名牌很难念，我觉得我没有办法正确地念出它们的名字。

- It always pumps me up to go shopping with my friends.
  跟朋友一起逛街购物让我觉得非常兴奋。
  ★ 短语 pump A up 让 A 感到兴奋、开心

- Before shopping, you can spend some time on doing research and comparing the prices, and make sure you don't pay too much for something.
  在购物之前，你可以先花点时间做好功课、比较价格，确保不会花冤枉钱。
  ★ 短语 do research 做调查，做研究

- My colleague needed someone else's advice on shoes, so she invited me to go with her tonight.
  我的同事需要别人给她一些对鞋子的意见，所以她邀请我晚上跟她一起去逛逛鞋店。
  ★ 语法 invite + 某人 + to... 邀请某人去做~

- This shopping mall is the place where I can buy high quality products and enjoy fine dining.
  在这家购物中心，我可以买到品质良好的商品以及享用一顿美餐。
  ★ 语法 关系副词 where 可以引导状语从句，但因其代替从句中的副词，因而称之为关系副词。

- The boutique offers one-of-a-kind dresses. You will never see the same thing on someone else.
  这家精品店提供独一无二的连衣裙。你绝对不会跟别人撞衫。
  ★ 短语 one-of-a-kind 独一无二的

在国外都说这几句

- What are the top 10 shopping places in California? I can't wait to explore all of them.

  加州十大购物天堂在哪里？我等不及要去一一探索它们了。

  ★ 短语 "top + 名词"是指"最棒的、最优良的～"。

- Compared to online shopping, I prefer to shop in real stores because I can try things on.

  比起网络购物，我更喜欢在实体店买东西，因为这样我可以试穿（试用）。

  ★ 短语 compare to　与～相比

- I am looking forward to updating my wardrobe with the spring collections.

  我很期待把我衣柜里的旧衣服淘汰，换成今年春天的新系列产品。

  ★ 语法 "look forward to + v-ing"是指"很期待……"的意思，后面接动词时，一定要使用动名词 v-ing 形式。

- Here's a list of tips you should follow when doing online shopping.

  这是一张清单，上面列有网络购物时你需要参考的小诀窍。

  ★ 短语 a list of...　～的清单，～的单子

- There is no way that I would quit my shopping habit. It's part of my life.

  我绝不可能戒掉我的消费习惯。这是我人生中不可或缺的部分。

  ★ 短语 no way　不可能，一点也不，绝不

- Susie is a compulsive buyer. She spends money even when she doesn't have any.

  苏西是个强迫性消费者。就算没钱，她还是要买东西。

  ★ 语法 "She spends money even when she doesn't have any."句中的最后一个单词 any，其实是"any (money)"的省略形式。

- Jennifer decided to spend all her savings on a designer name bag.

  珍妮弗决定拿所有的存款来买一个有设计师签名的包。

  ★ 语法 "spend... on + n."是指"花费…在 n. 上"的意思。

- If the act of buying makes you feel good, it is very likely that you are a shopaholic.

  如果只是买东西这个行为让你感到开心，你有可能是个购物狂。

  ★ 短语 make A feel...　让 A 感到～

在国外都说这几句

- I'd like to go to the shopping center tonight so I could buy a new pair of boots.
  今晚我想要到购物中心买一双新的靴子。
  ★ 短语 a pair of + 复数名词，一对～，一双～，一副～

- Meg sometimes feels insecure without her credit cards.
  没有信用卡，梅格有时会感到没有安全感。
  ★ 语法 feel 在此作动词，后面接形容词（不管是原级或比较级），表示"感到～"。

- Do you sometimes feel guilty or ashamed after buying all the things you don't need?
  在你花钱买了一堆你不需要的东西之后，你会有罪恶感或感到羞愧吗？
  ★ 语法 after 在此是表示时间的连词，用来表示句中两个动作发生的时间先后顺序，表示"在～之后"。

- Shopping is a good way to get the stress out of your system, but we should do it rationally.
  购物是减压的好方法，但我们应该理性购物。
  ★ 短语 get... out of your system 将～宣泄、释放出体外

- Victoria's addiction to shopping is out of control. She will be in big trouble if she keeps acting like this.
  维多利亚的购物瘾已经失控了。她如果一直这样下去会惹上大麻烦。
  ★ 短语 out of control 失去控制，不受控制

- In my opinion, shopping is fun but you have to learn to do it responsibly and to not overspend.
  我认为，购物非常有趣，但是你必须为你的购物方式、行为负责，避免超支。
  ★ 短语 in A's opinion 对 A 来说

- Monica is invited to a charity party tomorrow night. That's why she has to shop for a new dress for it.
  莫妮卡受邀参加明天晚上的慈善舞会。为此，今晚她必须买一件新的连衣裙。
  ★ 语法 That's why... 这就是为什么，因此

- This online shop offers a great selection of beautifully designed dresses in all different sizes.
  这家网店有许多好看的礼服款式并且提供各种尺码。
  ★ 短语 a great selection of... 许多～的选择

 Finish!!

Dialogue 在国外都说这几句

- Christmas is around the corner. I have a lot of shopping to do and need to decorate the house for the party.

  圣诞节就要到了。我有很多东西要买，还要为办派对布置房子。

  ★ 短语 "around the corner" 有两个不同的意思，一个是指"即将来临"，另一个是指"就在街角"的意思。

- The beautiful coat is for sale. It has never been worn before. If you want it, I can give you discount.

  这件美丽的大衣待出售。它还没被穿过。如果你想要的话，我可以给你折扣。

  ★ 短语 for sale 待出售，供出售

- This dress looks amazing and comfortable. The most important is that it slips right on.

  这件连衣裙看起来很棒也很舒服。重点是它很好穿。

  ★ 短语 slip on / off （匆忙地）穿／脱

- These formal two-piece suits are designed for businesswomen.

  这些正式的两件式套装是专为职场女性设计的。

  ★ 短语 be designed for... 为～设计的

- Angela feels like a princess in this breath-taking ball gown.

  穿上这件超赞的舞会礼服后，安吉拉觉得自己像个公主。

  ★ 短语 feel like... 觉得像个～

- This store covers a wide range of styles of clothing that will surprise you!

  这间店提供许多不同款式的衣服，一定会给你惊喜。

  ★ 短语 a wide range of... 多款风格／款式的～

- This traditional cheongsam is strikingly vivid and practical.

  这件传统旗袍色彩鲜艳、十分抢眼，而且很实用。

  ★ 语法 strikingly 在此为副词，修饰形容词"vivid"。

- Excuse me. I would like to try this dress on. Does it come in different colours?

  不好意思。我想要试穿这件礼服。请问它有别的颜色吗？

  ★ 短语 try on 试穿

049

在国外都说这几句

- The fitting rooms are on your right hand side. Let me know if there is anything else I can help you with.
  试衣间就在你的右手边。如果有什么其他需要帮忙的，请告诉我。
  ★ 短语 on the right / left hand side 右手 / 左手边

- How much does this scarf cost?
  这条围巾多少钱？
  ★ 语法 "how much" 在此为 "问金钱多少" 的疑问词，意思是 "多少钱"。

- This leather jacket might be too tight for me. Do you have this in a bigger size?
  这件皮衣对我来说太紧了。你们有尺寸再大一点的吗？
  ★ 语法 too... for A 对 A 来说太～

- I'm looking for a pair of jeans that will go well with my new shoes.
  我正在找一件可以搭配我新鞋子的牛仔裤。
  ★ 短语 "look for..." 的意思是 "寻找～"，通常表示还在寻找、还没找到。

- Do you offer tailoring service? I need to make this dress smaller.
  你们提供更改尺寸的服务吗？我需要把这件连衣裙改小一点。
  ★ 语法 smaller 在此是 small 的比较级，表示 "比较小"。

- When you try on clothes, you need to be careful not to get a lipstick stain on them.
  当你试穿衣服时，小心不要把口红沾到衣服上。
  ★ 短语 be careful 小心，注意

- If you're shopping for underwear, normally the clerk will not allow you to try them on.
  如果你要买贴身衣物，通常店员不会让你试穿。
  ★ 短语 shop for... 要买～东西

- When I pulled the shirt on and off, I broke the zipper by accident.
  当我穿脱上衣时，不小心把拉链弄坏了。
  ★ 短语 by accident 偶然地、意外地、不是故意地，等于 "accidentally"。

- I am afraid that you have to pay for the shirts you ruined.
  恐怕你必须要买下你弄坏的上衣。
  ★ 语法 afraid 这个词后面可以接名词、动词不定式 to + v. 或 that + 从句。

在国外都说这几句

- Shopping can make people feel satisfied and it can also boost the economic growth.
  购物可让人们感到满足，此外，还可以帮助经济增长。
  ★ 短语 be/feel satisfied　感到满足

- In a word, the reasons that can change the way people shop are convenience, price and customer service that the stores offer.
  总之，人们的消费习惯是会因为店家所提供的方便性、价格以及顾客服务而有所改变。
  ★ 短语 in a word　简言之、一言以蔽之

- What is your refund policy?
  退款的规定是什么？
  ★ 短语 refund policy　退款规定

- Providing the product is not damaged, you can return it and get your refund within 30 days of purchase.
  只要商品没损坏，你可以在 30 天内退回商品，我们会退款给你。
  ★ 短语 providing...　只要～，如果～

- Most stores in Australia will give you a refund with no questions asked if you wish to return the product within 30 days.
  如果你想要在 30 天内退货，澳大利亚的大部分商店都会无条件退款给你。
  ★ 短语 no questions asked　无条件的，不须理由的

- When you purchase something online, we hope our service can reach your satisfaction completely.
  当您线上购物时，我们希望我们的服务能让您满意。
  ★ 语法 completely 在此是副词，用来修饰形容词 satisfied（满足的），表示"完全满意"。

- Customers can return an undamaged mobile phone with all its accessories within 30 days of purchase for a full refund.
  购买物品后 30 天之内，顾客都可以将未损坏的手机以及所有原有的配件退回，即可享有全额退款。
  ★ 短语 a full refund　全额退款

- Most customers are more comfortable buying things from shops that offer return policies.
  大多数的顾客在提供退货服务的店家消费会感到比较安心。
  ★ 短语 "most + 名词"的意思是"大部分的～"。

在国外都说这几句

- If the laptop does not meet your expectations, you can bring it back. If possible, please let us know what the problem is.
  若笔记本电脑不符合您的期待，您可以退货。如果方便的话，也请告知我们是哪里出了问题。
  ★ 短语 bring... back 把～带回，在此则是指"退货"的意思。

- All products are returnable as long as they are in the same condition as when purchased.
  只要物品与购买时的状态一样，所有物品都可退货。
  ★ 语法 若要说明两个动作或两种情况同时发生，有三个词可用，分别是 when, while, as，中文解释都是"当～的时候"。有些情况，它们可通用。

- This pair of pants does not fit me. If you don't have the right size for me, can I exchange them for something else?
  这条裤子与我的尺寸不合。如果你们没有适合我的尺寸，我可以换成其他的商品吗？
  ★ 短语 exchange A for B 用 A 交换 B

- The majority of stores will request a receipt if you wish to return or exchange the product.
  如果你想要退换货的话，绝大部分的商家都会要求你出示发票。
  ★ 短语 the majority of... 绝大部分的～

- I went back to the store because some threads are falling out. The clerk apologized for it and asked me if I want to get a refund or exchange it for something else.
  因为衣服上有些线头脱落了，所以我把衣服拿回了店里。店员感到非常抱歉，并且询问我想要退款还是要换其他的商品。
  ★ 短语 apologize for... 对～感到抱歉

- I'd like to return this flat screen TV. There are some malfunctions with it so I'm just not happy with it.
  我想退这台平板电视。它好像有点故障，所以我不是很满意。
  ★ 短语 be happy with... 对～感到高兴，对～感到满意

- The clerk said this item is not refundable because it was on clearance and the refund policy for this particular item was stated on the receipt.
  这件商品购买的时候已经是最后折扣，所以店员说无法办理退款，详细的退款条款也都标注在发票上面。
  ★ 短语 on clearance 商品出清。在国外买东西一般来说只要是 30 天以内都可以办理退货。但如果店家对该商品做了商品出清，那么店员通常都会告知顾客要仔细地检查商品，因为该商品一旦售出就无法办理退换货了。

在国外都说这几句

- Just bring the receipt in and show it to customer service, and they will **take care of** it for you as soon as possible.
  只要把收据带来，然后出示给客服，他们就会尽快帮你解决。
  ★ 短语 take care of... 照顾~；处理~

- The refund policy usually is not too strict, but customers should not **take it for granted**.
  退款规定通常不会太严格，但顾客还是不应该视为理所当然。
  ★ 短语 take... for granted 把~视为理所当然

- If the store does not offer a refund, I will not **let it go** without an explanation.
  如果商店不肯办理退款，又不给我一个合理的解释，我是不会就轻易罢休的。
  ★ 短语 let it go 算了，罢休

- Always keep receipts and make sure to put them somewhere safe.
  一定要留着收据，并且要把收据放好，以免遗失。

- I don't remember when exactly I purchased the oven. Can you check a purchase record **in the system** and see if the warranty is still valid?
  我不记得什么时候买这个烤箱的。你可以查一下你们系统的购买记录，并看看是否还在保修期吗？
  ★ 短语 in the system （在）系统中

- Our refund policy may not **allow you to** return a product or get a refund if the product is damaged.
  若商品已经受损，我们则无法提供退换货的服务。
  ★ 短语 allow sb. + to... 允许某人做~

- Let us know if you have any problem with the product or our service and we will make it right.
  若您对商品或服务不满意，请让我们知道，我们会改善。
  ★ 语法 if 是连词，中文意思是"假如"。

- If you are not satisfied with your product, make sure you return it **as soon as possible**.
  若您对商品不满意，请确保尽快退还。
  ★ 短语 as soon as possible 尽快

跟任何人都可以用英语聊聊天

Unit 6 令人小鹿乱撞的约会

[生活便利贴]

约会是一门大学问，尤其是第一次约会总是让你心头小鹿乱撞，所以需要非常注意，像地点的选择、适宜的服装都需要细心规划。除此之外，准时赴约、带着愉快的心情出门、表现体贴以及注重礼貌都非常重要，要给对方留下美好的第一印象。让我们来看看怎么用英语规划出美好的约会吧！

Vocabulary 在国外都用这些词

MP3 02-11

restaurant
['rɛstrɒnt]
n 餐厅

photo
['fəʊtəʊ]
n 照片

equipment
[ɪ'kwɪpmənt]
n 装备，工具

topnotch
['tɒpnɒtʃ]
a 最高级的

reservation
[,rezə'veɪʃn]
n 预定，预约

pistol
['pɪstl]
n 手枪

stingy
['stɪndʒɪ]
a 吝啬的

casino
[kə'siːnəʊ]
n 赌场

makeup
['meɪk,ʌp]
n 化妆品

roller coaster
n 过山车

planetarium
[,plænɪ'teərɪəm]
n 天文馆

compliment
['kɒmplɪmənt]
n/v 赞美

adventurous
[əd'ventʃərəs]
a 具有冒险精神的

mountain
['maʊntən]
n 山

humor
['hjuːmə]
n 幽默感

stressful
['stresfl]
a 紧张的，压力重的

enjoyment
[ɪn'dʒɔɪmənt]
n 享受

anxiety
[æŋ'zaɪətɪ]
n 忧虑

 Finish!!

 在国外都说这几句

- When planning a first date, it's a good idea to pick a nice restaurant and get to know each other over a dinner.

  在计划第一次约会的时候,可以考虑选择一家好餐厅,并通过晚餐来好好认识对方。

  ★ 短语 get to... 开始~,着手于~

- When taking a woman out on a date, you should do your best to plan it well and always be on time.

  带女生出去约会时,你应该要好好规划约会行程并且要准时。

  ★ 短语 on time 准时

- Do you have any topnotch suggestions to help make my date perfect?

  你有什么好建议可以帮助我有个美好的约会吗?

  ★ 语法 "help (to) + v." 后面接动词时,可省略 to。

- I'm planning something special for my date because I want to give her a nice first impression.

  我正在为我的约会对象计划一些特别的东西,因为我想要给她留下好的第一印象。

  ★ 短语 plan... 计划~

- If your date is interested in art or history, it might be a good idea to take him/her to the museum.

  如果你的约会对象对艺术或历史有兴趣的话,那么带他/她去博物馆也许是个很好的选择。

  ★ 短语 take A to... 带 A 去~

- Taking your date to the museum is risky because it's not everybody's cup of tea.

  带你的约会对象到博物馆是有风险的,因为不是每个人都对博物馆有兴趣。

  ★ 短语 one's cup of tea 合某人的胃口、兴趣

- Do not be too stingy on the first date; otherwise, it is likely that you will blow it.

  第一次约会的时候不要太吝啬,不然的话,你很有可能会搞砸。

  ★ 短语 blow it 搞砸

- My boyfriend planned a movie night. We are going to see a chick flick in the cinema.

  我的男友计划了一个电影之夜。我们要到电影院去看爱情片。

  ★ 短语 chick flick 以年轻女性为主要观众的电影,通常以爱情为主题。

在国外都说这几句

- My girlfriend and I are going away for the weekend.
  我和我女朋友周末要出去度假。
  ★ 短语 go away 外出（指度假）

- Would you like to grab some coffee at my favourite café and get to know each other?
  你想要去我最喜欢的咖啡馆喝杯咖啡，然后聊聊天多认识对方吗？
  ★ 语法 each other 彼此，互相、一般用于两个之间的关系。

- We are about to go to the beach and try to cool down on this hot day, care to join us?
  这么热的天，我们正准备要去海边消暑，你想要跟我们一起去吗？
  ★ 短语 care to 喜欢、想要

- Going on the roller coaster in the theme park can be a good idea to establish your relationship.
  去游乐园坐过山车，是个让感情加温的好主意。
  ★ 短语 theme park 主题乐园

- It's so embarrassing to find out that I forgot to bring my wallet with me when checking out.
  我要结账的时候才发现忘记带钱包，真的是很难为情。
  ★ 语法 it's embarrassing... ～很丢脸的，～很难为情的

- My girlfriend and I are both adventurous. We have made up our minds to try some extreme sports.
  我和我的女友都充满冒险精神，我们下定决心要去尝试一些极限运动。
  ★ 短语 make up A's mind A下定决心

- As we are both animal lovers, do you feel like going to the zoo with me?
  既然我们都喜爱动物，你想要跟我一起去动物园吗？
  ★ 短语 animal lover 喜爱动物的人

- Let's go to the park. We can fly a kite or take a walk.
  我们一起去公园吧。我们可以放风筝或是散步。
  ★ 短语 fly a kite 放风筝

- Yesterday, we strolled through the weekend market hand in hand.
  昨天我们手牵着手一起逛假日市场。
  ★ 短语 stroll through 散步、闲逛

在国外都说这几句

- **Commenting** on the current political issue with your boyfriend/girlfriend is not recommended.
  建议最好不要跟你的男朋友／女朋友评论现今的政治议题。
  ★ 短语 comment on　发表意见，评论

- My boyfriend and I are both rock fans and we love going to rock concerts and **singing out loud** with the band.
  我和我男朋友都是摇滚乐迷，我们喜欢去摇滚演唱会并且跟着乐团一起大声唱歌。
  ★ 短语 sing out loud　大声唱出来

- We should **take a hike** in the woods as an adventure and experience Mother Nature.
  我们应该去森林徒步探险并且体验大自然的美好。
  ★ 短语 take a hike　去健行，去徒步旅行

- My boyfriend is crazy about history. I'm going to show him some of the famous **historical sites**.
  我的男友对历史很感兴趣。因此我要带他去探索几个著名的历史景点。
  ★ 短语 historical site　历史景点，遗迹

- Would you like to **go bowling** with me tomorrow night?
  明天晚上你想和我去打保龄球吗？
  ★ 短语 go bowling　打保龄球

- We went to a diner last night and shared a strawberry milkshake. Isn't that romantic?
  我们昨晚一起吃饭，还共享一杯草莓奶昔。是不是很浪漫？
  ★ 语法 "and" 是连词，用于连接前后两个意思相同的从句，或有时间先后顺序的两个句子。

- Do you **feel like going** to the local art galleries? They have really good installation art.
  你想去看看当地的画廊吗？那里有很棒的装置艺术。
  ★ 语法 feel like + v-ing　想要做～

- How about **going for a spin** and getting some fresh air?
  我们出去兜兜风，呼吸一些新鲜的空气，你觉得怎么样？
  ★ 短语 go for a spin　开、骑车去兜兜风

在国外都说这几句

- My boyfriend loves *Resident Evil* so we spend most of our time playing video games.
  我男友超爱《生化危机》。所以我们大部分时间都是在一起玩电玩。

- First dates can be stressful. All you need to do is be yourself and hope for the best.
  第一次约会压力可能会很大。你只需要做自己，然后希望有好的结果。
  ★ 短语 hope for the best　希望获得好结果

- Don't look at your phone all the time when you are on a first date. Eye contact is very important.
  第一次约会的时候，不要老是盯着手机。跟对方的眼神接触非常重要。
  ★ 短语 all the time　老是，总是

- Do you want to take a road trip with me to the country? It's gonna be fun.
  你想要和我一起开车到郊外旅行吗？一定会很有趣的。
  ★ 短语 "road trip" 的意思是 "开车旅游"。通常没有特定的目的地，只要开车沿路有好玩的景点，就会停车下来游玩的旅游。

- I am in the mood for something different. Let's try the drive-in theater instead of the cinema in the shopping center.
  我想尝试不一样的东西。我们不要去购物中心里面的电影院，改去露天的汽车电影院试试看。
  ★ 短语 in the mood for　有做~的心情、有心情做~

- I just filled up a picnic basket with sandwiches, wine, cheese and crackers. We are going to have a great afternoon.
  我刚把野餐篮装满了三明治、葡萄酒、奶酪和饼干。我们下午一定会玩得很开心。
  ★ 短语 fill up　装满，填满

- What do you think of going on a city tour on the horse carriage?
  你觉得坐马车游览市区怎么样？
  ★ 短语 city tour　市区游览，导览

- Let's not act like tourists and only go to those commercial tourist sites. Can you take me somewhere that only the locals know?
  我们不要像游客一样只去那些很商业化的观光景点。你可不可以带我去一些只有当地人知道的地方？
  ★ 短语 act like...　扮演~，举动像~一样

在国外都说这几句

- We should take a photo here to remember this perfect moment.
  我们应该在这里拍张照，留下美好的回忆。
  ★ 短语 take a photo　拍照，照相

- We can go on a bike ride by the river and enjoy the beauty of nature.
  我们可以沿着河边骑自行车，好好地享受大自然之美。
  ★ 短语 bike ride　骑自行车

- A nearby paint ball facility just opened. It looks very exciting. Do you want to go with me?
  附近一家新的彩弹射击场刚开业。看起来非常有趣。你想要跟我一起去吗？
  ★ 短语 paint ball　彩弹射击

- Last night, my boyfriend and I camped out and had our very first kiss under the stars.
  昨晚，我和我男友到户外露营，并在星光下第一次亲吻对方。
  ★ 短语 under the stars　在星光下，在夜空中

- Most people think of a candle light dinner, a movie and gazing at the stars as the ideal romantic date.
  大部分的人都觉得烛光晚餐、电影以及看星星是理想的浪漫约会。
  ★ 短语 think of A as...　把 A 看作是～

- We always go out for dinner if there is something special to celebrate.
  如果遇到特别的事情需要庆祝，我们都会出去吃晚餐庆祝一下。
  ★ 短语 go out for...　出去做～

- On our first date, we participated in a wine tasting day tour.
  第一次约会时，我们参加了一日品酒团。
  ★ 短语 participate in...　参加～，参与～

- We went to the sea world yesterday. It was the very first time I saw a whale in person.
  昨天我们去海洋世界，这是我第一次亲眼看见鲸鱼。
  ★ 短语 in person　亲身，亲自，本人

- I made a reservation for a couple's full body massage at a spa.
  我已经在水疗中心预订了伴侣全身按摩。
  ★ 短语 make a reservation for...　预订～，预约～

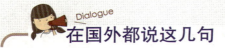 在国外都说这几句

- There is nothing better than bonding with someone you have feelings for.

  没有什么比与心仪的对象交流谈心更好了。

  ★ 短语 bond with...　与～交流，与～连结

- Most people do the same things on a date. How about we volunteer for something meaningful to do and help the people who are in need?

  大多数人的约会都千篇一律。我们何不当义工做些有意义的事？也可以帮助需要帮助的人们。

  ★ 短语 volunteer for...　自愿服务～，自愿做～

- I want to spend time with my girlfriend, but I also want to make time for myself every now and then.

  我想花时间跟女友在一起，但有时候我也想要好好地享受一个人的时光。

  ★ 短语 make time　腾出时间

- Let's go to Las Vegas and try our luck at a casino.

  我们去拉斯维加斯的赌场试试运气吧。

  ★ 短语 try A's luck　试试A的运气，赌赌A的运气

- My boyfriend is taking me out to a romantic candlelit dinner for our anniversary.

  我男友在饭店为我准备了浪漫的烛光晚餐庆祝我们的周年纪念日。

  ★ 短语 take A out to...　带A出去（做）～

- I am not an outdoor type of person. Can we head to the planetarium to explore the great universe?

  我不喜欢户外活动。我们可以去天文馆探索宇宙伟大的奥秘吗？

  ★ 短语 head to...　出发～，前往～

- If you are into tennis, we should go to Melbourne to watch the Australian Open.

  如果你喜欢网球，我们应该去墨尔本看澳洲网球公开赛。

  ★ 短语 A be into...　A对～有兴趣

- Rock climbing is not only fun but also helps couples build trust.

  一起攀岩不只有趣，还能增进情侣之间的信任感。

  ★ 短语 build trust　增进信任感

Dialogue 在国外都说这几句

- Doing the same thing over and over again on your dates can be boring. Sometimes we should think outside the box and plan something special to create a memorable moment.
  约会的时候老是做同样的事情会变得很无聊。有时候你要跳脱平常的思维模式，做一些特别的计划，这样才会让对方印象深刻。
  ★ 短语 think outside the box　反向思考，跳脱框框的思考模式

- Sometimes my girlfriend and I will go out separately to a club and meet each other as if we were strangers. It creates a different kind of sparkle.
  我跟我女朋友有时候会分头去夜店，然后假装彼此不认识，重新邂逅。这样可以制造不一样的火花。
  ★ 语法 "as if"的意思是"仿佛、似乎、好像"。可用于陈述语气，表示说话者所描述的是真的或是极有可能发生的情况。但当说话人认为句子所陈述的不是真实的或几乎不可能发生的情况时，谓语动词需用一般过去式或者过去完成式。

- I am going to surprise my girlfriend with a hot air balloon ride for her birthday.
  我女朋友生日的时候，我准备要带她去坐热气球，给她一个惊喜。
  ★ 短语 hot air balloon　热气球

- When going on the late night dates, I love going to a late movie and then having some late night snack.
  深夜约会时，我最爱去看一场午夜场电影，接着去吃夜宵。

- I like to watch the sunrise from a mountain and view the entire city which is illuminated by the sun.
  我想到山上看日出并且看整个城市被阳光笼罩的景色。

- Do you want to go fishing? I have all the equipment here, and we can go right away.
  你想去钓鱼吗？我这边什么装备都有，我们可以马上就去。
  ★ 短语 right away　立刻，马上

- Let's have a snow ball fight. You can team up with me and I'm sure we can defeat the other couples.
  我们来打雪仗吧，我相信我们两个合作一定可以打败其他情侣。
  ★ 短语 team up with...　跟~合作

在国外都说这几句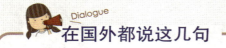

- Water pistol shootouts can be a lot of fun, but make sure you bring extra clothes, otherwise you might catch a cold easily when you get soaked.
  射击水枪非常好玩，但要记得多带几件衣服，不然全身湿透时会很容易感冒。
  ★ 短语 a lot of...　很多～

- Having high tea at a fancy tea house with your loved one is enjoyable.
  跟心爱的另一半到高级的茶馆享用英式三层下午茶真是一大享受。
  ★ 短语 high tea　（英式）三层式下午茶

- I love my boyfriend because he has a great sense of humour and always makes me laugh.
  我爱我的男友，因为他非常有幽默感而且总是能逗我笑。
  ★ 短语 make A laugh　逗 A 笑，使 A 发笑

- You don't need put on any makeup. I love the way you are.
  你不需要上任何的妆。我就是爱你原本的样子。
  ★ 短语 put on　在皮肤上涂某物

- Stars may brighten the night, just like your eyes can brighten up my life.
  星辰照亮夜空，就像你的双眼可以照亮我的人生。
  ★ 短语 brighten up　照亮

- Your smile always makes my day.
  你的笑容总是让我每天都很开心。
  ★ 短语 make A's day　令 A 很开心

- I like it when you stand up for yourself.
  我喜欢你总是能够捍卫自己的权利。
  ★ 短语 stand up for　支持～，捍卫～，维护～

- Where would you like to spend your vacation? We should plan ahead.
  你想要去哪里度假呢？我们应该提前计划。
  ★ 短语 plan ahead　提前计划

- Complimenting your date is an art. You have to wait for the right moment.
  赞美你的约会对象是一门艺术，你必须选择适当的时机。
  ★ 短语 wait for...　等候～

在国外都说这几句

- **Talking to you takes** my anxieties and worries **away**.
  跟你说话让我的忧虑和烦恼都消失了。
  ★ 短语 take... away 带走～，拿走～

- I **am madly in love with** you. Would you please go on a date with me?
  我疯狂地爱上你。你愿意跟我约会吗？
  ★ 短语 be in love with A 爱上～，与～陷入爱河

- I'm so **proud of** being a part of your life.
  我很骄傲能成为你生活的一部分。
  ★ 短语 be proud of... 为～感到骄傲，为～感到自豪

- **Thanks for** always being there for me when I need you.
  谢谢你总是在我需要你的时候陪在我的身边。
  ★ 短语 thanks for... 感谢～

- Is there anything that you would want to do **by yourself**?
  有什么事情是你想自己一个人做的吗？
  ★ 短语 by oneself 自己，单独地，独自地

- I want to be with you **forever and ever**. Nothing can tear us apart.
  我想永远永远和你在一起。没有什么可以把我们分开。
  ★ 短语 forever and ever 永永远远

- Your smile **lights up** my life, I will never get bored of it.
  你的微笑照亮我的人生，我永远不会看腻。
  ★ 短语 light up 点燃，照亮，容光焕发

- I love talking to you. You have **a** great **sense of humour**.
  我很喜欢跟你说话。你真的很有幽默感。
  ★ 短语 a sense a humour 幽默感

- I think we **have a connection** here. I'd like to know more about you.
  我觉得我们很来电，我想要进一步多认识你一点。
  ★ 短语 have a connection 来电，心动

- You seem to have lost some weight. Have you been **working out**?
  你似乎瘦了一点。最近有在健身吗？
  ★ 短语 work out 健身，锻炼

跟任何人都可以用英语聊聊天

Unit 7 友谊是人生的调味品

[生活便利贴]

朋友，是人际关系中非常重要的交际对象。真正的朋友通常会对彼此诚实、为对方着想、互相信任、聆听对方的烦恼并适时给予建议。对于大部分的人而言，朋友是可以信任的伙伴，因此朋友在人的一生中扮演着非常重要的角色。让我们来看看有什么英语句子是可以应用在朋友这个部分。

Vocabulary 在国外都用这些词

MP3 02-21

friendship
['frendʃɪp]
n 友情，友谊

classmate
['klɑːsmeɪt]
n 同班同学

coworker
['kəʊˌwɜːkə]
n 同事

jeopardize
['dʒepədaɪz]
v 使濒临危险境地；冒～的危险；危及

pop culture
ph 流行文化

awkward
['ɔːkwəd]
a 尴尬的

coincidence
[kəʊ'ɪnsɪdəns]
n 巧合

over the top
ph 过头，过火

tied up
ph 忙得不可开交

science fiction
ph 科幻小说；科幻电影

solution
[sə'luːʃn]
n 解决方式

clingy
['klɪŋɪ]
a 过度依赖别人的

music
['mjuːzɪk]
n 音乐

drawing
['drɔːɪŋ]
n 画画

elementary school
ph 小学

multi-national
a 跨国的

billionaire
[ˌbɪljə'neə]
n 亿万富翁

influence
['ɪnfluəns]
n 影响

在国外都说这几句

- Friendship plays an important role in everyone's life.
  友情在每个人的人生中扮演着很重要的角色。
  ★ 短语 ...play an important role ～扮演很重要的角色

- Friendships will fade away over time if you do not make the effort to maintain them.
  如果你不用心好好经营友谊，那么它会随着时间慢慢消逝不见。
  ★ 短语 fade away 慢慢消失，凋零

- Have you been in contact with your elementary school classmates?
  你跟你的小学同学一直有联系吗？
  ★ 短语 in contact with 与～有联系

- Unfortunately, I lost touch with one of my best friends three years ago.
  不幸的是，我3年前跟我一个很要好的朋友失去了联系。
  ★ 短语 lose touch with... 与～失去联系

- Communicating with your friends regularly is no doubt one of the best ways to maintain a good friendship.
  常常与朋友通话无疑是维持友谊最好的方法之一。
  ★ 短语 communicate with... 与～交往；通话

- How is everything going with you? I haven't seen you in a while.
  你一切都还好吗？我好久没看到你了。
  ★ 短语 in a while 一段时间

- How is your new job treating you? I hope everything is going well.
  你的新工作还好吧？希望一切都很顺利。
  ★ 短语 "某事 treat 某人"的原意是指"某事对待某人如何"，引申为"某事还好吧"。

- Did something bad happen on your way to work? You don't look very good.
  你去上班的路上，有什么糟糕的事情发生吗？你看起来不大好。
  ★ 短语 on A's way to... 在 A 去～的路上

- A coworker told me the funniest joke. It certainly cracked me up.
  一个同事给我讲了个最好笑的笑话。这个笑话让我捧腹大笑。
  ★ 短语 crack A up 让 A 捧腹大笑

- You are always there for me; I cannot thank you enough.
  你总是在我有需要的时候陪伴在我身边，让我非常感激不尽。
  ★ 短语 cannot thank you enough 感激不尽

065

在国外都说这几句

- You can tell your best friends everything as long as it doesn't jeopardize your friendship.

  你可以告诉最好的朋友所有的事情，只要不危害你们的友谊。

  ★ 语法 "as long as" 除了引导条件状语从句，表示"只要，既然"以外，也可以引导时间状语从句，表示"像～一样长"。

- You might find the story hilarious, but chances are that other people might think it's offensive.

  你觉得这个故事很好笑，但其他人很可能对它很反感。

  ★ 短语 chances are that （极）可能

- Out of topics to discuss with your friends? Try pop culture. It can always spice up the conversation.

  不知道要跟朋友谈论什么话题吗？试试看流行文化吧，它总能让你们的谈话更有趣。

  ★ 短语 discuss with... 与～讨论

- My best friend always gives the best pieces of advice. That's why I love her so much.

  我最好的朋友总是给我最好的忠告。这就是为什么我那么爱她。

  ★ 短语 a piece of advice 一则忠告

- The other day, I had the opportunity to catch up with an old friend and we talked about what we used to be when we were kids.

  前几天，我有机会与老朋友叙叙旧，并一起回忆小时候的事情。

  ★ 短语 "catch up with" 的原意是"赶上"，在此则引申为"与（朋友）叙旧"的意思。

- I don't want to ask tricky questions because they might put my friend in an awkward position.

  我不想问棘手的问题，因为可能会让我的朋友陷入尴尬的窘境。

  ★ 短语 put A in an awkward position 让A陷入窘境

- I was in the railway station waiting for a train, and I ran into an old friend from high school. What a coincidence!

  我在火车站等车，然后遇见了高中时的老友。真是巧啊！

  ★ 短语 run into... 撞到～；偶遇～

- Did you read about the over-the-top acts of that famous actress? It's all over the news.

  你看到有关那个知名女演员夸张行径的报道了吗？到处都是对这件事的报道。

  ★ 短语 read about 读到有关～

在国外都说这几句

- I love anything that relates to fashion, especially before-and-after topic.
  我喜欢有关时尚的一切，尤其是前后相关的主题。
  ★ 短语 relate to...　关于～、与～相关

- I'm so happy that all your dreams come true. Who do you want to share the joy with?
  我很高兴你所有的梦想都成真了。你想要跟谁分享这些喜悦呢？
  ★ 短语 ...come true　实现～，～成真

- You can talk about all your concerns with me. I'm all ears.
  你有什么烦恼都可以跟我说。我洗耳恭听。
  ★ 短语 be all ears　洗耳恭听

- My close friend is about to give birth to a baby girl and she asked me to be the godmother.
  我的闺蜜即将生个女孩。她请我当小孩的干妈。
  ★ 短语 give birth to...　生产～，生（孩子）

- If you need to talk about the problems you have at work, I'm only a phone call away.
  如果你想找人倾诉工作上的问题，我很愿意帮忙。
  ★ 短语 a phone call away　表示"一个电话的距离"，在此引申为"很愿意帮忙"。

- My friend and I used to see each other everyday, but now we are both tied up with our lives.
  我跟我朋友以前每天都会见面，但现在我们都各自忙于自己的生活。
  ★ 短语 used to　过去常常

- Even if you are good friends, it's probably better not to talk about politics.
  即使你们是好朋友，也最好不要讨论政治话题。
  ★ 语法 even if　即使

- My friends and I like to get together and talk about what's going on with our lives.
  我和我的朋友们喜欢聚一聚，并谈谈我们彼此的生活过得怎么样。
  ★ 短语 get together　聚集，聚在一起

在国外都说这几句

- What do you mostly do for fun in your free time?
  你空闲的时候喜欢做些什么好玩的事情？
  ★ 短语 for fun 开玩笑的，为了好玩的

- Hey, I haven't seen you for a while. Where do you work now?
  嘿，我好久都没有看到你了，现在在哪里高就啊？

- I always spend lots of time reading novels. Science fiction is my favourite.
  我喜欢花很多时间看小说。科幻小说是我最喜欢的。
  ★ 语法 "spend" 后可接名词或动词，但若接名词，则需使用 "spend + on"，若后接动词，动词则改成动名词形式："spend + v-ing"。

- When I find myself in a stressful situation, I will call my friends and have a girls' night out.
  当我处于压力大的状况时，我会打电话给我的朋友，和一群女孩子出去玩一个晚上。
  ★ 短语 a girls' night out 仅女性朋友出外玩乐的一个晚上

- My best friend always knows how to turn an incredibly frustrating aspect into something much more positive.
  我最好的朋友总是有办法将极端沮丧的情况转变成正面思考。
  ★ 短语 turn into... 使变成～，转变成～

- When are you free next? Let's catch up soon.
  你下次什么时候有空？我们赶快聚聚吧。

- My friends asked me tons of questions because it's been ages since the last time we met.
  我的朋友们问了我一大堆问题，因为距离上一次见面已经隔了好久了。
  ★ 短语 it's been ages 已经很久

- We should get together soon, I want to update you on all of the new gossip.
  我们要赶快约时间见面，我有好多新的八卦想要跟你说。
  ★ 短语 update A on... 更新（信息）给 A

- My best friend always helps me to tell right from wrong.
  我最好的朋友总是帮我明辨是非。
  ★ 短语 tell right from wrong 明辨是非

在国外都说这几句

- My friends and I always **laugh about** those reality TV shows. Some of the people on the show are acting crazy.
  我跟我的朋友们总是取笑那些电视真人秀节目。节目里的人有些会表现得很夸张。
  ★ 短语 laugh about... 嘲笑（有关）～

- Different interpretations of movies often **lead to** fun conversations among friends.
  关于电影的不同解读总是能让朋友间讨论得很开心。
  ★ 短语 lead to... 通向～、导致～

- Actually, I don't think this problem is **worth discussing**. The solution is pretty obvious; you just have to accept it.
  事实上，我觉得这个问题没有什么值得讨论的。解决方式已经非常明显了，你必须要接受它。
  ★ 短语 worth discussing 值得讨论

- I like hanging out with my friends because it always helps me **get my thoughts off my chest**.
  我喜欢跟朋友在一起，因为那总是能让我感到轻松。
  ★ 短语 get thoughts off A's chest 让A松一口气，让A如释重负

- It's still early. Do you want to **grab a bite** to eat with me?
  时间还早。你想跟我一起去吃个东西吗？
  ★ 短语 grab a bite 简单吃些东西

- I have never **struggled to** start a conversation with my best friends. We can talk about everything.
  我从来没有遇过不知道该跟老朋友聊什么话题的时候。因为我们什么都可以聊。
  ★ 短语 struggle to 挣扎地做～

- Tell me 3 secrets that you've never **shared with anyone** before.
  告诉我3个你从来没有跟别人说过的秘密。
  ★ 短语 share with A 跟A分享～

- **How long** have you lived here? Do you like this neighborhood?
  你在这里住多久了？你喜欢这一区吗？
  ★ 短语 "how long" 的意思是"多常，多久"，可表示距离，也可表示时间。

在国外都说这几句

- Are you seeing someone at present?
  你现在有交往的对象吗？
  ★ 短语 at present　现在，目前

- I heard that you got involved in an accident. Is everything okay?
  我听说你卷入一场意外。一切都还好吗？
  ★ 短语 get / be involved in　牵涉到～，卷入～

- Where are you originally from? You don't look like you are from here.
  你的家乡在哪里？你看起来不像本地人。

- What's your dream job?
  你梦想的职业是什么？
  ★ 短语 dream job　理想的职业

- What is your favourite movie of all time? We should watch it together.
  你一直以来最喜欢的电影是什么？有机会我们可以一起看。
  ★ 短语 of all time　一直以来

- What turns you on when you are in a relationship with someone?
  与人交往的时候，对方的哪些特点会吸引你？
  ★ 短语 turn... on　使～兴奋，使～高兴

- Is there anything that will turn you off, such as too clingy?
  有什么事会让你倒尽胃口吗，像是太黏人？
  ★ 短语 turn... off　让～倒尽胃口，让人～扫兴

- What do you do in your free time? Maybe we can plan something together.
  休闲时间你喜欢做什么？也许我们可以一起计划一些行程。
  ★ 短语 in A's free time　在 A 的空闲时间

- It depends on the weather. If it's a rainy day, I like to stay in and surf the Internet.
  要看天气状况怎么样。如果是雨天的话，我喜欢在家里上网。
  ★ 短语 stay in　待在家里、室内

- Tell me the most embarrassing thing you've done before. I promise I won't make fun of you.
  告诉我你做过的最令你最尴尬的事情。我保证不会嘲笑你。
  ★ 短语 make fun of A　嘲笑 A，嘲弄 A

在国外都说这几句

- I've never heard of such a weird thing. Are you sure you are not exaggerating?

  我从来没有听说过那么奇怪的事情。你确定你没有夸大？

  ★ 短语 ▶ hear of　听说过

- What types of books do you never get tired of reading?

  你对哪一类书籍绝不会厌倦？

  ★ 短语 ▶ get / be tired of...　厌倦做～，厌烦～

- How did you cope with break-ups in the past? It seems like you are very confident about such issues.

  过去你是怎么处理分手状况的？看起来你对这方面非常有自信。

  ★ 短语 ▶ cope with...　对付～，巧妙处理～

- I know you have wanted to start your own business since high school. How's that going?

  我知道你高中时就想开创自己的事业。进行得如何了？

  ★ 短语 ▶ start a business　创业，开公司

- If you meet someone that you love, would you prefer tell her in person or over the phone?

  如果你遇到自己爱的人，你会直接面对面跟她表白还是会在电话中跟她倾诉你的爱意？

  ★ 短语 ▶ over the phone　透过、经由电话表达

- I asked my friend about her first kiss and she started to blush.

  我问朋友有关她初吻的事情，她就开始脸红了。

  ★ 短语 ▶ "start to..."是指"开始（做）～"；通常也等于"start + v-ing"。

- Is there anything, other than the things you are already doing, you would like to pursuit in your life?

  除了你现在已经在做的事之外，在你的人生中还有想追求的事情吗？

  ★ 短语 ▶ other than　除了～

- How often do you surf the Internet a day?

  你一天当中上网的频率是多少？

  ★ 语法 ▶ "often"是频率副词，"how often"则是问某个动作发生的次数及频率，意思是"多常、多久一次"。

- What other places outside of Beijing would you like to visit the most?

  北京之外有哪些地方是你最想去游览的？

  ★ 语法 ▶ outside (of)　在～外；除了～外

071

在国外都说这几句

- How long have you been working for your current company?
  你在现在这家公司上班多久了？
  ★ 短语 work for　为~工作，为~做事

- Are you happy with your life for the most part? If not, what would you like to change?
  你对于现在生活大致上满意吗？如果不满意的话，你想要改变什么？
  ★ 短语 for the most part　主要地；大多数情况下；通常

- What is the worst prank you have ever played on someone?
  你对人做过最糟糕的恶作剧是什么？
  ★ 短语 play a prank on...　对~恶作剧

- If money were not a problem and you could go anywhere in the world, where would you go?
  如果钱不是问题，而且你可以到全世界的任何地方，你会去哪里？
  ★ 短语 in the world　全世界

- Did you watch *American Idol*? Who is your favourite performer so far?
  你看了《美国偶像》吗？目前你最喜欢哪个演员／选手？
  ★ 短语 so far　到目前（为止）

- What would be the most difficult thing for you to give up?
  你觉得哪一件事对你来说是最难放弃的？
  ★ 短语 give up...　放弃~；让出~；戒绝~

- What is that music you are listening to right now? It sounds so familiar.
  你现在在听什么音乐？听起来很熟悉。
  ★ 短语 listen to...　听（从）~

- I know you are good at drawing. I might need your expertise for something.
  我知道你很会画画。我可能会需要借用你的这个才能。
  ★ 短语 be good at...　擅长~，精于~

- My friends and I can watch *The Devil wears Prada* over and over again and never get tired of it.
  我和我的朋友们可以一直重复看《穿普拉达的女王》，而且不会腻。
  ★ 短语 over and over again　一再；反复；一而再，再而三

在国外都说这几句

- Have you ever stolen anything from a store or from someone? Did you feel guilty afterwards?
  你曾经顺手牵羊或偷过别人的东西吗？事后你会不会感到内疚？
  ★ 短语 ▶ steal from...　偷～的东西

- I cheated on exams quite often when I was in elementary school.
  我小学的时候考试常常作弊。
  ★ 短语 ▶ cheat on...　～作弊；对～不忠

- My best friend is in trouble. I am going to help her by any means necessary.
  我最好的朋友遇上麻烦。我无论如何都要帮她。
  ★ 短语 ▶ by any means necessary　无论如何

- Christmas is coming. I want to celebrate it with my best friends. We can play Secret Santa.
  圣诞节来了。我想要与我最好的朋友们一起庆祝。我们可以玩交换礼物。
  ★ 短语 ▶ Secret Santa　秘密圣诞老人，一种欧美人送圣诞礼物的游戏。

- My friends often embarrass me in public, but I know they mean no harm.
  我的朋友们总是喜欢在公共场合让我难堪。但我知道他们无意伤害我。
  ★ 短语 ▶ mean no harm　无意伤害

- Why are you always so quiet and shy in private? People might think you don't like them.
  你私底下为什么总是这么安静又害羞呢？其他人可能会觉得你不喜欢他们。
  ★ 短语 ▶ in private　私下，秘密地

- My top ambition in life is to own a multinational business and become a billionaire.
  我生命中最大的目标就是拥有一个跨国企业，并且成为亿万富翁。
  ★ 短语 ▶ in life　生命中

- My friends and I sometimes like to badmouth others.
  我和我的朋友们有时候喜欢说别人坏话。
  ★ 短语 ▶ badmouth...　说～的坏话

跟任何人都可以用英语聊聊天

Unit 8 家是永远的避风港

[生活便利贴]

周末在家可以好好放松、休息，消除累积了一个星期的疲劳。在家除了看电视、上网、补觉之外，需要抽出时间整理家务，像是打扫、洗衣服等。无论如何，宅在家里就是希望可以让自己好好地休息，然后迎接下个星期的挑战。让我们来看看这个单元可以学到什么样的实用英语句子。

Vocabulary 在国外都用这些词

MP3 02-31

chore
[tʃɔː]
n 家庭杂务

mail
[meɪl]
n 邮件

nightstand
['naɪtstænd]
n 床头柜

dirty work
ph 苦活、没人愿意做的事情

odor
['əʊdə]
n 气味

tile
[taɪl]
n 瓷砖、地砖

sink
[sɪŋk]
n 水槽、洗碗槽

guest room
ph 客房

lottery ticket
ph 彩票

suit
[suːt]
n 西装

housekeeper
['haʊskiːpə]
n 管家

brew
[bruː]
v 酿造（酒）

glove
[glʌv]
n 手套

sanctuary
['sæŋktʃuəri]
n 避难所、庇护所

recipe
['resəpɪ]
n 食谱

recycling
[ˌriːˈsaɪklɪŋ]
n 资源回收

extra
['ekstrə]
a 额外的

brownie
['braʊnɪ]
n 布朗尼蛋糕

在国外都说这几句

- **When it comes to** grocery shopping, it's better to make a list so that you don't forget what you need.
  要去买日常生活用品时，最好把要买的东西列一张清单，这样才不会忘记需要买什么东西。
  ★ 短语 when it comes to... 当涉及～，当谈到～时

- Everyone should be in charge of at least one chore, and the house will be spotless **in no time**.
  每个人都该负责一件家事，这样家里立刻就会一尘不染。
  ★ 短语 in no time 很快、立即

- The study is messy. **It's time to** have a thorough cleanup.
  书房好脏，是时候该大扫除一下了。
  ★ 短语 it's time to... 是时候应该～

- You should **tidy** things **up** in your room, don't expect other people to do your dirty work.
  你应该要好好地整理自己的房间，不要期望其他人会帮你做这些事情。
  ★ 短语 tidy up 整理，收拾

- You need to come up with a more organized way to **sort** things **out**.
  你需要想个方式，能够更加条不紊地整理这些东西。
  ★ 短语 sort out 整理某事物

- Hiring a housekeeper can take care of most of the chores that need to be done **on a daily basis**.
  请一位女管家可以帮你打理每天的打扫工作。
  ★ 短语 on a daily basis 每天，每日

- It is disgusting to have a sink that **is full of** dirty dishes and awful smells.
  洗碗槽内满满的脏盘子又充满异味，真的令人觉得很恶心。
  ★ 短语 be full of... 充满～，满满的～

- Those dirty dishes will **result in** horrible smells, stains and fungus so wash them now. Don't just leave them in the sink.
  那些脏盘子会滋生恶臭、污垢跟真菌。所以现在马上就去洗碗，不要把它们放在洗碗槽。
  ★ 短语 result in 导致，结果是

在国外都说这几句

- Doing housework is without doubt very hard work, but you must do it. No one likes a messy environment.

  做家务确实是非常辛苦，但是你必须做，因为没有人喜欢肮脏的环境。

  ★ 短语 without doubt　无疑的

- They always point fingers at each other for the mess. I suggest that you make a rule on the chores, so no one can get away with it.

  他们总是喜欢互相推卸责任，怪对方把房子弄得乱糟糟的。我建议你可以制订做家事的规则，这样每个人都有责任。

  ★ 短语 get away with...　不因某事受惩罚

- Please stack the dishes after washing them.

  洗完碗盘后，请把它们堆好。

  ★ 短语 stack...　堆叠～

- Washing dishes will prevent cockroaches and rats from invading your kitchen.

  洗碗盘能够防止蟑螂跟老鼠入侵你家厨房。

  ★ 短语 "prevent A from..." 的意思是"预防 A 做～，防止 A ～"，是指利用某种障碍阻止某人、某个行动或某件事情的发生。若"prevent"后接名词或代词，则是阻止某个对象，from 后面可接名词或动名词，表示需要阻止的事物或是动作。

- Do I have to do the laundry everyday? I think twice a week should be enough.

  我一定要每天都洗衣服吗？我觉得一个礼拜洗两次就够了。

  ★ 短语 do the laundry　洗衣服

- There is no doubt that a clean environment can put you in a good mood.

  毋庸置疑，干净的环境可以让你保持好心情。

  ★ 短语 there is no doubt that...　毫无疑问～，～毋庸置疑

- My suit cannot be hand washed, so I need to send it to the dry cleaners.

  我的西装不可以手洗，所以我要送去干洗店。

  ★ 短语 dry cleaner　干洗

- Wear gloves to protect your skin from the chemical detergent.

  戴手套可以保护肌肤，免于化学清洁剂的伤害。

  ★ 短语 protect A from B　保护 A 免于 B 的伤害

在国外都说这几句

- Doing a little clutter control everyday can keep your home tidy.
  每天整理脏乱可以维持家中整洁。
  ★ 短语 clutter control　脏乱控制、做些措施以预防脏乱

- This is a disaster. Pick up your toys right now, otherwise I will throw them all away.
  这真的是乱七八糟，现在就马上收拾你的玩具。不然我就把它们都丢掉。
  ★ 短语 throw away　丢掉

- Give me 20 minutes, then I can make my living room ready for visitors.
  给我 20 分钟的时间，我就可以让我的客厅干净到可以让客人来访。

- If I don't file my papers today, they will be piled up everywhere and become a mess eventually.
  如果我今天不将文件归档，它们就会堆得到处都是，最终变得很杂乱。
  ★ 短语 pile up　堆放，累积

- Junk mail, letters and receipts are taking over our room.
  垃圾邮件、信件和收据占据了我们的房间。
  ★ 短语 take over　占（地方）；费（时间）

- It only takes a few minutes to sort out all your papers. All you need is a more efficient way.
  你需要有个更有效率的方式，这样一来每天只需要花几分钟的时间就可以将文件好好地分类。
  ★ 短语 it takes + 时间　花费~（时间）

- I am going to set up a more organized recycling system in my room.
  我要在我的房间设立一个更有秩序的回收方式。
  ★ 短语 set up...　竖立~；建造~；创立~

- I check my mail box everyday, because I cannot stand having that junk mail lying in there.
  我每天都会检查我的信箱，因为我没有办法忍受信箱里面有一封垃圾邮件。
  ★ 短语 cannot stand...　无法忍受~

- I try to keep my house clean so that it's ready for visitors at any time.
  我努力让家保持清洁，这样才能随时接待访客。
  ★ 短语 at any time　任何时候，总是

Chapter 2 娱乐与休闲　Unit8

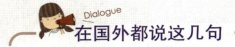

在国外都说这几句

- You cannot cover up bad odors with perfume. That just won't work.
  你无法用香水掩盖臭味。那是行不通的。
  ★ 短语 cover up... 掩盖～，遮住～

- I try to remove the bad odors first by opening the windows and lighting a scented candle.
  我试着打开窗户并点香氛蜡烛以去除臭味。

- The bad odors in my room do not go away; I don't know what else I can do.
  我房间的臭味总是散不掉，我不知道我还可以做些什么。
  ★ 短语 go away 离开、停止、变淡

- Take a minute to look around your apartment. How can you live in such a messy place?
  花1分钟看看你的公寓。你怎么有办法住在这么脏乱的地方？
  ★ 短语 look around... 看看～，环顾～

- Your cousin is visiting us next week. Please spend some time tidying up the guest room.
  你的表哥下星期要来拜访我们，请花一点时间整理一下客房。

- It's your turn to vacuum the floor.
  轮到你吸地板了。
  ★ 短语 vacuum the floor 用真空吸尘器吸地板

- Vinegar can be used on cleaning windows, mirrors and glasses. It will save you a lot of money.
  醋可以用来清洁窗户、镜子和玻璃。它可以帮你省下一大笔钱。
  ★ 短语 be used on... 用在～上，使用在～

- It's time to do the laundry. Get your coins ready and let's go to the laundromat.
  洗衣服的时候到了，把你的零钱准备好，我们一起去自助洗衣店吧。
  ★ 短语 get... ready 把～准备好

- If you really have no time for housework, hiring a housekeeper might be a good option.
  如果你真的没有时间做家务的话，那么请一位管家帮忙整理是一个好的选择。
  ★ 短语 have no time for... 不愿或不能为～花时间

在国外都说这几句

- I will let you pick the movie tonight, if you promise to do the dishes.
  如果你保证会洗碗的话，我就让你决定今天晚上看什么电影。
  ★ 短语 ▶ pick... 挑选出～，辨认出～

- Who is in charge of taking out the rubbish today?
  今天谁负责倒垃圾？
  ★ 短语 ▶ in charge of.. 照料～，负责～

- My bedroom is my sanctuary and a place where I rest. No one should barge in for no reason.
  我房间是我的避难所，也是我休息的地方。如果没有事的话，任何人不可以进来打扰我。
  ★ 短语 ▶ barge in 闯入，打扰

- Each detergent has its own purpose; don't just use one for everything.
  每一种清洁剂都有不同的用途，不要只拿一种来清洁所有东西。
  ★ 短语 ▶ A has its own purpose A 有特定用途

- It's time to clean the refrigerator and toss out trash and bad food.
  该整理冰箱并清出垃圾和坏掉的食物了。
  ★ 短语 ▶ toss out... 清出～，打扫～

- Make sure you dust the table and TV off before vacuuming the floor.
  吸地板之前，要记得先把桌子跟电视上的灰尘扫下来。
  ★ 短语 ▶ dust off... 除去～的灰尘

- Turn off the TV and the laptop and see what you can do to help around house.
  关掉电视和笔记本电脑，看看家里还有什么需要你帮忙的事情。
  ★ 短语 ▶ turn off... 关掉～

- I always put extra pillows on the top of my bed.
  我总是在床头多放几个枕头。
  ★ 短语 ▶ the top of... ～的头部

- I want to stay at home and cuddle with my husband.
  我想在家中依偎着老公。
  ★ 短语 ▶ cuddle with... 与～依偎，与～拥抱

在国外都说这几句

- My wife is looking for a nightstand that can **fit into** our bedroom.
  我老婆正在找跟卧房搭配的床头柜。
  ★ 短语 ▶ fit into... 与～适合，与～搭配

- We should just **throw** this stuff **away**. I don't think we will use it again.
  我们应该把这些东西丢掉。我觉得我们之后不会再用到了。
  ★ 短语 ▶ throw away... 抛弃～，丢掉～

- I'm exhausted. It's time to **take a** bubble **bath** and wash away my tiredness.
  我累坏啦。是时候做个泡泡浴，洗去一天的疲劳了。
  ★ 短语 ▶ take a bath 泡澡，洗澡

- I'm going to hire a designer and let him **figure out** what style of décor suits my apartment.
  我要请一个设计师来看看我的公寓适合哪种装潢风格。
  ★ 短语 ▶ figure out... 想出～；理解出～

- I **am** very **sensitive to** chemicals. I prefer all natural products.
  我对化学用品非常敏感。我倾向用纯天然产品。
  ★ 短语 ▶ be sensitive to... 对～敏感，对～过敏

- I'd rather not have a fireplace in my house. It will be a **pain in the neck** to clean it up.
  我宁愿不要在家里装火炉，因为打扫起来真的很麻烦。
  ★ 短语 ▶ pain in the neck 令人厌烦的人或事物

- I want to **put** the wooden tile **on** all the floors, so that it won't get too cold in winter.
  我想要在我家地板上铺上木头的地砖，这样冬天才不会太冷。
  ★ 短语 ▶ put on... 放在～上面

- I am going to the backyard and **waiting for** the shooting stars.
  我要到后院等流星到来。
  ★ 短语 ▶ wait for... 等待～，等候～

- You can find the answer to that question **on the net**.
  你可以在网络上找到这个问题的答案。
  ★ 短语 ▶ on the net 在网络上

在国外都说这几句

- If you have a problem with a technical issue, you should call their customer service hotline.
  如果你有技术方面的问题，你应该拨打他们的客服热线。
  ★ 短语 have a problem with... 在～方面遇到问题

- Hey, look at these old photos. I can't believe it was 10 years ago.
  嘿，看看这些旧照片。我真不敢相信已经过了10年了。
  ★ 短语 look at... 看看～；观察～

- I love to curl up in a sofa and watch a TV series.
  我喜欢窝在沙发上看电视剧。
  ★ 短语 curl up 卷成一团，窝着坐

- I'm teaching my pet dog to shake hands with me.
  我正在教我的宠物狗怎样与我握手。
  ★ 短语 teach A to... 教 A 做～

- Flipping through a fashion magazine does not require too much thinking.
  翻翻时尚杂志不需要动太多脑筋。
  ★ 短语 flip through... 草草翻阅～，快速翻阅～

- You should frame this picture if you love it so much.
  你如果真的那么爱这张照片的话，你应该把它表框起来。
  ★ 短语 frame the picture 把照片裱起来

- I sat on the couch and started to daydream about winning the lottery.
  我坐在沙发上开始做起中彩票的白日梦。
  ★ 短语 daydream about... 做～的白日梦

- When I'm bored, I invite my friend over and we play video games together.
  无聊时，我会邀请我的朋友来我家一起玩电动游戏。
  ★ 短语 invite A over 邀请 A 到家中做客

- Let's have a garage sale and make some extra bucks.
  让我们一起办一个车库拍卖，还可以赚一点外快。
  ★ 短语 garage sale 车库拍卖，在家中车库进行的旧货出售

在国外都说这几句

- I am going to lie back and read a great book.
  我准备躺着放松一下并读本好书。
  ★ 短语 lie back 休息，放松

- My brother decided to build a tree house in the backyard.
  我哥哥决定在后院盖一个树屋。
  ★ 短语 tree house 树屋

- My neighbor tried to blow up a firecracker with a magnifying glass.
  我的邻居试着用放大镜让鞭炮爆炸。
  ★ 短语 blow up... 炸毁～，使～爆炸

- Look at your nails! You need a manicure. There is a store on the corner that I highly recommend.
  看看你的指甲，你需要修剪它们了。转角有一家店我非常推荐。

- I don't know what to do to get rid of my boredom.
  我不知道要怎么做才不会无聊。
  ★ 短语 get rid of... 摆脱～

- Today I'm going to plot out a housewarming party for my best friend.
  今天我要好好地帮我朋友策划一场乔迁派对。
  ★ 短语 plot out... 策划～

- If you are good at handicrafts, you should try to make some furniture for your house.
  如果你对手工艺很在行，你应该试着为你的家里做一些手工家具。
  ★ 短语 be good at... 对～很在行，很会做～

- Playing computer games is definitely going to drive your boredom away.
  玩电脑游戏一定不会让你无聊。
  ★ 短语 drive away 驱走，赶走

- For a foodie, cooking is likely to be the happiest thing to do at home.
  对美食家来说，做菜可能是待在家中最开心的事情。
  ★ 短语 be likely to... 很可能～

- I am addicted to wine. I should brew some wine on my own.
  我嗜喝葡萄酒。我应该自己酿些酒。
  ★ 短语 on one's own 自己来

在国外都说这几句

- These cookies are out of this world! You have to give me your recipe.
  这些饼干真的好吃到无法用言语形容！你一定要把食谱给我。
  ★ 短语 out of this world　无法用言语形容

- I'm going to enjoy some ice cream and put lots of strawberries on it.
  我要好好地享用冰激淋，并在上面加很多草莓。
  ★ 短语 put... on A　在A上加～，加～在A上

- Let's call up friends to have afternoon tea together.
  让我们给好友打电话，一起喝下午茶。
  ★ 短语 call up...　打电话（给）～

- I'd like to invite everyone I know and have slumber party in my house.
  我想邀请我认识的每个人来我家开睡衣晚会。
  ★ 短语 slumber party　睡衣晚会（少女穿着睡衣通宵闲谈的聚会）

- Do you think we're too old to play hide and seek?
  你认为我们玩捉迷藏，会有点太老了吗？
  ★ 短语 hide and seek　捉迷藏

- My wife is having fun making some brownies.
  我老婆正在开心地烤着布朗尼。
  ★ 短语 have fun　玩得很开心

- Please set the table. Our guests are on their way.
  请把餐桌摆好。我们的客人马上就到了。
  ★ 短语 set the table　摆餐桌

- I am inviting my friends over to play poker.
  我要邀请朋友来一起打扑克牌。

- I just want to take a nap. Wake me up in an hour.
  我只想睡个午觉，一个小时之后叫我起床。
  ★ 短语 take a nap　打盹，小睡，午睡

跟任何人都可以用英语聊聊天

Unit 9 大自然就是我的家

[生活便利贴]

露营、烤肉、游泳都是假日休闲的好方式。为了让大家玩得尽兴，行前的准备工作，像地点的选择、食物的采买或是天气的确认可是一点都不能马虎。另外，出去玩也要注意自身的安全，若遇到危险的告示牌，千万要遵守上面的指示，不要一味地逞强，安全至上。这个单元让我们一起学习出去玩的英语单词跟句子吧！

Vocabulary 在国外都用这些词

MP3 02-41

entertain
[ˌɛntɚˈteɪn]
v 娱乐

classic
[ˈklæsɪk]
a 经典的

marshmallow
[ˌmɑːʃˈmæləʊ]
n 棉花糖

technology
[tɛkˈnɒlədʒɪ]
n 科技

flashlight
[ˈflæʃlaɪt]
n 手电筒

spin
[spɪn]
v 旋转

cater
[ˈkeɪtə]
v 满足需求或欲望

canoeing
[kəˈnuːɪŋ]
n 滑独木舟

camper
[ˈkæmpə]
n 露营车

outdoor
[ˈaʊtdɔː]
a 户外的

rafting
[ˈrɑːftɪŋ]
n 泛舟

extravagant
[ɪkˈstrævəgənt]
a 奢侈的，浪费的

itinerary
[aɪˈtɪnərərɪ]
n 旅程，路线

spyglass
[ˈspaɪglɑːs]
n 望远镜

trouble
[ˈtrʌbl]
n 麻烦

bathroom
[ˈbɑːθruːm]
n 浴室，厕所

mosquito
[məˈskiːtəʊ]
n 蚊子

dessert
[dɪˈzɜːt]
n 甜点

在国外都说这几句

- How do you keep everyone entertained while you are in the middle of the woods without modern technology?
  在树林中，没有现代的科技，要如何让大家都觉得好玩有趣呢？
  ★ 短语 in the middle of... 在～中间，在～当中

- There are all sorts of camping activities that can cater to different people's needs.
  各式各样的露营活动可以满足人们的不同需求。
  ★ 短语 all sorts of 各式各样的

- There is no substitute for a good camping trip because it's one of the best ways to get closer to nature.
  露营是无可取代的，因为它是亲近大自然最好的方式之一。
  ★ 短语 substitute for... ～的代替品

- Once we decide on the campsite, then we can pitch the tent.
  一旦我们决定好露营的地点，我们就可以开始扎营了。
  ★ 短语 pitch the tent 扎营

- Preparation is essential for any kind of outdoor activities.
  不管要做哪种户外活动，准备工作都非常重要。
  ★ 短语 any kind of... 任何一种的～

- Having the necessary supplies and equipment can make a difference in your camping experience.
  准备足够的补给和装备会让你的露营经验大大不同。
  ★ 短语 make a difference 有影响，有关系

- Depending on the location and the weather, the camping list will be varied.
  露营的准备清单会根据露营的地点及天气状况而有所不同。
  ★ 短语 depend on 视～而定，取决于～

常识补给站

在水中泡太久，为什么手指的皮肤会变皱呢？现在有科学家表示，手指或脚趾皮肤起皱是为了更稳固地抓取同在水中的物体，以及提供稳定的抓地力。皮肤表面起皱后，当你抓住一件湿湿的物品时，皮肤表面的凹槽会为被你手指挤开的液体提供了一个疏散的通道。

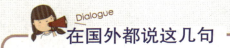

在国外都说这几句

- Give me the details of your camping itinerary and the contact number that you can be reached on.

  把你的具体露营行程和你的电话号码告诉我。

  ★ 短语 detail of... ～的细节，～的详情

- I will take a first aid class and a CPR class before we go camping just in case.

  露营前，我会去上急救以及心肺复苏术的课程以防万一。

  ★ 短语 take a class 上一堂课，上一门课程

- There are many things to be taken into consideration when you look for a good place to camp.

  当你要找地方露营时，有许多事情需要考量。

  ★ 短语 take into consideration 考虑到

- We should call the camp manager and inquire about the availability.

  我们应该打电话给营区经理，询问营区还有没有位置。

  ★ 短语 inquire about... 询问～；调查～

- Would you please let us know how often the bathrooms are cleaned?

  可不可以让我们知道，浴室多久清理一次？

  ★ 语法 "how often" 是要问"某件动作、事情发生的频率或次数"，"often" 在此是"频率副词"。

- I can't live without a hair dryer, so I am going to take a portable one with me.

  没有吹风机，我活不下去，所以我要带一个便携式吹风机去。

  ★ 短语 can't live without... 没有～就无法活下去

- It's probably a good idea to bring some drinking water with us.

  也许我们应该带一些饮用水。

  ★ 短语 drinking water 饮用水

It's nice out here!

Indeed!

在国外都说这几句

- I'm going to check out the activity program as soon as we arrive at the campsite.
  一到露营地点，我就去看看有什么活动可以参加。
  ★ 短语 as soon as...　一～，就～

- Kids, don't travel too far from the campsite without your parents' company.
  孩子们，不要在没有家长陪同的情况下，到离营区太远的地方。
  ★ 短语 far from...　离～很远、距离～远

- The best views and sights are usually located in a remote area.
  最好的景色通常都位于偏远地区。
  ★ 短语 remote area　偏远地区

- The greatest thing about going camping is that you get to spend more time with your loved ones.
  露营最棒的地方就是可以花更多时间跟你爱的人们在一起。
  ★ 短语 spend time with...　花时间与～在一起

- Setting up a campfire is the most classic outdoor activity when it comes to camping.
  篝火是去露营时最经典的户外活动。
  ★ 短语 when it comes to...　当涉及～时，谈到～时

- Don't you want to go mountain biking with us?
  你难道不想跟我们一起骑越野自行车吗？
  ★ 短语 go mountain biking　骑越野自行车

- I wanted to go bike riding, but I didn't bring a bike with me.
  我想要骑自行车，但我没带自行车来。
  ★ 短语 bring... with A　A没有（携带）带～

- Don't worry. There is a bicycle shop where you can hire one.
  别担心。那边有一家自行车店，你可以去那里租自行车。
  ★ 短语 hire...　租～

- If you want everyone to stay interested in fishing, you need to get everyone involved.
  你如果想要让大家享受到钓鱼的乐趣，那么你需要让大家都有参与感。
  ★ 短语 be / get involved　有参与感

在国外都说这几句

- My dad **taught** me how **to** tie a knot.
  我爸爸教我如何打绳结。
  ★ 短语 teach A to...　教 A 做～，指导 A 做～

- For the fish to **take the bait**, you need to put worms on the hook.
  为了要让鱼上钩，你需要在鱼钩上放些虫子。
  ★ 短语 take the bait　上钩

- I'm not **enthused over** fishing. You guys go ahead, and I will wait here.
  我对钓鱼一点都不热衷，你们去吧，我在这里等你们。
  ★ 短语 enthuse over...　对～很热衷

- After the sun **goes down**, we will need flashlights when going out on an adventure.
  太阳下山后，我们出去探险的时候会需要手电筒。
  ★ 短语 go down　（太阳、月亮、星辰等）落到地平线下

- Playing games is a great way to **kill time**.
  玩游戏是打发时间的好方法。
  ★ 短语 kill time　消磨打发时间

- Let's team up and have a **treasure hunt**. Whoever finds the treasure first doesn't have to wash dishes for a week.
  我们组队来玩寻宝游戏，无论谁先找到宝藏，都可以一个星期不用洗碗。
  ★ 短语 treasure hunt　寻宝游戏

- Camping is a great activity for **team building**.
  露营可以让大家建立团队精神。
  ★ 短语 team building　建立团队精神

- The guide showed us the **importance of** using limited resources to solve problems.
  导游教我们使用有限资源解决问题的重要性。
  ★ 短语 importance of...　～的重要性

- Don't be shy! Go and **mingle with** the other campers. You will make a lot of good friends.
  不要害羞！去跟其他露营的人交流一下。你可以交到很多好朋友。
  ★ 短语 mingle with...　与～往来，与～交流

在国外都说这几句

- After hiking around the campground, I'm going to have a ride on the swing.
  在营地附近健步走之后，我要去荡秋千。
  ★ 短语 have a ride on the swing　荡秋千

- Since we have a guitar player in our group, why don't we sing around the campfire?
  既然我们的团体中有人会弹吉他，为什么不围着篝火唱歌呢？
  ★ 短语 around the campfire　围绕着篝火，在篝火周围

- Depending on the age of the campers, some of the activities are supervised by adults.
  依照露营者的年龄，有些活动会有成人在旁监督。

- Let's spice things up at the camp and make it unforgettable.
  我们让露营刺激一点吧，这样大家才会永远记得。
  ★ 短语 spice up...　让～变得更有趣，使～更有趣味

- Wow! Are they canoeing? I always wanted to try that. Where do I line up?
  哇！他们在滑独木舟吗？我从以前就一直很想试试看。我要去哪里排队？
  ★ 短语 line up　排队

- Raymond is always very adventurous and willing to try new things.
  雷蒙总是很有冒险精神，而且喜欢尝试新的事物。
  ★ 短语 be willing to...　愿意～，乐意～

- Rafting is available in this area. Just sign up here and be there at 9 o'clock for the safety session first.
  这个地区可以泛舟。你只要在这边登记，然后早上9点先去参加安全说明会。
  ★ 短语 sign up　注册、报名登记

常识补给站

参加野外活动时，经常会在野外露营。到达目的地后，在搭建营地的同时，建一个简易的野外厕所是极为必要的。野外厕所应选择在营地的下风处，地点要比营地稍低一些，并应远离河流（20米以外），以免污染干净的水源。

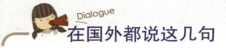 在国外都说这几句

- Have you ever tried whitewater rafting? It's not as dangerous as it looks.
  你之前有试过激流泛舟吗？它没有看起来那么危险。
  ★ 短语 as... as 像～一样

- Make sure you take safety precautions when swimming.
  下水游泳前，确保你做好了安全的防范措施。
  ★ 短语 take precautions 做好预防措施，做好防范措施

- My dad is hesitant about taking me on an adventure. He thinks I am still too young.
  我爸爸不太想带我去探险。他觉得我年纪还太小。
  ★ 短语 be hesitant about... 对～迟疑，对～抱着踌躇的态度

- In fact, a jet boat excursion is a thrilling activity. People with heart disease should not do it.
  事实上，玩喷射艇是很刺激的一项活动。有心血管疾病的人不要尝试。
  ★ 短语 heart disease 心脏病

- The kids are going to have a great time with each other on the slide.
  小朋友在滑梯那边可以一起玩得很开心。
  ★ 短语 have a great time 很开心

- Depending on your location, you may see a lot of stars with the spyglass.
  根据你所在地点，你也许可以用望远镜看到很多星星。

- I might lose interest doing a long hike. It sounds boring.
  我可能会对长途步行失去兴趣。因为这听起来很无聊。
  ★ 短语 lose interest doing... 对～失去兴趣

- Let's look around and see if there are any landmarks. That would come in handy if we get lost.
  我们到处看看附近有没有什么比较大的地标，这样之后迷路也不用怕了。
  ★ 短语 come in handy 迟早有用

- May I borrow your portable DVD player?
  我可以跟你借便携型的 DVD 播放器吗？
  ★ 语法 "borrow"的意思是"借，借入"。若加介词"from"，"borrow... from A"的意思是"向 A 借～"。

Dialogue 在国外都说这几句

- Sure. But my DVD player is about to run out of battery.
  当然。但是我的 DVD 播放器快要没电了。
  ★ 短语 run out of 用完，耗尽

- There's nothing wrong with telling a ghost story, just make sure everyone agrees with it.
  讲鬼故事没什么问题，但是要确保每个人都同意。
  ★ 语法 there is nothing wrong with... ～没什么不好的

- I hate mosquitoes. I have to put up a mosquito net before I go to bed.
  我讨厌蚊子。睡觉之前我一定要把蚊帐挂起来。
  ★ 短语 mosquito net 蚊帐

- We've decided to go for a noctivagation. It should be very exciting.
  我们决定要去夜游，应该会很刺激。
  ★ 短语 go for + 活动 进行活动

- It's time for truth or dare. Who wants to go first?
  我们来玩真心话大冒险。谁想第一个来？
  ★ 短语 truth or dare 真心话大冒险

- I love camping because it can make me forget about the hustle and bustle of my life.
  我喜欢露营，因为它可以让我忘记忙碌的生活。
  ★ 短语 hustle and bustle 吵闹喧嚣

- I simply want to lie back and have some time to myself.
  我只是想要躺下来好好享受一个人的悠闲时光。
  ★ 短语 have time 花时间，费时间

Chapter 2 娱乐与休闲 Unit9

Let's catch a big fish!

It'll make a perfect dinner!

在国外都说这几句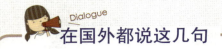

- There is nothing better than sitting around a bonfire and having some marshmallows with friends.
  和朋友坐在篝火边然后吃着棉花糖，没有什么可以比这个更好的了。

- Are you guys playing spin the bottle? That reminds me of my high school days so much.
  你们在玩转瓶子吗？这个游戏让我想起我的高中生活。
  ★ 短语 spin the bottle 转瓶子。年轻人常玩的一种游戏。

- Anyone want to play hide and seek? I'm going to count to 10.
  有人想要玩捉迷藏吗？我数到10就要来抓你们了。
  ★ 短语 hide and seek 捉迷藏

- Look at those mouth-watering lobsters! They will go so well with a glass of white wine.
  看看那些令人口水直流的龙虾！与白酒就是绝配。
  ★ 短语 go well with... 跟～很搭配

- We danced around the bonfire with music and had a wild night.
  我们随着音乐，围着篝火跳舞，度过了一个狂野的夜晚。
  ★ 短语 dance around... 围着～跳舞

- What kind of food should we cook at a bonfire?
  生篝火的时候应该煮什么样的食物呢？
  ★ 短语 what kind of... 哪一种～，哪一类型～

- I can't wait to have some sausages on toast.
  我已经等不及要吃一些香肠配吐司了。
  ★ 短语 can't wait to... 等不及要～

常识补给站

颗粒状的棉花糖(Marshmallow)源自古埃及。从约公元前2000年前开始，古埃及就有现在我们称为棉花糖的甜点。当时只有皇室及祭祀神明时才有机会享受到这种特殊的甜点。棉花糖是由生长在野地沼泽的葵类植物药蜀葵（Athaea Officinalis）所制成。所以棉花糖Marshmallow这个字就是由它本身的植物名称（Mallow）及其所生长的环境（Marsh）组合而成的。

在国外都说这几句

- May I also have a medium steak? It looks juicy and tender.
  我可不可以也来一份五分熟的牛排？它看起来鲜嫩又多汁。

- Knock yourself out. We have plenty of beef.
  你自己来，不要客气。我们还有很多牛肉。
  ★ 短语 knock yourself out 请便，不要客气

- I would kill to have some beer with these delicious foods.
  我很想要一些啤酒来配这些美食。
  ★ 语法 would kill to... 极度渴望去~

- What about me? I'm a vegetarian. What options do I have?
  那我怎么办？我吃素，这边有什么东西是我可以吃的吗？
  ★ 短语 what about... ~如何，~怎么办

- We have all kinds of vegetables here. Which ones do you want? I'm at your service.
  我们有很多不同种类的蔬菜。你想要吃哪一种？我可以为你服务。
  ★ 短语 at your service 为你服务

- Thank you. It's very nice of you to do so.
  谢谢。你这样做真的太好了。
  ★ 短语 It's very nice of you to do so. 你这样做真的太好了。

- Okay, it's dessert time. Who wants some marshmallow on cookies?
  好，接下来是甜点时间。有谁想要吃棉花糖饼干吗？
  ★ 短语 it's time for... 到了~的时间

- Duh. Like you even had to ask.
  那当然，你根本连问都不用问。
  ★ 语法 "Duh"属于较口语的用法，意思是"这还用说，这本来就是，废话（更强烈的用法）"。

- It might be worth it to invest in a camper if you go camping a lot.
  如果你常常去露营的话，那么你可以考虑花钱买一台露营车。
  ★ 短语 invest in... 投资~；耗费~

- Nothing extravagant here, we simply do some cooking over a fire.
  这里没有什么很奢侈的东西，我们只是很简单的在火堆上面做饭。
  ★ 短语 over a fire 在火（堆）上，在炉火上

在国外都说这几句

- I don't want to cook soup at all. It takes too much time.
  我一点也不想煮汤。它太花时间了。
  ★ 短语 not at all 一点也不

- Everyone is struggling with making a fire because the wood is wet.
  每个人生火时都碰到困难，因为木材是湿的。
  ★ 短语 struggle with... 奋斗～；挣扎地做～

- I made some soup at home in advance. It will save us a lot of trouble.
  我在家里已经先煮好了汤。这样可以减少不少的麻烦。
  ★ 短语 in advance 事先，预先

- Can you slice onions, garlic and some carrots up for me?
  你可以帮我把洋葱、大蒜和一些胡萝卜切片吗？
  ★ 短语 slice... up 把～切片

- I think you are burning the meat up.
  我觉得你把肉烤焦了。
  ★ 短语 burn up... 把～烧坏，烤焦

- I brought along food that doesn't need to be cooked, such as salad and crackers.
  我带了一些不需要烹饪的食物，像是沙拉跟饼干。
  ★ 短语 bring along 带来，拿来

- The milk you brought will not hold up much longer. We should drink it up ASAP.
  你带的牛奶没办法放太久。我们应该马上把它喝光。
  ★ 短语 hold up 支撑，保持不错（的状态）

- It's not easy to carry uncooked eggs into a campsite without breaking them by accident.
  把生鸡蛋带到营区，并小心不打碎它们，这不是件容易的事。
  ★ 短语 by accident 意外地

常识补给站

美国为全世界最大乳酪生产国家，其产量约占全世界25%～30%。在美国的饮食当中，常见的起司种类有摩兹瑞拉起司（Mozzarella）、切达起司（Cheddar）和巴马臣干酪（Parmesan）等。

Chapter 3 让身心放松的出国旅游
Going Abroad

Unit 10 | 没有它，你就出不了国
Unit 11 | 完美的旅行计划
Unit 12 | 准备飞向云端
Unit 13 | 过了海关就能到另一个国家
Unit 14 | 关于饭店与迷路
Unit 15 | 旅行是梦想的实践
Unit 16 | 优雅地处理突发状况

跟任何人都可以用英语聊聊天

Unit 10 没有它，你就出不了国

[生活便利贴]

出国旅游人人都爱，但事前准备非常重要。办护照、签证等，样样不能少。另外，机票和饭店的选择，需要多花点时间比较，选择经济实惠的方案，毕竟货比三家不吃亏。解决了旅游需要的文件后，就可以开始做行程的规划，列出自己想去的地点或想做的事情，想想如何将每天的时间充分利用。让我们看看有什么英语句子是对旅游有帮助的吧！

Vocabulary 在国外都用这些词

visa
['vi:zə]
n 签证

sightseeing
['saɪtsi:ɪŋ]
n 观光

temporary
['temprəri]
a 暂时的

interview
['ɪntəvju:]
n/v 面试；对~进行面谈

Visa Waiver Program
ph 免签证计划

EAST (Electronic System for Travel Authorization)
ph 旅游许可电子系统

embassy
['embəsi]
n 大使馆

non-refundable
[nɒn rɪ'fʌndəbl]
a 不可退还的，不可偿还的

revoke
[rɪ'vəʊk]
v 取消，撤回

niece
[ni:s]
n 侄女，外甥女

deposit
[dɪ'pɒzɪt]
n/v 订金，押金

enrich
[ɪn'rɪtʃ]
v 使丰富

spot rate
ph 补差额、差价

popularity
[,pɒpju'lærəti]
n 流行，大众化

ATM
ph 自动取款机

trip
[trɪp]
n 旅行，旅程

withdraw
[wɪð'drɔ:]
v 提取（现金）

receipt
[rɪ'si:t]
n 收据

在国外都说这几句

- I'm going to the USA next month. Do I need to apply for a visa?
  我下个月要去美国。我需要申请签证吗？
  ★ 短语 apply for...　申请～；请求得到～

- Visas can be divided into different categories. Please apply for a certain one based on the purpose of your visit.
  签证可以分为很多不同种类。请依照你出行的目的来申请不同的签证。
  ★ 短语 divide into...　把～分成、划分成～

- A tourist visa is granted for sightseeing purposes only.
  旅游签证专为观光的用途而核发。
  ★ 短语 A be granted for...　A 因为～被授予

- It's only a temporary stay in this country. Does that mean I should make an application for a non-immigrant visa?
  我只会在这个国家短暂停留，这是否表示我应该申请非移民签证？
  ★ 短语 make an application　申请、请求

- In order to apply for a visa, you have to have a valid passport.
  为了申请签证，你必须要有一本有效护照。
  ★ 短语 in order to　为了～，以便～

- Please be aware of the penalties for bringing in prohibited items.
  请注意带违禁品入境会受到刑罚。
  ★ 短语 be aware of　意识到～

- As an applicant, please make sure all the information provided is accurate.
  作为一位申请人，请确认你提供的所有资料准确无误。
  ★ 短语 make sure　确定

- After submitting the application, you might be requested to make an appointment to have an interview.
  申请表递出之后，你有可能会被要求预约面试。
  ★ 短语 make an appointment　预约

- Under no circumstances can you be late for the interview.
  无论如何，面试绝对不可以迟到。
  ★ 短语 under no circumstances　无论如何 / 在任何情况下都不

在国外都说这几句

- Remember to smile when you meet the visa officer **for the first time**.
  第一次见到签证官时，记得要微笑。
  ★ 短语 for the first time 第一次

- Try to relax. Just **greet** the officer **with** a smile. There is nothing to worry about.
  别紧张，只要以微笑跟官员打招呼。没什么好担心的。
  ★ 短语 greet with... 以～招呼，以～问候

- Will the interview **be conducted in** English?
  面谈会以英语进行吗？
  ★ 短语 be conducted in... 以～进行、以～处理

- Do I need to **make** any **preparations for** the interview?
  我需要为面试做什么准备吗？
  ★ 短语 make preparations for... 为～做准备

- You won't **be able to** have any one accompany you when you're having an interview.
  当你面试的时候，其他人不能够跟你一起去。
  ★ 短语 be able to 能够

- Make sure you are prepared to **express yourself** clearly.
  确保你能够清楚地表达你要说的事情。
  ★ 短语 express oneself 表达自己的思想或观点

- Most countries have introduced **e-visas**, so there will be no visa label on your passport.
  很多国家都已经采用电子签证，所以你的护照上面不会有签证贴纸。
  ★ 短语 e-visa 电子签证

- Are you sure you applied for the correct visa for the purpose of your visit?
  你确定申请的是与出行目的符合的正确签证吗？
  ★ 语法 "A + be + sure (that) + 从句" 的意思是 "A 确定～"。

- You must **comply with** all the visa conditions; otherwise, it will be cancelled.
  你必须遵守所有签证有关的条约，否则你的签证会被取消。
  ★ 短语 comply with... 遵守

在国外都说这几句

- Having a visitor visa **allows you to** enter the U.S.A. However, you are not allowed to undertake any type of work.
  拥有旅游签证可以让你到美国旅游。但是你无法从事任何工作。
  ★ 短语 allow A to... 允许 A ～，准许 A ～

- I **intend to** visit England in October. I don't think I need to make an application for visa because Hong Kong is included in England's Visa Waiver Program.
  我打算十月份去一趟英国。由于香港列于英国的免签证计划内，所以我不需要申请签证。
  ★ 短语 intend to... 打算～，想要～

- When you **plan a** trip to the United States, you need to go on the Internet and apply for a travel permit through ESTA.
  当你计划到美国旅游时，你需要上网通过免签程序认证系统获得旅行许可。
  ★ 短语 plan a... 计划～、安排～

- My father doesn't speak English. Can we make a **request for** an officer who speaks Mandarin?
  我爸爸不会说英语。我们可不可以要求一位会讲中文的签证官？
  ★ 短语 make a request for 要求，请求

- You must **fill in** all the mandatory fields; otherwise your application is very likely to be rejected.
  你必须填写所有必填项目，否则你的申请很有可能会被拒绝。
  ★ 短语 fill in 填写

- You should **bring** the entire application and any supporting documents with you **to** the interview.
  去面试的时候你应该携带所有的申请文件以及任何相关文件。
  ★ 短语 bring to... 带去～、带到～

- I am **traveling with** my family. Can I include them on the same application?
  我和家人一起旅游。我可以把他们一起放在同一个申请文件吗？
  ★ 短语 travel with... 与～一起旅游

- I arrived there before my appointed time and was not allowed to **be let into** the building.
  我比预约时间更早抵达那里，而且无法获准进入。
  ★ 短语 be let into... 允许进入～，进到～

跟任何人都可以用英语聊聊天

在国外都说这几句

- Sometimes you will **be asked to** go though an X-ray machine before entering the embassy.
  有时候进入大使馆之前，会要求你通过 X 光扫描检查。
  ★ 短语 ▶ be asked to...　被要求～

- How far in advance should I apply for a visa if I plan to go to Italy?
  如果准备到意大利旅游，我应该在多久之前就开始申请签证？

- My passport **is valid for** ten years.
  我的护照有效期是十年。
  ★ 短语 ▶ be valid for...　有效期～（时间）

- My visa allows me to stay in Australia for 5 years with **multiple-entries**.
  我的签证允许我在澳洲待五年，并可多次进出澳洲。
  ★ 短语 ▶ multiple-entries　多次入境鉴证

- The visa application fee is non-refundable. Even if your visa is refused, you still won't be able to **get** your money **back**.
  签证费用是无法退款的，即使你的签证被拒，你仍然没有办法把申请费拿回来。
  ★ 短语 ▶ get... back　把～要回来，拿回

- If you have questions about **filling out** the forms, please refer to our FAQ page.
  如果你有关于填表的问题，请参考我们的常见问题网页。
  ★ 短语 ▶ fill out...　填写～，填空～，通常指表格和申请书等。

- **How many** photos should be included with my visa application?
  申请表需要附上多少张照片？
  ★ 语法 ▶ "how many + 可数复数名词" 的意思是 "多少～"。

- **What size** photo should be attached to the form?
  表格上面的照片需要什么尺寸的？
  ★ 短语 ▶ what size　什么尺寸

- You will be contacted by the visa office **via e-mail** if your application is incomplete.
  如果你的申请表不完整的话，签证处会以电子邮件方式跟你联系。
  ★ 短语 ▶ via e-mail　以电子信件的方式联系

Dialogue 在国外都说这几句

- You do not need a visa if you are only a transit passenger.
  如果你只是从这个国家过境的话，就不需要签证。
  ★ 短语 transit passenger 过境旅客

- Sometimes you might need a transit visa if you stay at the airport for more than 48 hours as a transit passenger.
  如果你过境时需要待在机场超过 48 小时，那你可能会需要过境签证。
  ★ 短语 transit visa 过境签证

- My primary reason for traveling to the United Kingdom is to participate in a language program.
  我到英国的主要原因是参加语言课程。
  ★ 短语 participate in... 参加～，参与～

- Am I required to pay a non-refundable visa application fee before submitting the document?
  申请签证时，在提交文件前，我就需要缴无法退款的申请费用吗？
  ★ 短语 be required to... 需要～，被要求～

- Breaking the law in our country may result in your visa being revoked.
  在本国犯法会导致你的签证被取消。
  ★ 短语 result in... 结果～，导致～，用来表示结局或结果。

- Please sign the declaration form at the bottom.
  请在表格最下方的声明栏签名。
  ★ 短语 at the bottom 最下方

- The only application fee payment method is by credit card.
  申请费的付款方式我们只接受信用卡。
  ★ 短语 by credit card 以信用卡的方式付费

- My grandfather is over the age of 80. Is an interview still compulsory?
  我外公已经超过 80 岁，必须要安排面谈吗？
  ★ 短语 over the age of + 数字 超过～岁

- Please note, applicants over the age of 75 are not required for an interview.
  请注意，超过 75 岁的申请人不需参加面谈。
  ★ 短语 please note 请注意

Dialogue 在国外都说这几句

- If you are a citizen of China, please bring along your household registration record.
  如果你是中国居民，请带上你的户口簿。
  ★ 短语 household registration record　户口簿

- My aunt accompanied my niece to her interview because she is under the age of 18.
  我阿姨陪我的侄女参加面谈，因为她未满18岁。
  ★ 短语 accompany A to...　陪同A到～，陪A去～

- It is more difficult to get a visa when you are outside of your own country.
  若你不在你所属的国家，签证会比较难核发。
  ★ 短语 be outside of...　在～外面，在～之外

- The photo for a visa application must be in color. Black and white photos will not be accepted.
  申请签证的照片必须是彩色的。我们不收黑白照片。
  ★ 短语 in color　彩色的

- If you cannot be identified from the photo on your current visa application, you will need to submit a new photo.
  如果你的签证申请所附的照片无法辨认是本人，你就需要交新的照片。
  ★ 短语 be identified from...　从～辨识出，从～识别出

- Before applying for a student visa, all students are required to be accepted and pay the deposit for their program.
  申请学生签证以前，所有学生必须先取得学校机构的录取许可并缴上课程订金。
  ★ 短语 student visa　学生签证

- A working holiday visa allows you to stay in Australia for one year.
  打工度假签证可以让你待在澳大利亚长达一年的时间。
  ★ 短语 working holiday visa　打工度假签证，这是一种可以一边打工、一边旅游的特殊签证

- Please read through the information and contact the immigration office if you have any questions about a working holiday visa.
  请详读打工度假签证的信息，若有任何的问题，请联系移民局。
  ★ 短语 read through　详细阅读

- The main purpose of this visa is to allow you to work for unlimited hours.
  这类型签证的主要目的是让你能够不限时数的工作。
  ★ 短语 the purpose of...　～的目的，～的用途

在国外都说这几句

- This visa is for people who are interested in enriching international views of vision.

  此签证是针对那些想要扩展国际视野的人的。

  ★ 短语 be interested in... 对～有兴趣，有兴趣～

- You must be over the age of 18 at the time of your visa application.

  申请这种签证，你必须年满 18 岁。

  ★ 短语 at the time of... 在～的时候

- You can study here for up to 12 months if you are granted this visa.

  若你的签证核发了，你最多可以在这留学 12 个月。

  ★ 短语 up to... 最多可至～，最高可至～

- If you are a working holiday visa holder, you can conduct any kind of work in the country.

  如果你持有打工度假签证，你可以在这个国家进行任何一种工作。

  ★ 短语 any kind of... 任何一～的，任何种类的～

- If you meet certain criteria, you can come to the country without a visa.

  如果你符合某些标准，你可以不用签证就来这个国家。

  ★ 语法 "meet" 最常见的意思是 "遇见，碰上，认识"，但在此句的意思是 "符合，满足"。"meet + (a) standard(s) / (a) requirement(s)" 的意思是 "符合水准、条件"。

- You will be requested to do a health examination for some visa applications.

  有些类型的签证申请会要求你进行体检。

  ★ 短语 health examination 体检

- Fill out the forms and return them to the visa office in your country by post.

  填写这些表格，并邮寄回你所在国家的签证处。

  ★ 短语 return to... 缴回～，归还～

- Can I exchange dollars for Australian dollars, please?

  我可以将美元兑换成澳币吗？

  ★ 短语 exchange for... 兑换～、交换～

- What is 1 pound to the dollar now?

  现在一英镑对美元汇率是多少？

  ★ 语法 "to" 在此句的意思是 "比对，比起"，也就是指出英镑比对美元的汇率。

在国外都说这几句

- The exchange rate can be found on most bank websites.
  外币兑换的利率可以在各银行的网站找到。
  ★ 短语 exchange rate　外币兑换利率

- The bank might charge you a service fee for exchanging currencies.
  银行可能会收取兑换币值的手续费。
  ★ 短语 service fee　手续费

- Traveler's checks are not commonly used, except for in the U.S.
  除了美国，旅行支票在其他地方没有那么广泛地使用。
  ★ 短语 traveler's check　旅行支票

- What face value of notes do you want? We have $20, $50 and $100.
  你想要哪一种面额的钞票？我们有 20 块、50 块跟 100 块的。
  ★ 短语 face value　面额

- I'm sorry, but I seem to have put in the wrong amount.
  很抱歉，但我似乎填错金额了。
  ★ 短语 seem to...　似乎～，好像～

- The exchange rate for cash was $1 to ￥6.63.
  美金兑换人民币的现金兑换汇率是 1：6.63。
  ★ 短语 for cash　现金

- The spot rate is usually better, but you have to pay the difference if you want to cash out.
  即期汇率通常比较划算，但是若你要拿现金的话就必须补差额。
  ★ 短语 pay the difference　补差额

- Broadly speaking, you should avoid exchanging money at a local exchange booth. The exchange rate is really bad there.
  一般来说，除非没有其他选择，否则你应该避免在当地的外币交换所换钱，因为汇率很不划算。
  ★ 短语 broadly speaking　一般来说

- Traveler's checks are fading in popularity because they're not convenient.
  旅行支票已经不流行了，因为它很不方便。
  ★ 短语 fade in popularity　逐渐不流行，慢慢不普及

- Can traveler's checks be reissued if they are lost or stolen?
  若旅行支票遗失或被偷，可以补发吗？
  ★ 短语 be reissued　重新补发

在国外都说这几句

- I would rather not carry a large amount of cash. I can withdraw money from an ATM if needed.
  我宁可不带那么多现金在身上。如果有需要的话我可以去提款机取钱。
  ★ 短语 a large amount of... 一大笔～，很大笔金额的～

- Visa debit cards are widely used in western countries.
  在西方国家，Visa 借记卡被广泛使用。
  ★ 短语 visa debit card　Visa 借记卡

- You should make compare exchange rates from different banks before purchasing other currencies.
  购买外币之前，你应该多比较不同银行的汇率。
  ★ 短语 make compare... 对～加以比较

- Before you leave for your trip, you need to contact your bank and confirm if you can use your credit card overseas.
  你旅行之前，需要先询问你的银行，确认一下你的信用卡在国外能不能用。
  ★ 短语 leave for... 动身到～，出发到～

- You should avoid using a credit card to withdraw cash in foreign countries because the interest rate is extremely high.
  你应该避免在国外使用信用卡提取现金，因为费用非常高。
  ★ 短语 credit card 信用卡

- Maybe you should talk to the bank teller at the foreign currency exchange counter.
  也许你应该和外币兑换银行的服务员谈一谈。
  ★ 短语 talk to... 与～谈谈，与～讲话

- Can I have the receipt, please?
  可以给我收据吗？

- My parents reminded me that we should have travel insurance.
  我父母提醒我们要购买旅游平安险。
  ★ 短语 remind A that... 提醒 A ～

> **常识补给站**
>
> 旅行支票可以用的货币有美金、加拿大元、英镑、日元、澳元、人民币以及欧元。大部分的面额为 20、50 或 100。旅行支票不会过期，所以可以先购买保存起来以备未来使用。

跟任何人都可以用英语聊聊天

Unit 11 完美的旅行计划

[生活便利贴]

解决了护照、签证这些事情，接下来就要好好规划旅游行程了！若是跟团旅行，就不需要花太多时间安排行程，但如果是自游行，那么就要开始好好做功课。依照自己的预算选择机票、饭店以及交通工具。另外，不管旅行的目的地是哪里，都要事先查询当地的天气以及了解一下文化风俗，避免因为不熟悉当地的文化，而闹一堆笑话。

Vocabulary 在国外都用这些词

MP3 03-11

weather
['weðə]
n 天气

luggage
['lʌgɪdʒ]
n 行李

time zone
ph 时区

facility
[fə'sɪləti]
n 设施

insurance
[ɪn'ʃʊərəns]
n 保险

overweight
[,əʊvə'weɪt]
a 超重的

finalize
['faɪnəlaɪz]
v 完成，结束

schedule
['skedʒuːl]
n 行程

by appointment
ph 按照约定的时间或地点践约

expensive
[ɪk'spensɪv]
a 昂贵的

frequent
['friːkwənt]
a 频繁的

layover
['leɪəʊvə]
n 转机时间

deluxe
[,də'lʌks]
a 豪华的

breathtaking
['breθteɪkɪŋ]
a 惊人的，美不胜收的

smoke free
ph 禁烟

special
['speʃl]
a 特别的

suite
[swiːt]
n 套房

 在国外都说这几句

- We are on a tight budget so we want to plan a vacation that doesn't cost too much.
  我们的预算有限，所以想要计划一个不需花太多钱的假期。
  ★ 短语 on a budget　缺钱，（经济）拮据

- Packing for a vacation is everybody's nightmare. I wish someone could do it for me.
  为旅行打包是每个人的梦魇，真希望有人能帮我。
  ★ 短语 pack for...　为～打包，为～（目的）装箱

- You should choose clothes that are appropriate for the local weather.
  你应该选择适合当地天气的衣服。
  ★ 短语 be appropriate for...　适合～，合适～

- It is a smart idea to place the things you use the most in your hand luggage.
  把最常用的东西放在手提行李是聪明的做法。
  ★ 短语 hand luggage　手提行李

- Always remember to adjust your watch if you are traveling to a country in a different time zone.
  如果你要去的国家在不同的时区，要记得调整手表的时间。
  ★ 短语 remember to...　记得去～

- I need a copy of my medicines' prescriptions because the custom's officer might ask for it.
  我需要药品的处方签，因为海关可能会要求我出示。
  ★ 短语 copy of...　～的影本，～的副本

- Lay out all the items you intend to take and mark a tick on your packing list when you put it in your luggage.
  把所有你想打包的东西摊开来，当你把它放到行李里面后，在你的打包清单上面打个钩。
  ★ 短语 lay out...　展出～，摆出～

- We should contact the travel agent about the hotel's in-room facilities.
  我们应该联络旅游专员，问问有关饭店的房内设施。
  ★ 短语 in-room　房内的

- When it comes to personal toiletries, travel kits are always the best choice.
  当谈到个人清洁用品时，旅行套装是最好的选择。
  ★ 短语 when it comes to...　当谈到～，涉及～

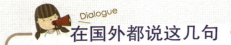

在国外都说这几句

- The travel kits always come in convenient sizes.
  旅行套装的尺寸一般都很方便。
  ★ 短语 travel kit　旅行套装

- Never pack items such as passports and plane tickets in checked luggage.
  像是护照和机票等物品，绝不要打包在托运的行李中。
  ★ 短语 checked luggage　托运行李

- You cannot take more than 100ml of liquids with you on board.
  你不可以带超过100毫升的液体上飞机。
  ★ 短语 on board　在飞机上；在船上

- My mother is struggling over if she should pack her coat or not.
  我妈妈还在纠结是不是要把大衣也装进行李箱。
  ★ 短语 struggle over...　挣扎；争斗

- If you are worried, you can keep all valuable items in the hotel safe.
  如果你担心的话，你可以把所有贵重物品放在饭店的保险箱内。
  ★ 短语 keep in...　置于～中，摆在～

- I would like to pay for my flight ticket by credit card, because then I will be covered by travel insurance.
  我想要用信用卡买机票，因为这样就可以享有旅游险。
  ★ 短语 be covered by...　被～覆盖

- You can find all sorts of travel information on the web.
  你可以在网络上找到各种不同的旅游信息。
  ★ 短语 on the web　网络上，上网

- Don't pack more than you need, or you will end up paying extra for overweight luggage.
  不要打包你不需要的东西，不然你最后会把钱都花在超重行李上。
  ★ 短语 more than...　多于～，超过～

- If you are flying with a budget airline and know that your luggage is going to be overweight, you can always purchase more luggage allowance on the website.
  如果你是飞廉价航空又知道你的行李一定会超重，那么你就可以先上网加购额外的行李公斤数。
  ★ 短语 luggage allowance　行李公斤数

在国外都说这几句

- You must conform to the security procedures.
  你一定要遵守这些安全措施。
  ★ 短语 conform to / with...　符合～，遵守～

- You should start packing at least a week prior to your departure.
  你应该在旅行前至少一个星期就开始打包。
  ★ 短语 prior to...　在～以前，在～之前

- Half of the fun of traveling is in the planning because you can picture yourself in those beautiful sites.
  旅游有一半的乐趣是在计划，因为你可以想象自己身处在那些美丽的景点里。
  ★ 短语 half of...　一半的～，二分之一的～

- Are you sure you want to stay in a five-star hotel? It's going to cost you a lot.
  你确定你要住在五星级酒店？这样会花你很多钱。
  ★ 短语 five-star hotel　五星级酒店

- I'm going to put you in charge of traffic. Make sure you are familiar with the public transportation when we get there.
  你负责交通的部分。我们抵达的时候，你要确保你对当地的公共交通工具很熟悉。
  ★ 短语 be familiar with...　对～很熟悉

- I want to travel as comfortably as possible while maintaining my budget.
  我想要尽可能舒舒服服地旅游，同时也要符合我的预算。
  ★ 短语 maintain A's budget　符合 A 的预算、经费

- You can get a much lower rate when taking a vacation during the off-season.
  选择淡季的时候旅行，你可以得到比较便宜的折扣。
  ★ 短语 off-season　淡季（的）

- It took us three weeks to finalize the schedule.
  我们花了 3 个星期才确定最终的行程。
  ★ 语法 "it takes us + 时间" 意思是 "花了我们多少时间"。

- We are heading off on a big adventure. I'm sure we will have a great time together.
  我们就要去探险了，我们一定会玩得很开心。
  ★ 短语 head off...　动身去～，出发到～

在国外都说这几句

- I will **pay a visit to** the pharmacy and buy some over-the-counter medicine.
  我会去一趟药店，买一些非处方药。
  ★ 短语 pay a visit to　去；拜访

- We should **divide up the work**; each of us should be responsible for different things.
  我们应该分工合作；每个人负责不同的事情。
  ★ 短语 divide up the work　分工

- You should **split up** your cash, traveler's checks and credit cards in different bags.
  你应该把现金、旅游支票和信用卡分开放在不同的包里。
  ★ 短语 split up...　分开～；划分～

- Are there any **special events** that are by appointment only?
  有哪些特别的活动是要预约才可以参加的吗？
  ★ 短语 special event　（平常没有）特殊场合才有的活动、庆典、庆祝

- Did you **figure out** what currency we will need?
  你清楚我们需要使用哪种货币了吗？
  ★ 短语 figure out...　想出～；理解～

- Did you **find out** which bank has the best exchange rate?
  你找到哪一家银行有最低的外币汇率了吗？
  ★ 短语 find out...　找出～

- The bank on the corner is **having a promotion**. We should go there.
  转角的那家银行现在正在做促销。我们应该去看看。
  ★ 短语 have a promotion　促销

- Let's **keep our eyes open** for deals advertised on the Internet.
  我们睁大眼睛找找网络广告上的旅游行程。
  ★ 短语 keep A's eye open　A 要张大眼睛；A 要注意

- Should we arrange **airport pick up** or do you prefer to go there by public transportation?
  我们是安排机场接送还是自己搭交通过去？
  ★ 短语 airport pick up　机场接送

在国外都说这几句

- It's time to print out our reservation confirmations.
  该把我们的订位／订房确认单打印出来了。
  ★ 短语 print out... 把～打印出来

- You cannot expect the rest of us to run on your schedule. That's very selfish.
  你不能期望我们大家都依照你的行程进行。那非常自私。
  ★ 短语 the rest of... 其余的～，其他的～

- I cannot wait to make plenty of memories by meeting the locals and enjoying their food!
  我迫不及待地想去认识当地人、好好享受他们的美食，并留下满满的回忆。
  ★ 短语 cannot wait to... 等不及～、迫不及待～

- It's important to take care of yourself when traveling. Going to a doctor overseas can be very expensive.
  旅行时，你要好好照顾好自己。在国外看医生是非常贵的。
  ★ 短语 take care of... 照顾～，照料～

- More and more frequent travelers choose to book their airfares online.
  越来越多经常旅行的人选择在网上订机票。
  ★ 短语 more and more 越来越多的

- Trust me. It pays to shop around to find the best flight ticket deals.
  相信我。找机票时货比三家是值得的。
  ★ 短语 it pays to... ～是值得的，～是划算的

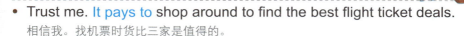

- If you know your travel plans well in advance, then you might be able to get early bird deals.
  如果你事先就知道旅游行程，你可能可以拿到早到早得的优惠。
  ★ 短语 early bird 早到优惠

常识补给站

廉价航空公司（Low-cost Carrier，也称 Low-cost Airline，No-frills Airline 或 Budget Airline，经常简称为 LCC），中文简称廉航，指的是将营运成本控制至比一般航空公司低的航空公司。这类航空公司一般在飞机上不提供餐饮服务（除非加价要求），行李的限制也会比较严格。

在国外都说这几句

- The earlier you book the ticket, the cheaper the price will be.
  你越早订票，价钱就会越便宜。

- You should search different travel sites for the lowest deals.
  你应该搜寻不同网站找出最便宜的价格。
  ★ 短语 search for... 寻找～，搜寻～，此短语表示希望得到想要的东西。

- Search several travel sites to see if there is any last-minute promotion that meets your needs.
  多搜寻一些旅游网站，看看是否有最后的网络促销折扣能满足你的需求。
  ★ 短语 last-minute 最后的，最后一分钟的

- Flying standby is risky as no one can promise that there will be a seat for you.
  候补机位风险很大，因为没有人可以保证你会有位置。

- A standby ticket means you only get a seat on a sold-out flight if someone doesn't show up.
  候补机票意味着班机上有乘客没出现，你才可以得到机位。
  ★ 短语 sold-out 卖光的，销售一空的

- The flight was overbooked, so the airline decided to upgrade me to business-class.
  这个航班超额订位，所以航空公司决定把我升级到商务舱。
  ★ 短语 business-class 商务舱

- I purchased the ticket through an airline website. However, I changed my mind. Can I change it to a later date?
  我从航空公司的网站上订票。然而，我改变主意了。可以改晚一点的日期出发吗？
  ★ 短语 change A's mind A 改变主意

常识补给站

手机漫游（roaming）指的是用户向移动通信运营商申请让自己的手机电话号码可以在国外使用，使通信可以保持而不中断。通常情况下，处于漫游状态的用户并不需要更换手机号码，但是在使用某些服务时可能会受到限制，费率也会明显提高，因此时常有用户因为在漫游时没有关闭非必需的服务（如数据网络等）而产生高额漫游费用的情况。

在国外都说这几句

- Flying at non-direct flight can save your money on airfare.
  选择非直飞的航班可以帮你省一点钱。
  ★ 短语 non-direct flight 非直飞的航班

- You'll receive your e-ticket by e-mail once the payment is settled.
  一旦费用付清之后，你将会收到电子邮件寄来的电子机票。
  ★ 短语 e-ticket 电子机票

- I'd like to book a flight from Beijing to Melbourne on March 1st.
  我想要订3月1日从北京飞往墨尔本的航班。
  ★ 短语 from A to B 从A到B

- Your connecting flight departs at 10:30. That means you will have a two-hour layover.
  你转乘的航班会于10点30分起飞。这代表你将有两个小时的时间转机。
  ★ 短语 depart at... ～出发，～启程

- During the layover, you can do some shopping in the duty-free shops at the airport.
  你可以利用转机的时间，在机场的免税店买点东西。
  ★ 短语 duty-free shops 免税商店

- Would you like to fly business class or coach?
  你想要搭乘商务舱还是经济舱？
  ★ 语法 Would you like to...? 你想要～？

- Could you please book me a first class direct flight to London for the 1st of May?
  您可以帮我订一张5月1日直飞伦敦的头等舱机票吗？
  ★ 短语 first class 头等舱

- I'd like to book two economy class round-trip tickets to San Francisco.
  我要两张飞往旧金山的经济舱往返机票。
  ★ 短语 round-trip ticket 往返票

- I'd like to book a premium economy open return, please.
  我要订一张回程尚未决定日期的特级经济舱来回机票。
  ★ 短语 open return 尚未决定回程日期的机票

- If possible, please avoid any red eye flights.
  如果可以的话，请不要订红眼航班。
  ★ 短语 red eye 红眼航班，指的是深夜飞、清晨抵达的班机。

在国外都说这几句

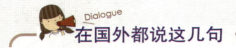

- **Making hotel reservations** on the Internet is very easy and convenient.
  在网上订饭店既简单又方便。
  ★ 短语 make a hotel reservation 预订饭店住房

- What **types of** rooms do they offer at this hotel?
  他们这家饭店提供哪些房型？
  ★ 短语 type of... ～的类型，～的样式

- Is there a gym in your hotel?
  你们的饭店有没有健身房？

- We have **single rooms**, twin rooms and executive suites available at the moment.
  我们目前尚有单人房、双人房和行政套房可供预订。
  ★ 短语 single room 单人房

- What's the rate for **presidential suite** per night?
  总统套房一个晚上的收费是多少？
  ★ 短语 presidential suite 总统套房

- I want to have a twin room with an **ocean view**.
  我想要一间有海景的双人房。
  ★ 短语 ocean view 可以看到海岸风景的

- At the moment, all the double rooms are fully booked. There is only one **standard** single **room** left.
  目前所有双人房都客满，只剩一间标准单人房。
  ★ 短语 standard room 标准房

- **Is** the Wi-Fi **free for** hotel guests?
  饭店住客可以免费使用无线网络吗？
  ★ 短语 be free for A A 可免费使用

- We know nothing about this area. Let's ask the receptionist to **get** us **a taxi**.
  我们对这一带一点都不熟悉。我们请饭店前台帮我们叫出租车吧。
  ★ 短语 get a taxi 叫出租车

- Do you offer any discounts if I **stay for** more than 10 days?
  如果我住超过 10 天，你们能够提供折扣吗？
  ★ 短语 stay for + 天数 待多少天

在国外都说这几句

- I would like to book a deluxe harbor-view room for 10 days.
  我想预订一间豪华港景房，住宿时间为 10 天。
  ★ 短语 harbor-view 可以看到海港景色的

- Is it possible to have early check-in if I arrive early on the day?
  若我当天提早抵达，我是否可以提前入住饭店？
  ★ 短语 early check-in 提早登记入住

- In that case, I recommend booking the room for the prior night to guarantee immediate access.
  若是这样的话，我建议一并预订前一晚的房间，这样才能保证快速入住。
  ★ 短语 in that case 既然那样，如果那样的话

- You can enjoy the breathtaking view of the entire city of Melbourne.
  你可以在房间里就享受到墨尔本全市美景。
  ★ 短语 view of... ～的景色，～的景致

- Our hotel provides barrier free access for people with special needs.
  我们的饭店提供无障碍通道给有这类特殊需求的房客。
  ★ 短语 barrier free access 无障碍通道

- All rooms are smoke-free. But a smoking area is available on the ground floor.
  所有的房间都禁烟房间，但是我们在一楼有设置吸烟区。
  ★ 短语 be available 有提供的；可得到的

- A credit card must be presented to the reception when checking in. This applies to all reservations made through the website.
  所有通过网络订位的旅客，在登记入住时，都必须在柜台出示信用卡。
  ★ 短语 be presented to... 出示给～

- Our spacious suites are ideal for both business and entertaining.
  我们宽敞的套房，对出差和玩乐的旅客都很适合。
  ★ 短语 be ideal for... 对～来说很完美；非常适合～

- All the hotel guests are entitled to enjoy our breakfast buffet.
  所有饭店的旅客都可享用饭店的自助式早餐。
  ★ 短语 be entitled to... 使有资格～

- I would like to set up a morning call service at 7:00 a.m.
  我想要预订早上 7 点的叫早服务。
  ★ 短语 morning call service 叫早服务

跟任何人都可以用英语聊聊天

Unit 12 准备飞向云端

[生活便利贴]

规划了那么久，终于可以开开心心地出国了！不过托运行李的公斤数可要先控制好，不然到了机场，还没出国就已经把钱花在不必要的事情上，那可真的是扎心啊！出国玩的同时，一定要小心自身的安全，以防在国外叫天天不应、叫地地不灵。事先做好功课，若该区晚上的治安欠佳，那么就要尽量避免晚上自己独自出门。

Vocabulary 在国外都用这些词

e-ticket
n 电子机票

queue
[kju:]
n 队伍

advise
[əd'vaɪz]
v 建议

ground crew
ph 地勤人员

seat
[si:t]
n 位置，座位

take off
ph 飞机起飞

catalogue
['kætəlɒg]
n 目录

smartphone
['smɑ:tfəʊn]
n 智能手机

inform
[ɪn'fɔ:m]
v 通知

trolley
['trɒlɪ]
n 手推车

postage charge
ph 邮资

constantly
['kɒnstəntlɪ]
ad 不断地；时常地

snore
[snɔ:]
v 打呼

violation
[ˌvaɪə'leɪʃn]
n 违反，违规

sock
[sɒk]
n 袜子

backpack
['bækpæk]
n 背包

aisle
[aɪl]
n 走道

blindfold
['blaɪndfəʊld]
n 眼罩

在国外都说这几句

- **Print out** the e-ticket you received before heading to the airport.
  出发前往机场前，把你收到的电子机票打印出来。
  ★ 短语 print out... 打印出～

- Our flight number is CX123, which **check-in counter** should we go to?
  我们的航班号是 CX123，我们应该要到哪个柜台报到？
  ★ 短语 check-in counter 报到柜台

- Look at the long queue! It will take forever for us to check in. I'm going for the **self-service check-in** kiosks.
  你看看这个队伍那么长！要等很久才会轮到我们。我决定去找自助报到服务亭。
  ★ 短语 "self-service check-in" 的意思是 "自助报到"，现在许多机场都开始提供这种便利的报到服务，通过自助报到服务柜台，只要几个简单的步骤，就可以立即完成报到和选位手续。

- Check-in counters are **on the ground floor**.
  办理登机手续的柜台在一楼。
  ★ 短语 "on the + 序数词（second, third...）floor" 的意思是第～层楼。

- **You are advised to** arrive at the airport 2 hours prior to departure time.
  建议你要在飞机起飞的两个小时前抵达机场。
  ★ 短语 A be advised to 建议 A ～，A 被建议～

- If you **are still unsure of check-in time**, please contact your airline directly.
  如果你不确定办理登机手续的时间，请直接与你的航空联络。
  ★ 短语 be unsure of + n. 不确定 n.，对 n. 没把握

- To save time, please **have your tickets and passport ready**.
  为了节省时间，请把（机）票和护照拿在手上准备好。
  ★ 短语 have + n. + ready 把 n. 准备好

- Please **be aware that** carry-on baggage limit is 5kg per person.
  请注意，手提行李的限制为每人 5 公斤。
  ★ 短语 be aware that... 注意～

- Self-service check-in **is open to** all passengers. If you have any problem operating the machine, please contact the ground crew.
  办理登机手续的自助机开放给所有乘客使用。若你对机器使用有任何问题，请与地勤人员联络。
  ★ 短语 be open to... 开放给～，公开供～使用

在国外都说这几句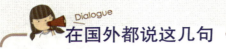

- After obtaining your boarding pass from the self-service kiosks, you can go directly to the baggage check-in counter.
  从自助办理登机台拿到登机证之后,你就可以直接去托运行李。
  ★ 短语 boarding pass 登机证

- Once your e-ticket is issued, you can make changes to your flight online.
  一旦你的电子机票已出票,你可以在线上更改你的航班信息。
  ★ 短语 make changes 做变动,做改变

- Airline staff will be around if you need any further assistance.
  若你需要进一步的协助,航空公司工作人员会在附近协助你。
  ★ 短语 be around 在旁边;在附近

- Before going to the airport, we can use online check-in to pick preferable seats via the Internet.
  前往机场前,我们可以使用线上办理登机的服务在网络上选择你想要的座位。
  ★ 短语 via the Internet 经由网络,以网络

- I'm so looking forward going shopping in the duty-free shops in the waiting lounge.
  我好期待在候机大厅的免税商店购物。
  ★ 短语 duty-free shop 免税商店,可简写成 DFS。

- You will be requested to show your boarding pass if you wish to make a purchase in the duty-free shops.
  在免税店买东西的时候,店员会要求你出示登机牌。
  ★ 短语 make a purchase 购物

- Please take your luggage and boarding pass to the express luggage line if you have already finished self-check in online.
  如果你已经在线上办理完登机,请拿着你的行李和登机牌到快速行李托运处排队。
  ★ 短语 take to... 拿到~、拿去~

- I should arrive at the boarding gate at least 30 minutes before the departure time.
  我应该在飞机起飞至少 30 分钟前抵达登机门。
  ★ 短语 arrive at... 抵达,到达

- Hurry up. We need to check in 2 hours ahead of the departure time.
  快一点。我们要在起飞前两小时办好登机手续。
  ★ 短语 ahead of... 在~之前

在国外都说这几句

- The food court is on the other side of the airport.
  美食区在机场的另一边。
  ★ 短语 on the other side of...　在～的另一边、侧

- Do you prefer a window seat or an aisle seat?
  你想要靠窗还是靠走道的座位？
  ★ 短语 awindow seat　靠窗的座位，an aisle seat　靠走道的座位

- When can we board the plane? Do I still have time to grab a coffee?
  我们什么时候登机？我还有时间去买杯咖啡喝吗？
  ★ 短语 board the plane / ship / train　上飞机 / 船 / 火车

- Excuse me, is our flight going to take off on time?
  不好意思，请问我们的航班会准时起飞吗？
  ★ 短语 excuse me　不好意思；请问

- Unfortunately, your flight is going to be delayed due to the weather.
  很不幸地，你们的航班由于天气原因延误了。
  ★ 短语 due to　由于

- Will you be traveling in business class or premium economy?
  你会搭乘商务舱还是特选经济舱？
  ★ 短语 travel in + 舱等　搭乘（舱）旅行

- On the day of your flight, please check the airline's website to make sure your flight is on schedule.
  班机起飞当天，请查询航空公司网站，确认你的航班会按原计划起飞。

- Please note that the check-in counter will be closed 20 minutes before departure.
  请注意，办理登机的柜台会在飞机起飞前的 20 分钟关闭。
  ★ 短语 please note that...　请注意～；请指明～

- If your luggage exceeds your allowance, you'll be charged for each extra kilogram.
  如果你的行李超重，针对超重的公斤数，你必须缴付超额费用。
  ★ 短语 charge for...　为～收费；索价～

 在国外都说这几句

- We are catching a domestic connecting flight. Therefore, we will have to recheck our luggage at the first port of entry.
  我们要赶国内转机航班。因此我们必须在入境国重新登记行李。
  ★ 短语 port of entry　进口港，入境港，报关港

- All the passengers will be requested to go through Customs and security.
  所有的乘客都会被要求通过海关跟安全检查。
  ★ 短语 go through...　通过～；进入～

- The ground crew will instruct you to take a shuttle bus to catch your connecting flight.
  地勤人员会指示你去搭乘转机接驳车去搭转乘的班机。
  ★ 短语 take a +（交通工具）　搭乘（交通工具）

- I don't mind flying economy, but the only problem is that there is not enough leg room for me.
  我不介意坐经济舱，但唯一的问题是经济舱没有足够的伸腿空间。
  ★ 短语 leg room　供伸腿的空间，腿的活动余地

- We will be showing you a safety demo before the airplane takes off. Please pay attention to it.
  我们将会在飞机起飞前，播放一段飞行的安全示范影片。敬请注意观赏。
  ★ 短语 pay attention to...　关心～，注意～

- The in-flight entertainment system allows you to watch the programs you like without having to share it with others.
  机上的娱乐系统让你们可以看自己喜欢的节目，而且不需要跟别人共用。
  ★ 短语 share with...　与～分享，与～共用

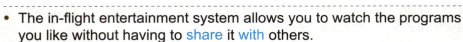

> **常识补给站**
>
> 　　飞机餐就是民航飞机在飞行中供应给旅客的餐饮，是长途飞行中一个重要的部分。飞机餐的餐点内容由航空公司来定。由于坐上飞机后，人们飞上万米高空后，味觉和嗅觉都会因为外在的干燥和气压而有所改变，所以航空公司也须费心研究出适合飞行时味蕾的餐点。

在国外都说这几句

- We have to run to the boarding gate! The airplane is about to take off in 20 minutes.
  飞机再有 20 分钟就起飞了！我们得跑着去登机门了。
  ★ 短语 ▶ be about to...　即将～，马上～

- Hey, look at the in-flight duty free shopping catalogues. It provides additional 10% off.
  嘿，看看机上免税商品的目录。它还提供了额外的九折优惠。

- My seat is right next to the emergency exit.
  我的座位在紧急逃生口的旁边。
  ★ 短语 ▶ next to...　在～旁边；几乎～

- The earphones and safety instructions are in the seat pocket in front of you.
  耳机和安全指南就在你座位前方的袋子中。
  ★ 短语 ▶ in front of...　在～前面

- You need to buckle up and turn off your smartphone.
  你要系紧安全带并关掉智能手机。
  ★ 短语 ▶ buckle up　系上安全带

- Please put up your tray and seat in the upright position. We are about to take off.
  请把你的餐盘收好，并将椅背竖直。我们即将起飞了。
  ★ 短语 ▶ put up...　升起～，举起～

- Can you show me how to plug in the earphones?
  你可以告诉我如何插上耳机吗？
  ★ 短语 ▶ plug in...　插上～（插头）以接通电源

- I am going to take a good rest on the plane.
  我要在飞机上好好休息一下。
  ★ 短语 ▶ take / have a rest　休息

- The passenger just passed out on the plane. Please inform the cabin crew to help him.
  有一名乘客在飞机上昏倒。请通知机组人员来帮忙。
  ★ 短语 ▶ pass out　昏倒，失去知觉

在国外都说这几句

- Please fill out the landing card if this country is your final destination.
  若此国家是你的旅游目的地，那么请填写入境卡。
  ★ 短语 final destination   最终目的地

- Could I have an extra pillow and a night kit, please?
  能多给我一个枕头和夜间盥洗套组吗？
  ★ 短语 night kit   夜间盥洗套组，一般包含了袜子、牙刷、牙膏以及眼罩。

- Welcome aboard. Would you like a copy of today's newspaper?
  欢迎登机。你需要一份今天的报纸吗？
  ★ 短语 welcome aboard   欢迎（请）登机

- Do you mind switching seats with me?
  你介意跟我换一下位子吗？
  ★ 短语 switch with...   与～交换；与～调换

- As a matter of fact, I don't mind changing seats with you as long as yours is a window seat as well.
  事实上，我不介意和你换位子，只要你的位子也是靠窗的位子。
  ★ 短语 as a matter of fact   事实上，实际上

- Can you assign my seat right next to my daughter? I prefer to sit with my daughter.
  你可以把我的位子安排在我女儿旁边吗？我想和我的女儿坐在一起。
  ★ 短语 sit with...   与～坐在一起

- Ladies and gentlemen, the cabin crew will be serving drinks shortly.
  各位先生、女士，机组人员将很快为您送上饮料。
  ★ 短语 ladies and gentlemen   各位先生、女士

- The lavatory is currently occupied.
  洗手间正在使用中。
  ★ 语法 飞机的洗手间通常有两个灯号，一个是"occupied"代表"有人使用中"，另一个则是"vacant"代表"无人使用"。

- The passenger who sits behind me keeps kicking my seat. Can you deal with it?
  坐在我后面的乘客一直踢我的椅子。你可以处理一下吗？
  ★ 短语 deal with...   处理～；应付～

 在国外都说这几句

- Please put your carry-on luggage in the bin that is on top of your seat.
  请将你的随行行李置于座位上方的柜子里。
  ★ 短语 on top of...　在～的上方

- I'm browsing through the in-flight entertainment catalogue.
  我正在翻阅机上娱乐系统的目录。
  ★ 短语 browse through...　浏览～；随便翻阅～

- The flight attendant will make an announcement when in-flight shopping is available.
  机上购物服务开始时，空乘人员将会广播通知。
  ★ 短语 flight attendant　空乘人员

- The flight attendant brought the trolley to me and asked me what kind of drink I would like to have.
  空乘人员将手推车推到旁边，并且询问我想要什么饮料。
  ★ 短语 bring to...　带到～、带来～

- Would you like me to show you the watch you're interested in?
  你想看一下那块你感兴趣的表吗？
  ★ 短语 be interested in...　对～有兴趣

- You can pay for this necklace with most major credit cards.
  你可以使用国内外主流信用卡付这条项链的费用。
  ★ 短语 pay for...　为～付款，付～费

- I'm sorry. The item you are looking for is not available anymore. Would you like to have a look at something else?
  很抱歉。你正在看的这件商品已经不再继续贩售了。你要不要再看看其他的东西？
  ★ 短语 not...anymore　不再～

- Are the items listed in the catalogue available for home delivery?
  目录上列出的所有商品都可以送货上门吗？
  ★ 短语 home delivery　送货上门

- Home delivery prices will be adjusted for tax and postage charges.
  送货上门服务的价格将因税金和邮资而有所调整。
  ★ 短语 be adjusted for...　调整～，调节～

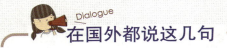 在国外都说这几句

- That kid is running around the entire plane and yelling at his brother loudly.
  那个小孩在飞机上跑来跑去又一直对他的哥哥大吼大叫。
  ★ 短语 yell at...　对～叫喊

- When the seat belt light is on, please return to your seat and fasten your seat belt.
  当安全带的警示灯亮起时，请回到你的座位，并请系上安全带。
  ★ 短语 return to　返回

- Stop constantly digging through the overhead bin.
  请不要一直在舱顶的置物箱翻翻找找。
  ★ 短语 dig through...　挖掘～，发掘～

- You should not get out of your seat when the plane is preparing to land.
  当飞机准备降落的时候，你不应该离开座位。
  ★ 短语 get out of...　逃避～；离开～

- People should not sit back in full recline when it's dining time.
  人们不应该在用餐的时候将椅背完全后调。
  ★ 短语 in full recline　（将座位的靠背）完全后仰

- The guy next to me snores. Can I sit somewhere else?
  坐在我旁边的这个人打呼。我可以换到别的位置去吗？
  ★ 短语 somewhere else　其他地方

- The passenger left his notebook on even though he was told to turn it off.
  即使空乘人员叫他把笔记本电脑关上，这位乘客还是一直开着电脑。
  ★ 短语 leave... on　将～保持开启／开机的状态

- I suggest that you steer clear of alcohol and caffeine. Otherwise, you might not be able to fall asleep.
  我建议你避免酒精和咖啡因。不然你很有可能会睡不着。
  ★ 短语 steer clear of...　避免～，避开～

- The mother is attempting to calm her baby down.
  这个妈妈试图要让她的小孩安静下来。
  ★ 短语 attempt to...　试图～；企图～

在国外都说这几句

- **Smoking is prohibited** on this airplane. Any violators will be fined.
  本航班为禁烟飞机。违者会被处以罚款。
  ★ 短语 A is prohibited A 是被禁止的

- The airline provides passengers with a pair of socks to **keep them warm**.
  这家航空公司为所有乘客提供一双袜子，以便保暖。
  ★ 短语 keep warm 保暖

- I hope I won't sit with an **armrest wrestler** this time.
  我希望这次我不会跟喜欢抢椅子扶手的人一起坐。
  ★ 短语 armrest wrestler 喜欢跟邻座的人抢椅子扶手的人，喜欢占据整个椅子扶手的人

- I wanted to go to the rest room. However, the person sitting next to me was in deep sleep and I didn't want to **wake him up**.
  我想去洗手间。但是坐我旁边的人睡得很熟，我不想吵醒他。
  ★ 短语 wake A up 把 A 叫醒

- The man's backpack has **taken up** all the space in the overhead bin. I have to put mine somewhere else.
  那个人的背包占用了舱顶置物柜所有的空间。我必须要把我的行李放在别的地方。
  ★ 短语 take up... 占用～（空间／时间），占去～（空间／时间）

- Please **keep** all of your personal belongings **out of** the aisle.
  请不要将你的个人物品放在走道。
  ★ 短语 keep out of... 使～不进入

- The passenger **made a** special **request** for vegetarian food.
  那个乘客提出素食餐的特别要求。
  ★ 短语 make a request 提出要求

- Every time I board a plane, I **am** always **greeted with** a great smile from flight attendants.
  每次我登机时，空服人员都会带着微笑欢迎我。
  ★ 短语 be greeted with... 受到～的欢迎

- The captain is **making an announcement** informing us of the weather at our destination.
  机长正在广播，告知我们目的地的天气。
  ★ 短语 make an announcement 广播；通知

跟任何人都可以用英语聊聊天

Unit 13 过了**海关**就能到另一个国家

[生活便利贴]

出入海关有许多需要注意的事情，比如身上不可以带超过 100ml 的液体或尖锐物品等。由于每个国家的规定不同，限制的物品也会有差异，一般都会限制肉、鱼类食品（生食）、种子及含种子的物品等。这些东西都需要在海关申报，由海关人员来告知此物品是否可以入境该国，如果不行，那就只能当场丢弃并销毁。

Vocabulary 在国外都用这些词

MP3 03-31

immigration
[ˌɪmɪˈɡreɪʃn]
n 移民（局）

plant
[plɑːnt]
n 植物

international
[ˌɪntəˈnæʃnəl]
a 国际的

escalator
[ˈeskəleɪtə]
n 手扶梯

seed
[siːd]
n 种子

reservation
[ˌrezəˈveɪʃn]
n 预约

London
[ˈlʌndən]
n 伦敦

photography
[fəˈtɒɡrəfɪ]
n 照相、摄影

hostel
[ˈhɒstl]
n 青年旅社

cigarette
[ˌsɪɡəˈret]
n 香烟

dairy products
ph 乳制品

common
[ˈkɒmən]
a 普及的，普遍的

language
[ˈlæŋɡwɪdʒ]
n 语言

checkpoint
[ˈtʃekpɔɪnt]
n 检查站

arrangement
[əˈreɪndʒmənt]
n 安排

verify
[ˈverɪfaɪ]
v 证明，证实

forbidden
[fəˈbɪdn]
a 被禁止的

medium
[ˈmiːdɪəm]
a 中型的；中间的

在国外都说这几句

- Before entering other countries, we must clear customs and immigration.

  进入其他国家前，我们必须通过海关和入境检查。

  ★ 短语 enter 进入～；着手～

- My grandparents are afraid of going through customs, because it's their first time going overseas.

  我的祖父母很担心通关，因为这是他们第一次出国。

  ★ 短语 be afraid of v-ing 害怕，恐惧，担心

- There is nothing to worry about. We will clear customs in no time.

  没有什么好担心的。我们很快就会通关。

  ★ 短语 in no time 很快，立即

- After the plane lands, we will be headed to the baggage claim area.

  飞机降落后，我们前往行李领取区。

  ★ 短语 baggage claim area 行李领取区

- Please go down through the escalator to the customs inspection.

  请搭手扶梯下去，进行海关检查。

  ★ 短语 go down... 下去～，沿着～下去

- Now, present your passport and any travel documents to the customs officer.

  现在，将你的护照以及任何旅游文件交给海关人员。

  ★ 短语 present to... 交给～，递交给～

- Most customs officers keep a poker face. They don't look very friendly.

  大部分的海关人员都是一副扑克脸。他们看起来不是很友善。

  ★ 短语 poker face 扑克脸（面无表情的样子）

- The officers asked me about the purpose of this trip.

  海关人员问我此行的目的是什么。

  ★ 短语 ask about... 询问有关～

- The officers usually check thousands of visitors a day.

  这些官员通常一天要审核几千名旅客。

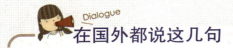 在国外都说这几句

- The customs agents will ask people to undergo strip searches randomly.
  海关官员会随机找旅客做搜身检查。
  ★ 短语 strip search （执法单位对嫌犯做的）脱衣搜身检查

- If you are not a citizen of this country, you will need to fill out a landing card and declaration form.
  如果你不是这个国家的居民，那么你就需要填写入境卡跟申报单。
  ★ 短语 landing card 入境卡

- Please fill out this customs declaration form if you have anything that needs to be declared.
  若你有任何东西需要申报的话，请填写这张海关申报单。
  ★ 短语 customs declaration form 海关申报表

- Please indicate where you are flying from and your flight number on the landing card.
  请在入境表上面标明你的出发地以及你的航班号码。
  ★ 短语 fly from... 从～飞来，从～搭机来

- What is the purpose of your visit? Are you here all by yourself?
  你旅游的目的是什么？你是自己一个人来吗？
  ★ 短语 purpose of... ～的目的，～的用途

- The purpose of my visit is sightseeing. I want to see the Statue of Liberty.
  我此行的目的是观光。我想要去看自由女神像。
  ★ 短语 Statue of Liberty 自由女神像

- I'm here for business. I am attending an education fair in three days.
  我来这里出差。我 3 天后要参加一个教育展览。
  ★ 短语 for business 因公出差

- How long do you plan to stay in London?
  你打算在伦敦停留多久？
  ★ 短语 plan to... 计划～，打算～

- I am going to stay here for three weeks.
  我将在这里停留 3 个星期。
  ★ 短语 stay for + 时间 待～（多久），停留～（多久）

在国外都说这几句

- I'll be staying at the Four Seasons Hotel.
  我将住在四季酒店。
  ★ 短语 stay at... 暂驻～，待在～

- Please come up to the immigration counter with your passport.
  请带着你的护照前往入境审查的柜台。
  ★ 短语 come up 到达～；前进～

- We should hand in our passports. Let the customs officer run the database and confirm the identity.
  我们应该交出护照，然后让海关人员核对资料库并确认身份。
  ★ 短语 hand in... 提出～；缴出～

- Do you have anything that needs to be declared?
  你有任何东西需要申报吗？

- Are two bottles of red wine in excess of the duty-free allowance?
  两瓶红酒超过了免税限额吗？
  ★ 语法 in excess of... 超过～，超出～

- I forgot to tell you that I bought 2 cartons of cigarettes.
  我忘了告诉你我买了两盒香烟。
  ★ 语法 forget + to + v. 忘了做

- If you are unsure about whether to declare something, you'd better go to the red aisle and declare it.
  如果你不确定是否要申报某样东西，你最好还是走红色通道并且申报。
  ★ 短语 be unsure about... 不确定～，没有把握～

- The immigration officer took me to a private booth to have a further inquiry.
  移民官员带我到隔离小房间进行更进一步的询问。
  ★ 短语 take A to... 带A到～

- The officer had to ask me some personal questions to make sure everything is all right.
  官员必须问我一些私人问题，以确保所有事情都没问题。
  ★ 短语 everything is all right 一切都好；没有问题

在国外都说这几句

- I have another connecting flight. I was told to contact the ground crew the minute I arrive.
  我还要转搭另一班班机。我被告知一抵达就要马上跟地勤人员联络。

- The landing card has different languages on it. Just pick the one that you understand to fill it out.
  入境卡提供各种不同的语言。请选择一张你看得懂的来填写。

- The officer had a look at my passport, scanned it, and verified it.
  官员看过、扫描并确认了我的护照。
  ★ 短语 have a look at　看一看～；检查～

- I ticked "no" on all the boxes on the declaration form and then turned it in because I do not have anything to declare.
  因为我没有什么东西需要申报，所以我在海关申报表上面全部勾选"否"，然后就交出去了。
  ★ 短语 turn in...　交出～，归还～

- Bringing plants or seeds into this country is prohibited.
  携带植物或种子进入这个国家是被禁止的。
  ★ 短语 bring A into...　将 A 带进～

- It is stupid to smuggle drugs into that country. It might result in the death penalty.
  走私毒品到该国是非常愚蠢的。这有可能会被判处死刑。
  ★ 短语 smuggle... into...　将～走私至～

- Be nice and smile to the officers. Maybe they will return the favor and be friendly.
  对海关官员好一点并多一点笑容。也许他们会对你有所回报并对你友善一点。
  ★ 短语 return the favor　回报

- If you get lost, just follow the indicators and then you will find your way.
  如果你迷路的话，只需跟着指示牌走，就可以找到你要去的地方。
  ★ 短语 be / get lost　迷路，迷失

在国外都说这几句

- Photography and talking on mobile phones are not allowed at customs.
  在海关不允许拍照及打电话。
  ★ 短语 A + be (not) allowed　（不）允许 A，A 是（不）被准许的

- Please do not make jokes about bombing or smuggling. You will get yourself into trouble.
  请不要开有关炸弹或走私的玩笑。你会让自己惹上麻烦。
  ★ 短语 make jokes about...　开～的玩笑，讲～的笑话

- I always carry a photocopy of my passport, and keep it separate from the passport.
  我总是携带一份护照的影印本，并把它跟护照分开放。
  ★ 短语 keep... separate from A　让 A 远离～，将 A 与～分开

- Customs and immigration officers are strict on the rules. Don't ever take chance on it.
  海关和出入境审查官员对于规定非常严格。不要心存侥幸。
  ★ 短语 be strict on...　对～严格，对～严谨

- The man is making a scene because he didn't follow the rules and declare all his items.
  那名男子因为没有遵守规定进行申报而大吵大闹。
  ★ 短语 make a scene　大吵大闹

- I feel uncomfortable when an officer of the opposite sex frisks me.
  我对于让异性官员对我搜身感到不舒服。
  ★ 短语 be / feel uncomfortable...　对～觉得不舒服，对～感到不安

- Did you fly to Greece on a private jet?
  你搭私人飞机到希腊吗？
  ★ 短语 private jet　私人飞机

- Did you take time to read the customs regulations on the airplane?
  在飞机上，你花时间阅读海关规章了吗？
  ★ 短语 take time to...　花时间～、需要时间～

在国外都说这几句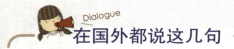

- My friend got caught when he attempted to bring in unauthorized dairy products. He is now under investigation.
  我的朋友在试图携带未被准许的乳制品时被逮到了。他现在正在接受调查。
  ★ 短语 be / get caught　被抓到，被发现

- By law, customs officers are authorized to conduct a personal search.
  依法，海关官员可以进行人身搜查。
  ★ 短语 by law　依法，依照法律

- When being asked for a personal search, it is wise to operate in coordination.
  当被要求要进行搜身时，好好配合是最聪明的做法。
  ★ 短语 to operate in coordination　配合

- Please have your passport ready and unlock your baggage for inspection.
  请准备好你的护照还有将行李解锁以备审查。
  ★ 短语 have... ready　把～准备好，把～放手边

- My passport was stamped and I had permission to enter the country.
  我的护照盖过章后，我就被允许进入这个国家。
  ★ 短语 have permission to...　被允许～，有做～的许可

- We must pass through the security checkpoints to access the arrival hall.
  我们必须通过安全检查关卡才能进入入境大厅。
  ★ 短语 pass through...　通过～，穿过～

- The two cartons of cigarettes have been confiscated as they exceeded the allowance.
  这两条烟因为超过免税限额，所以被没收了。
  ★ 短语 be confiscated...　被没收，被充公

- Follow the signs and go to the ground floor to claim your luggage.
  依照指示到达一楼去领取行李。
  ★ 短语 claim luggage　取行李，认领行李

- You don't need to claim your luggage yet because you have another flight to connect with.
  因为你还要转机，所以你先不用取回托运的行李。

- Let me check the screen to see which baggage carousel my baggage has been assigned to.
  让我看看屏幕显示我的行李被分配到哪个行李转盘。
  ★ 短语 assign to 分配到，指定到

- Be patient. Let's wait for our bags to appear. They should be here very soon.
  有点耐心。我们等行李出现。它们应该马上就来了。
  ★ 短语 wait for... 等候～，等待～

- A customs officer is walking a black dog through the baggage area.
  一位海关官员正带领一只黑狗经过行李区。
  ★ 短语 walk through 行经，步行经过

- The dog is searching for forbidden fruits or products with a high sense of smell.
  这只狗正在用敏感的嗅觉来寻找禁止携带的水果或农产品。
  ★ 短语 search for... 寻找～，搜寻～

- My husband and I marched down to the baggage claim as soon as we got off the plane.
  一下飞机，我老公和我就尽快走向行李提领区。
  ★ 短语 march down 走向～

- If you have the checked luggage, please remember to pick it up in the baggage claim area.
  如果你有托运行李，请记得要去行李提领区拿行李。
  ★ 短语 pick up... 拾起～，拿取～

- My mother tied a pink ribbon to the handle so that we can recognize it as soon as we see it.
  我妈妈绑了一个粉红色缎带在把手上，所以我们只要一看到就认得出来。
  ★ 短语 tie A to... 把 A 绑在～，将 A 系在～

- I put a tag with my contact details on my luggage.
  我在我的行李箱上面放了一个有联系方式的标签。
  ★ 短语 put... on 放在～的上面

在国外都说这几句

- **Hurry up**. I want to get to the baggage claim area before it gets too crowded.
  快一点。我想要赶在人多之前去行李提领区拿行李。
  ★ 短语 hurry up　赶快，快一点

- **A crowd of** people had gathered at the baggage claim area by the time we got there.
  我们抵达行李提领区时，一群人已经聚集在那边等候行李了。
  ★ 短语 a crowd of...　一大群～，一伙～

- We lost our luggage so now we need to talk to the airline and try to **track** it **down**.
  我们的行李丢了，所以现在要去问航空公司看看它们现在在哪里。
  ★ 短语 track down　经追踪或搜索而发现

- In order to avoid the trouble of losing luggage, we should make our bags **stand out** and purchase extra insurance on them.
  为了避免行李遗失的麻烦，我们应该让袋子显眼一些，并额外进行保险。
  ★ 短语 stand out　引人注目，突出

- We should stay alert and **keep a close eye on** our luggage.
  我们应该保持警惕，而且随时注意我们的行李。
  ★ 短语 keep a close eye on　密切注视；密切关注

- The more connections you make, the greater chance that your bags may be lost.
  转机次数越多，行李弄丢的机会就越大。
  ★ 语法 "the + 比较级，the + 比较级" 这种句型称为双重比较级，意思为 "越～，就越～"。

- We are in the international arrivals hall. Where should we **meet up with** our family?
  我们在国际到达大厅了。我们应该在哪里跟家人会面？
  ★ 短语 meet up with...　遇到～；与～见面

- I have arranged for a taxi to pick us up **on arrival**.
  我已经安排出租车在我们到达的时候来接我们。
  ★ 短语 on arrival　到达的时候

- Did you **inform the taxi driver of** our expected time of arrival?
  你告知出租车司机我们预计抵达的时间了吗？
  ★ 短语 inform A of...　告知 A ～，让 A 知道～

在国外都说这几句

- Did you agree on a set price or metered tariff with the taxi driver?
  你跟出租车司机讲好了吗？是直接收一个价钱还是要按表收费？
  ★ 短语 metered tariff　按表收费

- There are a number of ways to arrange airport pick-up.
  有一些方法可以安排机场接送。
  ★ 短语 a number of...　一些～，若干～

- I will take a taxi because I don't want to drag my luggage all the way along to the hotel.
  我要搭出租车，因为我不想沿路拖着行李到饭店。
  ★ 短语 drag along　拖着

- The driver will meet us at the gate and drive us directly to the hostel.
  司机将在大门接我们，并直接带我们前往青年旅社。
  ★ 短语 drive A to...　载 A 去～，接送 A 到～

- Taxi by far is the most common means of airport pick-up.
  出租车显然是目前最普遍的机场接送方法。
  ★ 短语 by far　目前

- Transfer between the hotel and the international airport is 1,500 per one-way trip.
  饭店到国际机场接送服务的价格是单程 1 500 元。
  ★ 短语 between A and B　A 和 B 之间

- Did you call to make arrangements and discuss the price of the shuttle in advance?
  你事先打电话安排并讨论班车的价钱了吗？
  ★ 短语 in advance　事先，预先

- The shuttle service took down our information and a credit card number to hold the reservation.
  班车接送服务处抄下我们的信息和信用卡号，以保留预约。
  ★ 短语 take down...　写下～，记下～

- Where can I hire or rent a car at the airport?
  机场哪里有租车服务？

Unit 14 关于饭店与迷路

跟任何人都可以用英语聊聊天

[生活便利贴]

抵达国外,首先要做的事就是到饭店登记入住,把行李放好,就可以开始已经规划好的行程了。登记入住饭店的时候,要算好入住的时间,才不会到达了饭店却只能待在饭店大厅浪费美好的时间。饭店内也有许多旅游信息,像地图、美食杂志或是一些旅游小册子,上面都还有一些优惠券或是近期的活动,这些资源都可以好好利用。

Vocabulary 在国外都用这些词

MP3 03-41

nudity
[ˈnjuːdətɪ]
n 裸露

mistake
[mɪˈsteɪk]
n 错误

bellboy
[ˈbelbɔɪ]
n 行李员,饭店大厅的服务生

reservation
[ˌrezəˈveɪʃn]
n 预定

pajamas
[pəˈdʒɑːməz]
n 睡衣裤

refrigerator
[rɪˈfrɪdʒəreɪtə]
n 冰箱

high-class
[ˈhaɪˈklæs]
a 高级的

automatically
[ˌɔːtəˈmætɪklɪ]
ad 自动地

agree
[əˈgriː]
v 同意

tip
[tɪp]
n v 小费;给小费

complimentary
[ˌkɒmplɪˈmentrɪ]
a 赠送的

helping hand
ph 帮助;援手

receptionist
[rɪˈsepʃənɪst]
n 柜台人员

girlfriend
[ˈgɜːlfrend]
n 女朋友

supermarket
[ˈsuːpəmɑːkɪt]
n 超级市场

building
[ˈbɪldɪŋ]
n 建筑物

snack
[snæk]
n 点心

nearby
[ˌnɪəˈbaɪ]
a 附近

在国外都说这几句

- My full name is Andrea Evans. I'd like to check in, please.
  我的全名是安德里亚·埃文斯。我想登记入住，谢谢。
  ★ 短语 check in　（到饭店）登记入住

- Welcome to our hotel. May I have your passport please?
  欢迎光临我们的饭店，护照可以借我看一下吗？
  ★ 短语 welcome to...　欢迎到～

- I could not find your reservation record. Do you have the confirmation letter with you?
  我找不到你的订房记录。请问你带了订房确认信吗？
  ★ 短语 reservation record　订房／订位纪录

- I booked a non-smoking room with a king-size bed.
  我订了一间有大床的非吸烟房间。
  ★ 短语 king-size bed　特大床，加长型的床

- Hi, Ms. Evans, your room is not available just yet. You can wait in the lobby, and we will inform you as soon as it's ready.
  嗨，埃文斯小姐，你的房间现在还没有整理好。你可以在饭店大厅等一下，房间一旦准备好了我们会马上通知你。
  ★ 短语 just yet　仍，现在还

- Would you like to sign up for our frequent guest program? It's free.
  你想登记参加我们饭店常客方案吗？此方案是免费的。
  ★ 短语 sign up for...　参加～（俱乐部、方案、课程），加入～

- We are staying at a five-star hotel. I'm so looking forward to it.
  我们住在五星级饭店。我对此非常期待。
  ★ 短语 look forward to　期待

- There is no dress code for staying at a five-star hotel. However, nudity is not allowed.
  住五星级饭店没有规定一定要穿什么衣服。不过，不可以脱光光什么都不穿。
  ★ 短语 dress code　穿衣法则，着装标准

- Hotel receptionists might be friendlier if you dress up nicely.
  如果你打扮得好看一些，饭店柜台可能会对你比较友善。
  ★ 短语 dress up　装扮

Dialogue 在国外都说这几句

- We will be **staying at** a high-class hotel. Tipping is necessary.
  我们会住在高级饭店。给小费是免不了的。
  ★ 短语 stay at...   停留在～，暂时住在～

- I **was surprised at** how little the single room costs.
  我很惊讶单人房的房价居然那么便宜。
  ★ 短语 be surprised at...   对～感到惊讶，讶异于～

- Don't **toss** your passport **around**. Put it in the hotel safe.
  护照不要乱丢，把它放进饭店的保险箱里面。
  ★ 短语 toss around   乱丢

- During the busy season, we **are less likely to** get an extra room.
  饭店入住旺季，再多订一个房间的希望甚微。
  ★ 短语 be less likely to...   比较不可能～

- The hotel just gave me a free upgrade to a business suite. That is something I never **dreamt of**.
  饭店刚刚免费帮我升级到商务套房。我真是做梦也没想过。
  ★ 短语 dream of   做梦，梦到

- Did you **do** any **research on** the hotel we are staying at?
  你事先对我们要住的这家饭店做了研究吗？
  ★ 短语 do research on...   对～做研究，调查～

- Because of the long wait at the reception, the receptionist felt sorry and gave us two buffet breakfasts **at no extra charge**.
  因为我们在柜台等了很久，柜台人员觉得很抱歉，然后给了我们两份免费的自助式早餐券。
  ★ 短语 at no extra charge   不须额外付费

- I requested an ocean view room, but all I can see through the window is the building next door.
  我要求入住的是一间海景房，但从窗外看出去我只看到饭店隔壁的建筑物。

- We are terribly sorry for the mistake. We will switch you to an ocean view right away and the first night is **on the house**.
  我们真的非常抱歉。我们会马上帮您换到海景房，并且第一个晚上不收费。
  ★ 短语 on the house   免费

在国外都说这几句

- Please keep the door closed. I don't want other people to see me in my pajamas.
  请把门关好。我不想别人看到我穿睡衣的样子。
  ★ 短语 ▶ keep... closed / locked 把～关好 / 锁上

- Why did you leave the TV on when you were out of the room?
  不在房里的时候，你为什么把电视开着？
  ★ 短语 ▶ be out of... 脱离～

- If you need your room cleaned, just place the "Please clean my room." sign on the doorknob.
  如果你需要人来清理房间，那就把"请打扫我房间"的牌子放在门把上。
  ★ 短语 ▶ place A on... 把 A 放在～上，将 A 放置在～

- The door will be locked up automatically. People from outside cannot open it without the key.
  这个门会自动上锁。房间外面的人没有钥匙是开不开的。
  ★ 短语 ▶ lock up 锁上

- The reservation is under Ryan Philips.
  预订的姓名是雷恩・菲利普斯。
  ★ 语法 ▶ "under..." 通常的意思是"在～下方"，但在此句的用法则是指"房间是以～的名义订的"。

- You are staying here for 2 nights, so you will be checking out the day after tomorrow. Is that correct?
  你预计在这里住两个晚上，所以退房时间是后天。对吗？
  ★ 短语 ▶ the day after tomorrow 后天

- I'm afraid you can't check in until after 3:00 p.m.
  恐怕你要到下午 3 点后才可以登记入住。
  ★ 语法 ▶ not...until... 不到～，无法～；要到～，才可～

- Complimentary breakfast is served in the restaurant between 7 and 11 a.m.
  饭店餐厅从早上 7 点到 11 点供应免费早餐。
  ★ 短语 ▶ between A and B 在 A 和 B 之间

- The gym is on the third floor at the end of the hall.
  健身房在三楼的走道尽头。
  ★ 短语 ▶ at the end of... 在～的尽头

在国外都说这几句

- **The spa and massage service are on the top floor. You can make a reservation here at the reception.**
  水疗跟按摩服务在顶楼。你可以在柜台预约这些服务。
  ★ 短语 make a reservation 预约

- **We made a reservation under the surname of Green.**
  我们以格林的名义订的房间。
  ★ 短语 under the (sur)name of... 以~的名字（姓氏）订房、订位的

- **Good afternoon, Mr. Green. May I see your photo ID, please?**
  下午好，格林先生。我可以看看你有照片的证件吗？
  ★ 短语 "ID"是"identification"的简称，意思是"（能够证明身份的）证件"。

- **What time will the breakfast buffet start?**
  自助式早餐几点开始供应？

- **The hotel will ask you to register your credit card when checking in so they will put the bill on the card.**
  入住的时候，饭店会要求登记你的信用卡资料。你的消费将会被记录在信用卡上。
  ★ 短语 put the bill on the card 将账单记录在信用卡上

- **How would you like to pay for your room?**
  你想要怎么付费？
  ★ 短语 pay for... 付费~，付款~

- **I'd like to speak to the hotel manager on duty.**
  我想与值班经理谈谈。
  ★ 短语 on duty 值班，上班，当班

> **常识补给站**
>
> 有些西方国家（如美国）都是有小费制度的，去餐厅用餐时，就必须额外再加上餐点总金额的 10%~20%，作为给服务生的小费。住在饭店，出门时也是要放 1~5 美元在床头柜上，当作给清洁人员的小费。出国前要先查清楚该国家是不是适用小费制度。如果忘记留下小费的话，人家会认为你非常不礼貌！

在国外都说这几句

- Good morning, ma'am. I'd like to check out of room 120. Here's the key.
  早安，女士。我想退房，房号是 120。这是房间钥匙。
  ★ 短语 check out of + 房号   从～（房间）退房

- I'm afraid that my boyfriend and I slept in, so we missed the breakfast.
  恐怕我和男友睡过头了，所以我们错过了早餐。
  ★ 短语 sleep in   晚起（床）、睡到很晚才起床

- The hotel we stayed in charged us for late checkout. We should be careful next time.
  我们住的饭店加收我们延迟退房的费用。我们下次要小心一点。
  ★ 短语 charge A for...   对 A 索取～的费用

- The hotel requires a one hundred dollar credit card deposit to hold the room. We can pay the rest in person.
  饭店要求 100 元订金才能保留订房。其他的费用可以等亲自到了现场再付。
  ★ 短语 in person   亲自，本人

- I want a room with the view of the city.
  我比较想要一个可以看到城市景的房间。
  ★ 短语 the view of...   ～的景观，～的景色

- The snacks in the minibar are extremely expensive. Don't even touch them.
  迷你吧台里面的点心非常贵。你连碰也不要碰。

- I made the booking through a travel website. Here's my booking reference number.
  我是通过旅游网站订房的。这是我的订房代码。
  ★ 短语 booking reference number   订房代码

- Could you spell your last name out for me, please?
  请您拼出您的姓氏好吗？
  ★ 短语 spell out...   拼出～；详加说明～

- I paid by credit card via the website in advance.
  我事先就通过网站以信用卡的方式付费了。
  ★ 短语 pay by...   以～的方式付款

 在国外都说这几句

- Welcome to the Starks Hotel. **How may I help you**?
  欢迎莅临史达克饭店。我可以为你服务吗？
  ★ 短语 how may I help you 有什么需要帮忙的吗，我可以为你服务吗

- My co-worker and I have a twin room **reservation for** today.
  我的同事和我今天订了一间双人房。
  ★ 短语 reservation for + 日期 （日期）有订房、订位

- Could you please tell me what services **are included in** the room rate?
  可以请你跟我说房间费用包含哪些服务呢？
  ★ 短语 be included in... ～包含，～包括

- The hotel provides room service **for an additional charge**. Here's the price list.
  饭店提供客房服务，需要额外付费。这个是价目表。
  ★ 短语 for an additional charge 额外付费

- We **are all set**. Your room number is 2043, and this is your key.
  手续都准备好了。你的房间号码是2043，这个是你的钥匙。
  ★ 短语 be all set 准备好了

- Use the elevator to go to 20th floor and then **turn right**.
  请坐电梯到20楼，然后右转。
  ★ 短语 turn right 右转

- Our room is the second to last one **on the left-hand side**.
  我们的房间是在左手边倒数第二间。
  ★ 短语 on the left (hand) side 左（手）边的

- A bellboy will bring your bags to your room **at your request**.
  行李员会将你的行李提上去。
  ★ 短语 at A's request 应A的要求、依照A的要求～

- Will you be paying by cash or credit card?
  你将以现金还是信用卡付费？

- You requested a room **away from** the restaurant. Is that right?
  你要求房间要离餐厅远一点，对吗？
  ★ 短语 away from... 远离～，离～远一点

在国外都说这几句

- If you have any further inquiries, feel free to dial 000 to contact the reception.
  如果你有其他要求，请随时拨打 000 与饭店前台联系。
  ★ 短语 feel free to...　随意～，随时～

- This is Jason Cooper in room 120. Could you send up a bottle of champagne and some strawberries?
  我是 120 房间的杰森・古柏。你可以送一瓶香槟跟一些草莓上来吗？
  ★ 短语 send up...　送上～，送到～

- I would like to set a wake-up call for 7:30 a.m.
  我想设定早上 7：30 的晨唤服务。
  ★ 短语 wake-up call　晨唤服务，也就是请饭店设定电话闹钟唤醒房客的服务。

- There is something wrong with the refrigerator in my room. It smells.
  我房间的冰箱有问题。它有怪味。
  ★ 语法 there is something wrong with...　～有问题

- The receptionist said they would send the maintenance to have a look.
  前台人员说会请维修人员来检查一下。

- In the meantime, the hotel manager apologized for the inconvenience.
  同时，饭店经理为给我们造成的不便感到很抱歉。
  ★ 短语 in the meantime　同时

- I'm fully satisfied with the way they handled it.
  我对他们处理的方式感到很满意。
  ★ 短语 be satisfied with...　对～感到很满意

常识补给站

出国旅游，电压常常是一大问题，美国的电压为 110～120V，有些国家的电压为 220～240V（像是英国、澳大利亚），要记得电压不同，绝对不可以勉强使用，不然可能会造成电路问题。不过，现在很多的电器都是使用国际电压（110～240V 通用），如此一来就不会有电压不同的问题。但为了保险起见，要再三地检查要带出去的电器用品，电压到底符不符合当地规格。

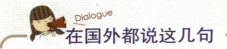

在国外都说这几句

- I'm lost. Can you help me out? I need to go to 5th Avenue.
  我迷路了。你可以帮帮忙吗?我需要去第五大道。
  ★ 短语 help A out   帮助 A,帮忙 A

- Of course. I'm more than happy to give you a hand.
  当然。我非常乐意帮助你。
  ★ 短语 give A a hand   助 A 一把臂之力,帮忙 A

- Everyone needs help from time to time.
  每个人偶尔都需要帮忙。
  ★ 短语 from time to time   偶尔,有时

- Most people are willing to give a helping hand when someone is in need.
  大多数人都愿意在(别人)有需要的时候给予帮忙。
  ★ 短语 be willing to...   愿意~,乐意~

- Could you please tell me how to get to the National Museum?
  你可以告诉我要怎么去国家博物馆吗?
  ★ 短语 get to...   到~,去~

- The supermarket is in the middle of the block, across from the park.
  超市就在街口中间,公园的对面。
  ★ 短语 across from...   在~的对面

- Pardon me. I'm lost. Could you please tell me how I can get to the cinema?
  对不起,我迷路了。你可以告诉我要怎么到电影院吗?
  ★ 短语 pardon me   对不起

- Just go straight; the cinema is just around the corner.
  只要直走,电影院就在转角附近。
  ★ 短语 around the corner   在附近

- Excuse me, Could you direct me to David Jones Department Store?
  不好意思,你可以告诉我到大卫琼斯百货公司的方向吗?
  ★ 短语 direct A to...   为 A 指路~,指引 A 到~

- The bakery is on Elizabeth Street, about 15 minutes on foot.
  面包店就在伊莉莎白街,步行大约 15 分钟可以抵达。
  ★ 短语 on foot   步行,用走的

在国外都说这几句

- The stadium is far away. It's impossible to walk from there.
  体育场离这里很远。你没有办法从这边走到那边。
  ★ 短语 far away 远处，很远

- Excuse me, I can't seem to find a supermarket. Do you know where one is?
  抱歉，我好像找不到超市，你知道哪里有超市吗？
  ★ 语法 "Do you know where one is?"的"one"是指"supermarket"，这是因为第一句已经提过"supermarket"，为避免重复，而用"one"代替。

- There are many supermarkets near by. Do you have a particular one in mind?
  这附近的超市还挺多的。你特别想找哪一家吗？
  ★ 短语 in mind 心中，脑海中

- Thank you so much for taking time to show me the way!
  谢谢你花时间解释跟我说怎么走！
  ★ 短语 take time to... 花时间～

- Is the theater far from the hotel?
  剧院离饭店远吗？
  ★ 短语 be far from... 离～很远，远离～

- If we get lost, we should ask a police for help.
  如果我们迷路，我们应该向警察寻求援助。
  ★ 短语 ask A for help 向 A 求助，请求 A 帮忙

- Don't worry. Just take a deep breath. Everything will be fine.
  别担心。深呼吸一下，一切都会没事的。
  ★ 短语 take a deep breath 深呼吸

- I have Google Map on my phone. I will have no problem finding my way back to the hotel.
  我手机上有谷歌地图。我一定可以找到回饭店的路。
  ★ 短语 find A's way back to... A 找到回～的路 / 方向

- I am lost because I don't have mobile data overseas.
  我迷路是因为我的手机在国外没有网络。
  ★ 短语 mobile data 手机网络

跟任何人都可以用英语聊聊天

Unit 15 旅行是梦想的实践

[生活便利贴]

在国外，使用交通工具是非常重要的一件事情。对地铁、公交车路线都要事先查询，最好直接在网上找到交通地图，这样可以避免迷路，避免不必要的麻烦。此外，也要搞清楚交通工具的运营时间，有些路线或是车站在假日是不营运的，千万不要傻傻地在车站等待，你很有可能等半天都不会有车来。

Vocabulary 在国外都用这些词

MP3 03-51

carriage
['kærɪdʒ]
n 四轮马车

explore
[ɪk'splɔː]
v 探索；探险；考察

pedestrian
[pə'destrɪən]
n 行人

playground
['pleɪɡraʊnd]
n 游戏场，运动场

seesaw
['siːsɔː]
n 跷跷板

mosquito
[mə'skiːtəʊ]
n 蚊子

vendor
['vendə]
n 摊贩

directory
[də'rektərɪ]
n 指南

royal
['rɔɪəl]
a 王室的

flashlight
['flæʃlaɪt]
n 闪光灯

elder
['eldə]
n 年龄较大者，长者

bottled water
ph 瓶装水

baby carriage
ph 婴儿车

mummy
['mʌmɪ]
n 木乃伊

underground
[ˌʌndə'ɡraʊnd]
n 地铁（英式用法）

subway
['sʌbweɪ]
n 地铁（美式用法）

Broadway
['brɔːdweɪ]
n 百老汇

parking space
ph 停车位

在国外都说这几句

- What a beautiful day! Does anyone care to go bike riding with me?
  天气真好！有没有人想要跟我一起去骑自行车？
  ★ 短语 care to... 想要～，喜欢～

- I made a reservation in advance to ensure that a city tour in a carriage is available.
  我事先有做预约，确保我们有城市导览的马车可以搭乘。
  ★ 短语 in advance 预先，事先

- Bike riding, without a doubt, is one of the best ways to explore a city.
  骑自行车无疑是游览这个城市最棒的方法之一。
  ★ 短语 without a doubt 无疑地，确实地

- You need to be careful with the pedestrians when riding a bike.
  骑自行车的时候你要小心行人。
  ★ 短语 be careful with... 当心，对～十分注意

- The horse carriage will go around the entire Central Park.
  马车会带我们走过整个中央公园。
  ★ 短语 go around 四处走动；探望

- The scheduled city tour has been canceled due to the bad weather.
  已安排好的城市游览因为天气不好而取消。
  ★ 短语 due to... 因为～，由于～

- My family and I took a walk in the Central Park last night.
  我的家人和我昨天晚上在中央公园散步。
  ★ 短语 take a walk 散步

常识补给站

有些国家地区（像是澳大利亚）交通工具计费方式与国内大不相同，他们会以区（zone）来计价，将整个都市分成 1~2 个区，在同一个区域里只会收一个价钱，一旦跨区，索取的费用就会是两个区的价钱，相对比较高。另外，当收取的交通费达到一定的金额，当日就不会再扣任何的交通费用，此称为 day cap。

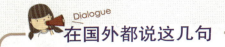

在国外都说这几句

- Do not catch butterflies or insects in the park. Please leave them alone.
  不要在公园捕捉蝴蝶或昆虫。请不要打扰它们。
  ★ 短语 leave A alone 请不要打扰 A

- There is a playground in the park. Let's go and play on the seesaw.
  公园里面有个游戏场。我们去玩跷跷板吧。
  ★ 短语 play on a seesaw 玩跷跷板

- We should take a Central Park walking tour. It looks like a lot of fun.
  我们应该要参加中央公园的步行游览之旅。看起来很有趣。
  ★ 短语 take a tour 参加游览

- I don't feel like going to a park because there are so many spiders and mosquitoes.
  我没有很想去公园，因为有很多蜘蛛和蚊子。
  ★ 短语 feel like 想要，意欲

- There is a sign in the park that says, "Keep off the Grass."
  公园里有"请勿践踏草坪"的标语。
  ★ 短语 keep off... 远离～，不接近～

- I always want to watch *Romeo and Juliet*. Do I line up here for the tickets?
  我一直都想看《罗密欧与朱丽叶》。请问我要这边排队买票吗？
  ★ 短语 line up 排队，整队

- My boyfriend and I sat on the bench by the lake.
  我男朋友和我坐在湖边的长椅上。
  ★ 短语 by the lake 在湖边（旁）

- If you want to feel like a New Yorker, you have to go to the stadium and watch a baseball game.
  如果你想体验纽约客的感觉，你一定要到运动场看一场棒球赛。
  ★ 短语 feel like 感觉像～

- There are so many street performers in the Central Square.
  中央广场那边有好多街头艺人在表演。
  ★ 短语 street performer 街头艺人

在国外都说这几句

- Let's grab a bite from the street vendor.
  我们去路边摊买些东西吃。
  ★ 短语 grab a bite （随便、匆忙）吃点东西

- The lady is walking her dogs in the park. They look adorable.
  那位妇人在公园遛狗。它们看起来好可爱。
  ★ 短语 walk dog(s) 遛狗

- I looked down from the bridge and saw some people rowing a boat.
  我从桥上往下看，看到一些人在划船。
  ★ 短语 row a boat 划船

- Enjoying a concert in the Central Park is also a great opportunity to experience New York.
  在中央公园欣赏音乐会也是体验纽约生活的好机会。
  ★ 短语 an opportunity to... ～的机会，～的良机

- Are you interested in going to the History Museum with me tomorrow?
  你明天有兴趣跟我一起去历史博物馆吗？
  ★ 短语 be interested in... 有兴趣～，对～有兴趣

- We'd better buy tickets online, or we may have to spend a lot of time waiting at the ticket booth.
  我们最好上网买票，不然会在售票亭等很久。
  ★ 短语 spend + 时间 + v-ing 花时间做～

- Let me take a closer look at the museum directory. The British Royal history exhibit should be on the second floor.
  让我仔细看一看博物馆指南。英国的皇家历史展应该在二楼。
  ★ 短语 take a look at... 看看

- Take your time. We have all day to make the best out of it.
  慢慢来。我们有一整天的时间，可以在这里好好利用。
  ★ 短语 take A's time A 慢慢来，A 不急

- How much is the entrance fee to this museum?
  这家博物馆的门票是多少钱？
  ★ 短语 how much 多少钱

- This queue is for the exhibition on the top floor.
  这个队伍是在排顶楼的展览。
  ★ 短语 on the top floor 顶楼，最高楼层

在国外都说这几句

- The opening hours of the museum are from 10 a.m. to 4 p.m.
  博物馆的开放时间是从早上的十点到下午四点。
  ★ 短语 opening hour 开放时间，营业时间

- Flashlights are not allowed in the museum.
  博物馆里面不可以使用闪光灯。
  ★ 短语 be not allowed 不被允许

- The MoMA Museum is closed on public holidays.
  纽约现代艺术博物馆在公假日不开放。
  ★ 短语 "MoMA" 是 "The Museum of Modern Art" 的缩写，意思是"现代艺术博物馆"。

- Audio tours can be rented at an additional cost.
  你可以额外付费，租用语音导览的服务。
  ★ 短语 audio tours 语音导览

- Admission is always free for children 12 and under.
  12岁（含）以下的孩童免费入场。

- The museum offers concessions for students and elders.
  这家博物馆向学生及年长者提供优惠。
  ★ 短语 offer... for A 提供 A ～、给予 A ～

- All personal belongings are subject to security inspection before entering the museum.
  进入博物馆前，所有个人物品都要接受安全检查。
  ★ 短语 be subject to... 受～的支配，需经～的

- The lines to purchase general entrance tickets are usually long.
  购买一般门票的等候队伍通常都很长。
  ★ 短语 general entrance ticket 一般票、大众票

- Videotaping without permission is illegal in the museum.
  博物馆内未经许可录影是违法的。
  ★ 短语 without permission 私自，未经允许

- Please keep your voice down when talking on a mobile phone.
  讲手机的时候请降低音量。
  ★ 短语 talk on the phone / mobile phone 讲电话 / 手机

在国外都说这几句

- Food and drinks are strictly prohibited in this area.
  这一区域严禁任何饮食。
  ★ 短语 be prohibited 被禁止

- Can bottled water be carried into the museum?
  瓶装水可以带进博物馆吗?
  ★ 短语 carry into... 带进~, 带入~

- Baby carriages are available at the Information Desk.
  服务台那边有婴儿车可供使用。
  ★ 短语 information desk 服务台

- Ellis Island was transformed into a museum years ago.
  几年前艾莉丝岛变成了博物馆。
  ★ 短语 transform into... 转变成~; 改变成~

- Ellis Island Immigration Museum is dedicated to educating people about the local immigrant history.
  艾莉丝岛移民博物馆致力于教育大众当地的移民历史。
  ★ 短语 be dedicated to... 奉献给~, 以~奉献

- The museum hosts a series of exhibits, please visit its website for details.
  这家博物馆主办一系列的展览,详情请至博物馆网站查询。
  ★ 短语 a series of... 一系列的~; 连续的~

- The Guggenheim Museum was designed by architect Frank Owen Gehry.
  古根海姆博物馆是由建筑师弗兰克•盖里设计的。
  ★ 短语 be designed by... 由~设计, 由~构思

- Over 2 million works of art from all over the world are stored at the museum.
  超过两百万件来自世界各地的艺术品都收藏在这座博物馆。
  ★ 短语 all over the world 世界各地

- The Mystic Ancient Egypt exhibition is showing at the moment. Shall we go and see the mummy?
  神秘的古埃及展现在正在展出。我们要不要一起去看看木乃伊?
  ★ 短语 at the moment 目前

在国外都说这几句

- I <u>am impressed by</u> the details of the artwork on display.
  我对于展出的艺术品细节感到印象深刻。
  ★ 短语 be impressed by...　对～感到惊艳，对～感到印象深刻

- Some museums <u>are</u> only <u>open to</u> guided tours.
  有些博物馆只开放给有导游的旅行团。
  ★ 短语 be open to　向～开放

- The <u>gift shop</u> is right next to the exit. Feel free to buy some souvenirs for your friends.
  礼品店就在出口的旁边。你可以买一些纪念品给朋友们。
  ★ 短语 gift shop　礼品店

- The Museum of the Motion Picture <u>focuses</u> mostly <u>on</u> multimedia.
  电影博物馆主要的展览是针对多媒体技术。
  ★ 短语 focus on...　集中～，聚焦～

- Unfortunately, the museum <u>is</u> now <u>closed for</u> renovations. It won't be open until next month.
  不幸的是，这家博物馆目前因装修而关闭。它要到下个月才会开放。
  ★ 短语 be closed for...　因～关闭，因～不营业

- The fare for the underground or a bus is $2.79 <u>one-way</u>.
  搭乘地铁或当地公交车的单程费用是 2.79 美元。
  ★ 短语 one-way　单程，单趟

- We should buy a <u>day pass</u> if we are traveling to many places today.
  如果今天要去很多地方的话，我们应该买一日票。
  ★ 短语 day pass　一日票

- What is the most affordable way to <u>get around</u> New York City?
  可以游遍纽约最省钱的方法是什么？
  ★ 短语 get around...　游遍～；到处跑～

- When does the subway <u>stop operating</u>?
  地铁什么时候停止营运？
  ★ 短语 stop + v-ing　停止～

- Because of the culture festival, the <u>metro system</u> is open 24 hours today.
  因为文化节的关系，今天地铁系统是 24 小时营运的。
  ★ 短语 metro system　地铁系统

在国外都说这几句

- How long does it take to Times Square by subway?
  搭乘地铁到时代广场需要多长时间？
  ★ 短语 ▶ by subway　搭乘地铁

- New York City public transportation generally includes buses and subways.
  纽约市大众运输通常分为巴士和地铁两种。

- Can I buy Metro Cards at subway stations with a credit card?
  我可以在地铁站用信用卡买地铁卡吗？
  ★ 短语 ▶ buy / purchase... with credit card(s)　用信用卡买～

- Where can I top up my Metro Card?
  我可以在哪里充值我的地铁卡？
  ★ 短语 ▶ top up　充值

- Don't forget to touch on and touch off when entering and exiting the station.
  进出车站的时候，不要忘记要刷你的地铁卡。
  ★ 短语 ▶ touch on/off　过地铁闸门时，刷卡进站 / 出站

- Did you double check the time for the Broadway show?
  你有再次确认百老汇表演的时间吗？
  ★ 短语 ▶ double check　仔细检查，再次检查

- New York's Broadway is famous for all sorts of shows.
  纽约的百老汇因有着各种不同的表演而出名。
  ★ 短语 ▶ famous for...　以～闻名，以～出名

- We started searching for Broadway show tickets when we were planing our trip to New York.
  计划要到纽约时，我们就开始搜寻百老汇表演的门票了。
  ★ 短语 ▶ search for　搜寻

- The tickets to *The Phantom of the Opera* sold out weeks ago.
  《歌剧魅影》的门票早在几星期前就卖完了。
  ★ 短语 ▶ sell out　卖光，卖完

在国外都说这几句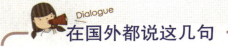

- You should check the websites of Broadway shows that you're interested in seeing.
  你应该上网找找有兴趣看的百老汇表演。
  ★ 短语 "be interested in + v-ing" 的意思是 "对～有兴趣"。

- Broadway show tickets cost a lot. Maybe I should try my luck at the TKTS booth.
  百老汇表演的票很贵。也许我该到折扣票亭试试运气。
  ★ 短语 "TKTS booth" 在此的意思是 "百老汇折扣票亭",专门售卖纽约百老汇歌舞剧剩余门票的售票亭,各家剧院通常会放出次日午场或当天的票给 TKTS 集中贩售,距离开演时间越近,票就越多,通常 TKTS 会以七五折到半价的优惠价格售卖百老汇表演门票。

- I don't care if I need to wait in line for more than an hour. I want to see this show badly.
  我不在乎我要排队等超过一个小时。我真的非常想要看这个表演。
  ★ 短语 wait in line 排队等候

- I fell in love with *The Lion King* from the moment I saw it.
  从我看到《狮子王》的那一刻起,我就爱上这个表演。
  ★ 短语 fall in love with... 爱上～

- I'm a big fan of *Wicked*. I will never get tired of watching it.
  我是《绿野仙踪前传》音乐剧的铁粉。不管看几次我都不会腻。
  ★ 短语 a fan of... ～的粉丝

- The tickets we purchased are very cheap. Therefore, our seats are miles away from the stage.
  我们买的票非常便宜。因此,我们的座位离舞台超远。
  ★ 短语 miles away from... 离～很远

- Madison Square Garden is home of the New York Knicks.
  麦迪逊广场花园是纽约尼克斯队的主场。
  ★ 短语 Madison Square Garden 麦迪逊广场花园

- I cannot wait to be at the stadium to cheer on my favorite team.
  我都等不及到运动场帮我最爱的球队加油啦!
  ★ 短语 cheer on... 帮～加油,鼓励～

在国外都说这几句

- My son is very excited about seeing his first baseball game at the stadium.
  我儿子对于要到球场看他人生的第一场棒球比赛感到很兴奋。
  ★ 短语 be excited about... 对~感到很兴奋

- Don't drive to the game. You will never find a parking space.
  不要开车去看比赛。你一定找不到停车位。
  ★ 短语 drive to... 开车到~，开车前往~

- I'm going to Yankee Stadium. Do you know which subway stop I should get off at?
  我要去洋基球场。你知道我应该在哪个地铁站下车吗？
  ★ 短语 Yankee Stadium 洋基（队）球场

- Entry gates open 2 hours prior to the scheduled game time on weekends.
  周末期间，入口大门会在预定比赛时间两个小时前开放。
  ★ 短语 on weekends 周末期间

- A security checkpoint is set up at every gate. Please cooperate with the staff.
  每一个入口都设置有安全检查站。请与工作人员配合。
  ★ 短语 cooperate with... 与~配合

- When we arrive at the stadium, I am so going to get a hot dog from the vendor.
  等我们到了运动场，我一定要去摊贩那边买个热狗。
  ★ 短语 hot dog 热狗

- You need to show your photo ID if you wish to get some beer at the stadium.
  如果你想在球场买啤酒的话，你需要出示证件。
  ★ 短语 wish to 想要

- Let's go and celebrate the Yankee's win. Dinner is on me.
  我们去庆祝洋基队的胜利。晚餐我请。
  ★ 短语 ...be on me ~由我来请客

跟任何人都可以用英语聊聊天

Unit 16 优雅地处理突发状况

[生活便利贴]

快乐的时光总是过得特别快，一转眼就到了该回家的时候了。玩得开心、满载而归的同时，还要注意托运行李的重量限制，免得花冤枉钱在超重费上。退房时也要注意跟饭店柜台再三确认是否有额外的消费以及消费金额是否正确，若是没有注意，信用卡账单上可是会多出一笔莫名的费用喔！

Vocabulary 在国外都用这些词 MP3 03-61

cancellation
[ˌkænsəˈleɪʃn]
n 取消

refund
[ˈriːfʌnd]
v 退款

modify
[ˈmɒdɪfaɪ]
v 修改

guest
[gest]
n 客人，顾客

affect
[əˈfekt]
v 影响

personal
[ˈpɜːsənl]
a 个人的，私人的

compensation
[ˌkɒmpenˈseɪʃn]
n 补偿，赔偿

finally
[ˈfaɪnəli]
ad 最后，终于

reimburse
[ˌriːɪmˈbɜːs]
v 偿还，归还

damage
[ˈdæmɪdʒ]
n 损害

suitcase
[ˈsuːtkeɪs]
n 公事包

panic
[ˈpænɪk]
n 恐慌，惊慌

elegant
[ˈelɪɡənt]
a 优美的，高雅的

exotic
[ɪɡˈzɒtɪk]
a 异国的

empty-handed
[ˌemptiˈhændɪd]
a / ad 空手的；空手地

radio
[ˈreɪdɪəʊ]
n 电台

fatigue
[fəˈtiːɡ]
n 疲劳

insomnia
[ɪnˈsɒmnɪə]
n 失眠

在国外都说这几句

- I would like to cancel my reservation. Could you please tell me what the cancellation policy is?
  我想要取消我的预约。可以请你告诉我取消订房的规定是什么吗？
  ★ 短语 cancellation policy　取消（订房）规定

- Cancellation must be made three days prior to arrival.
  取消订房须于入住前 3 天通知。
  ★ 短语 prior to...　在～之前，在～前

- Once a reservation has been made and paid for by credit card, you are fully obligated to pay for your entire stay.
  一旦订房确认，信用卡也付款后，就必须保证入住。
  ★ 短语 be obligated for + n.　对～有义务，对～有责任

- Stacey, please cancel my room reservation at the Four Seasons Hotel. I've changed my mind; I don't want to stay there this time.
  史黛西，请把我在四季酒店的订房取消掉。我改变主意了，我这次不想住那边。
  ★ 短语 cancel (a) reservation　取消订房 / 位

- I don't think Mrs. Johnson made a reservation at all.
  我认为约翰逊太太根本就没有订位。
  ★ 短语 not at all　一点有不，一点也没有

- Your credit card has been charged at the time you made the reservation.
  在您订位的同时，您的信用卡也交易成功了。
  ★ 短语 at the time...　在～时候，在～时间

Thank you!

Have a great day!

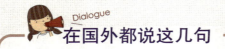

在国外都说这几句

- Nothing will be refunded to you if you are a no-show.
  如果你无法入住的话，费用是不会退还给你的。
  ★ 短语 no-show 预订座位却没出席的人；未能如约出席的人

- Can I modify the date of my reservation via the Internet?
  我可以在线上修改预约入住日期吗？
  ★ 短语 via... 经由～，经过～

- You are obliged to contact the hotel directly to make any changes to your reservation.
  你必须直接与饭店联系以便更改订房信息。
  ★ 短语 be obliged to... 必须～，不得不～

- You can cancel or change your booking via our self-service online booking system.
  你可以使用我们的线上自助订房系统取消或更改预订信息。
  ★ 短语 self-service 自助

- Sir, I need to cancel my reservation for tomorrow night.
  先生，我需要取消明晚的预订。
  ★ 短语 cancel for... 取消了～

- 48 hour advance notice is required for hotel cancellations.
  要取消酒店预订，请提前 48 小时通知。
  ★ 短语 be required for... ～需要

- Cancellations made within 24 hours of the booking will result in a $1,200 cancellation fee.
  如果在 24 小时内取消预订，将收取 1200 美元的手续费。
  ★ 短语 result in... 导致～，结果是～

- No-shows affect us greatly because of our size. Therefore, please be sure to inform us if you decide to cancel your reservation.
  因为本餐厅规模不大，预约没出席对我们影响较大。因此，若你决定要取消预约，请务必通知我们。
  ★ 短语 be sure to 务必

- A 48-hour advance notice for cancellation is required for tables up to 4 guests.
  若预订人数为四位以上，请于 48 小时前通知取消预订。
  ★ 短语 up to... （时间／人数）多于～，高于～

在国外都说这几句

- I'd like to cancel my reservation for tickets to the tennis game, please.
  我想取消网球比赛的订票。
  ★ 短语 cancel a reservation for... 取消～的订位

- No refund will be issued for cancellations within 12 hours of the reservation.
  12 小时内取消订票将无法退款。
  ★ 短语 be issued for... ～的核发，～的配给

- Ticket cancellation might lead to a fine.
  取消订票可能会导致罚款。
  ★ 短语 lead to 导致，引起

- Cancellations made one week in advance will qualify for a full refund.
  提前一星期取消订票可以全额退款。
  ★ 短语 qualify for... 有资格～；合格～

- I cancelled the reservation because I had to deal with personal matters.
  我取消订位是因为我必须要处理一些私人事情。
  ★ 短语 personal matter(s) 私人事情，个人事件

- I lost my luggage. Who should I talk to about this?
  我遗失了行李，这个问题我需要跟谁讨论？

- If my luggage is nowhere to be found, will I be eligible to apply for any compensation?
  如果我的行李怎么样都找不到，那我可以申请任何形式的赔偿吗？
  ★ 短语 be eligible to... 有资格做～

- If your bag was lost on a domestic flight, then it should be tracked down in 3 days.
  如果你的行李在国内航线丢失，那么应该可以在 3 天之内找到。
  ★ 短语 domestic flight 国内班机，国内飞行

- Can I bring back some medicine as long as it is for my personal use?
  如果只是我私人使用，我可以带回一些药品吗？
  ★ 短语 as long as 只要

在国外都说这几句

- My checked luggage is nowhere in sight. I'm worried that it is lost.
  我完全没看到我的托运行李。我有点担心它已经不见了。
  ★ 短语 in sight　看得见，在视线范围内

- My bags finally showed up, but I had to wait more than 30 minutes.
  我的行李终于出现了，但我等了超过 30 分钟。
  ★ 短语 show up　出现；露面

- Your bags are on the next flight. We will have them delivered to your house tomorrow morning at the latest.
  你的行李在下一班班机。我们最晚会在明天早上将它们送到你家。
  ★ 短语 deliver to...　送到～；运到

- My bags were taken by someone else by mistake. Could you please contact the person as soon as possible?
  我的行李被别人误拿了。你可以帮我尽可能联系那个人吗？
  ★ 短语 by mistake　搞错，错误地

- Will the airline company reimburse the expenses before my luggage arrives?
  在我的行李送达之前，航空公司会赔偿这中间任何的花费吗？

- The airline company will contact you once your luggage is found.
  一旦找到你的行李，航空公司会跟你联络。

- I headed directly to the baggage carousel when I got off my flight because other people might take my luggage by mistake.
  一下飞机，我就直接前往行李传送带，因为其他人很有可能误拿我的行李。
  ★ 短语 head to...　出发前往～，往～出发

> **常识补给站**
>
> 　　机场退税：到国外旅游，在大部分的国家都可以办理退税。每个国家的退税规定大不相同，一般来说消费要达到一定的金额才可符合退税的门槛，退税额约为商品总价值 10%。不过要注意的是，有些国家只允许旅游签证的持有者办理退税。另外，退税的时候，要记得把商品带在手边，不要放入托运行李，不然，办理退税人员没有看到商品实物，可能不会让你享有退税的服务！

在国外都说这几句

- You should check your luggage for any damage right at the moment you get them.
  当你拿到行李时，你就应该检查行李是否有毁损。
  ★ 短语 check for... 检查～；核对～

- I reported the damage to the airline customer service. Hopefully they will come up with a solution soon.
  我向航空公司的客服中心报告了行李毁损。希望他们很快会想到解决办法。
  ★ 短语 report to... 向～汇报；向～报到

- Make sure you take a photo of the damaged area just in case.
  为了保险起见，要记得把损坏的部分拍照留存。
  ★ 短语 take a photo 拍照

- Can you please point out the damage?
  请问你可以指出毁损（部分）吗？
  ★ 短语 point out... 指出～；提出～

- Ninety-eight percent of all missing luggage eventually turns up. So don't worry.
  遗失的行李中有百分之九十八最后都会出现。不用担心。
  ★ 短语 turn up... 出现～，露面～

- The airline informed me that they take no responsibility for any prohibited items.
  航空公司通知我，他们不负责违禁品的赔偿。
  ★ 短语 take no responsibility for... 不对～负责，不对～承担责任

- Did you take a picture of your luggage with your mobile phone?
  你用手机给你的行李拍照了吗？
  ★ 短语 mobile phone 手机

- I am going to wait for the baggage claim carousel to circle one last time.
  我要再等行李转盘转最后一圈。
  ★ 短语 wait for... 等候～

- Give up. Your luggage is lost for sure. Let's talk to the airline staff about compensation.
  放弃吧。你的行李一定是丢了。我们去跟航空公司的工作人员谈赔偿吧。
  ★ 短语 give up 放弃

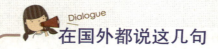

在国外都说这几句

- The airline offered me some cash on the spot after realizing my bags were lost.
  航空公司在知道我遗失行李后，立刻赔偿我了一些现金。
  ★ 短语 on the spot 立刻；当场

- If your luggage is not delivered on arrival, please contact the Lost & Found office.
  如果你的行李没有在你抵达时送达，请和失物招领处联络。
  ★ 短语 Lost & Found 失物招领处

- Did you describe what your luggage looks like to the airline personnel?
  你向航空公司的员工描述了行李大概的样子吗？
  ★ 短语 describe to... 向～描述

- Please present the luggage receipt to the ground crew.
  请把行李票据交给地勤人员。
  ★ 短语 present to... 交给～，呈交给～

- The airline representative promised to deliver the delayed baggage to my doorstep.
  航空公司代理人承诺会将延迟抵达的行李送到我家门口。
  ★ 短语 deliver A to... 将 A 送到～，将 A 运送给～

- Did you also ask for the contact number in case you need to call them and follow up?
  你顺便问了他们的联络方式吗，以防你需要打电话追踪？
  ★ 短语 follow up 追踪后续行动

- Why didn't the airline reply to my complaint? I've been waiting for 3 days.
  为什么航空公司不回复我的投诉？我已经等了3天了。
  ★ 短语 reply to... 回复～，回答～

- The airline company tried to negotiate a reasonable compensation.
  航空公司试着和我协商，希望能谈到合理的赔偿金额。
  ★ 短语 negotiate... 谈判～；协商～

- Don't panic. Take a deep breath. Everything will be OK.
  别恐慌。深呼吸。一切都会好的。
  ★ 短语 take a deep breath 深呼吸

- Please **fill out** this form and we will contact you as soon as we have any information.
  请填写这张表格，一有消息我们会马上通知你。
  ★ 短语 fill out 填写

- Before I **left for** Paris, my friends asked me if I could buy a few things for them.
  我出发前往巴黎前，我朋友问我可不可以帮他们买几样东西。
  ★ 短语 leave for... 前往～，动身到～

- I **picked out** the elegant necklace as a souvenir for my mother.
  我为妈妈挑选了这个优雅的项链当纪念品。
  ★ 短语 pick out... 挑选～；拣出～

- Let's go to the city center and have a look. I'm sure there will be **plenty of** stores.
  我们一起去市中心看看吧。我保证那里一定会有许多商店。
  ★ 短语 plenty of... 很多～，大量～

- You can **walk around** the neighborhood of your hotel, you might find something special as gifts.
  你可以在饭店附近逛逛，说不定你会找到特别的东西当礼物。
  ★ 短语 walk around... 在～附近走走；逛逛

- In case you really don't have time to go shopping here, you can consider buying souvenirs at the airport.
  万一你在这里真的没有时间买东西，那你可以考虑去机场买纪念品。

That one is beautiful!

It is!

 **在国外都说这几句**

- Are you sure you want to buy key chains as souvenirs? Most people would just throw them away.
  你确定你要买钥匙扣当纪念品吗？大部分的人应该都会把它丢掉吧。
  ★ 短语 ▶ throw away　丢掉

- I bought you a souvenir. However, I forgot to put it in my checked luggage so it was confiscated by the customs.
  我给你买了纪念品。但是我忘记把它放进托运行李，所以被海关人员没收了。
  ★ 短语 ▶ be confiscated by...　被～没收，被～征收

- I'm really grateful for the exotic vase you bought me.
  我真的很感激你买这么有异国情调的花瓶给我。
  ★ 短语 ▶ be grateful for...　感激～，感谢～

- You should have bargained with the vendor. He charged you too much for this watch.
  你应该要和小贩讲价的。这支手表他卖你太贵了。
  ★ 短语 ▶ bargain with...　与～讨价还价，与～杀价

- I don't want to return home empty-handed. Otherwise, I would probably be considered a Scrooge.
  我不想两手空空地回家。不然的话，我一定会被认为是个铁公鸡。
  ★ 短语 ▶ "Scrooge"是狄更斯（Charles Dickens）的小说《小气财神》（Christmas Carol）中的人物，现在意思引申为"守财奴、吝啬鬼、铁公鸡"。

- Being stuck in traffic is such a nightmare.
  被困在堵车的车流中真是噩梦。
  ★ 短语 ▶ be / get stuck in...　困在～；被～阻塞

Face the reality!

Back to work!

在国外都说这几句

- Check your smartphone, and then you can know what the hold up ahead is.
  查一下你的智能手机，这样你可以知道前方为什么堵住。
  ★ 短语 hold up　阻碍～；拦截～

- I do not want to drive on the main roads during the rush hours.
  我不想在高峰时刻开车到主路上。
  ★ 短语 rush hour　（上下班期间的）交通拥挤时间；高峰时间；高峰时刻

- The traffic isn't moving at all. I wish I could get out of the car and stretch out a bit.
  车流一点都没有动。我真希望我可以下车伸展一下。
  ★ 短语 stretch out...　伸直～，拉长～

- If you are bored, why not sing along with the music?
  如果你很无聊，为何不跟着音乐唱歌呢？
  ★ 短语 sing along with...　跟着～一起唱

- That driver won't lay off his horn. It's so annoying.
  那个司机一直按喇叭。真的是很烦。
  ★ 短语 lay off...　停止使用～；停止骚扰～

- I don't think we will be able to get there on time.
  我认为我们不会按时抵达目的地。
  ★ 短语 on time　准时

- I told my boss that I am going to be late due to the traffic congestion.
  我告诉老板我因为交通堵塞而会迟到。
  ★ 短语 traffic congestion　交通堵塞

- This traffic jam was caused by an accident.
  这次的堵车是交通事故所造成的。
  ★ 短语 be caused by...　因～造成，因～导致

- Turn on the radio when you drive so you can keep up with the traffic status.
  开车时，把广播打开，这样你才能了解最新路况。
  ★ 短语 keep up with...　跟上～；与～保持联系

- Jet lag is a temporary condition that causes fatigue or insomnia because of travelling across time zones.
  时差综合征是暂时的功能失调，是因为经过不同时区而导致的疲劳或失眠。
  ★ 短语 jet lag　时差

在国外都说这几句

- I took a mild sleeping pill to help me fall asleep.
  我吃了一粒温和的安眠药帮助我入睡。
  ★ 短语 fall asleep 睡着

- Why did you get on a long flight with a hangover? It must make you feel miserable.
  你为什么要在长途飞行时宿醉？你这样一定非常不舒服吧。
  ★ 短语 get on 登上（交通工具）

- Please get plenty of rest and do not drink any alcohol the night before departure.
  出发前一晚，请尽量多休息，并且不要喝任何含酒精的饮料。

- Are these no-jet-lag tablets made from natural herbs?
  这些消除时差的药丸是天然草药提炼的吗？
  ★ 短语 be made from... 由～制造，尤其指经过（化学）加工制造，已看不出原材料原本的样子。

- I am still recovering from my jet lag, so I am going back to sleep again.
  我还在倒时差，所以我要再回去睡觉。
  ★ 短语 recover from... 从～恢复，恢复～（健康）

- Some passengers will take a sleeping pill and try to sleep through the whole flight.
  有些乘客会在飞机上吃安眠药，然后试着整个旅程在睡眠中度过。
  ★ 短语 sleep through... 一直睡到～

- My mother does not take any medications she is not familiar with.
  我妈妈不吃她不熟悉的药物。
  ★ 短语 be familiar with... 熟悉～（某物），通晓～

- One of the best ways to fight jet lag is to stay up until bedtime.
  对抗时差最好的方法之一就是等到就寝时间再睡。
  ★ 短语 stay up 不睡觉，熬夜

- Normally, it takes at least one to two weeks to get the jet lag out of your system.
  通常，要完全摆脱时差的问题，至少需要 1～2 个星期。
  ★ 短语 get A out of your system 摆脱 A

Chapter 4 求学与就职
School & Work

Unit 17 | 留学生活的点点滴滴
Unit 18 | 校园与房屋租赁
Unit 19 | 面试就像是一台舞台剧
Unit 20 | 做个有活力的职场人
Unit 21 | 职场就像社会的缩影
Unit 22 | 沟通是最好的桥梁
Unit 23 | 增长见识的贸易博览会
Unit 24 | 接待礼仪很重要
Unit 25 | 没有一个辞职是真的说再见

跟任何人都可以用英语聊聊天

Unit 17 留学生活的点点滴滴

[生活便利贴]

在国外独自求学的过程是非常辛苦的，不但要以新的语言来学习新知识，还要适应新的环境，结交新朋友。但是，这些人生的洗礼，可以训练自己独立自主以及面对压力的能力，每一个小小的经验对未来都有极大的帮助，所以要趁着这段时间，多学、多听、多看，丰富自己的经验，为自己的未来做最好的投资。

Vocabulary 在国外都用这些词

 04-01

thrilled [θrɪld]
a 非常兴奋的，极为激动的

congratulation [kən,grætʃu'leɪʃn]
n 祝贺

deadline ['dedlaɪn]
n 截止日期，期限

tuition fee
ph 学费

parent ['peərənt]
n 父母之一

scholarship ['skɒləʃɪp]
n 奖学金

applicant ['æplɪkənt]
n 申请者

major ['meɪdʒə]
n 主修

student residence
ph 学生宿舍

orientation [,ɔːrɪən'teɪʃn]
n 新生训练

curriculum [kə'rɪkjələm]
n 课程

semester [sɪ'mestə]
n 学期

permit [pə'mɪt]
v 允许

sign [saɪn]
v 签名

accommodation [ə,kɒmə'deɪʃn]
n 住处

stressed [strest]
a 紧张的，有压力的

open day
ph 学校、机构等开放公众参观的开放日

magazine [,mægə'ziːn]
n 杂志

在国外都说这几句

- My sister was admitted to Harvard University.
  我姐姐刚被哈佛大学录取。
  ★ 短语 be admitted to...   获准进入～；录取进入～

- Last week, my brother received letter of offer from Harvard University.
  上星期，我哥哥收到了哈佛大学的录取通知书。
  ★ 短语 letter of offer   入学许可

- He is thrilled because going to law school at Harvard University has always been his dream.
  他非常兴奋，因为进入哈佛大学法学院一直是他的梦想。
  ★ 短语 law school   法学院

- Congratulations on your acceptance to NYU! All your hard work finally paid off.
  恭喜你被纽约大学录取！你的辛苦总算有了结果。
  ★ 短语 congratulations on...   恭喜～，恭贺～

- You have been accepted to the University of Washington — Well done!
  你被华盛顿大学录取了，做得好啊！
  ★ 短语 be accepted to...   获准进入～；录取进入～

- What separated my brother from other applicants was his passion for science and thirst for knowledge.
  跟其他申请人相比，我哥哥对科学的热情以及对事物的求知欲让他脱颖而出。
  ★ 短语 separate from...   分隔～；区别～

- When is the deadline for submitting the letter of acceptance?
  提交接收函的截止日期是哪天？
  ★ 短语 deadline for...   ～截止日期，～最后期限

常识补给站

大部分航空公司（廉价航空除外），都会为到国外求学的学生提供"学生票"，学生提供国外学校的入学许可或国际学生证，即可购买学生票。学生票的优惠可分为两种，一种是让出外念书的游子可以以较优惠的价格购买机票，另外一种则是提供行李公斤数的优惠，将行李公斤数提升至 30 或 40 公斤。

在国外都说这几句

- My brother needs to think about how he will pay for his tuition.
  我哥哥需要思考一下他要如何付学费。
  ★ 短语 pay for... 为～付钱，付～的钱

- My brother is discussing the payment options with our parents.
  我哥哥正在和父母讨论要用什么方式来付学费。
  ★ 短语 discuss with... 与～讨论，与～商谈

- Factors such as tuition fees and personal expenses need to be taken into consideration.
  像学费和个人花费这些因素都需要考虑。
  ★ 短语 take into consideration 纳入考量

- When will I find out if I am being offered a full scholarship?
  我什么时候能知道有没有申请到全额奖学金？
  ★ 短语 find out... 知道～，发现～

- The results of the scholarship will be mailed to the applicant in a week.
  奖学金的结果会在一个星期之内邮寄给申请者。
  ★ 短语 be mailed to... 邮寄给～，邮寄到～

- You need to make a payment of US $1,000 in advance as a deposit to secure your place.
  你需要事先缴 1000 美金来当作保留位置的押金。
  ★ 短语 make a payment 付款，付费

- What are the chances of getting admitted to Harvard?
  被哈佛录取的机会有多大？
  ★ 短语 the chance(s) of... ～的机会，～的可能性

- I would like to have a shot with Yale University.
  我想试试看申请耶鲁大学。
  ★ 短语 have a shot 有机会；试试看

- If you would like to change your major, you need to notify the admissions department in writing.
  如果你想换专业，你必须要以书面的方式通知招生处。
  ★ 短语 in writing 以书面的方式

在国外都说这几句

- Who can I speak with about my study plan?
  我可以跟谁讨论我的课程规划？
  ★ 短语 speak with... 与～讨论，与～谈

- If you would like to do a double major, you will need to speak with your advisor.
  如果你想修双学位，你将必须跟导师谈谈。
  ★ 短语 double major 双专业

- How can I apply for student residence?
  我要怎么样申请学生宿舍？
  ★ 短语 apply for 申请

- How much does it cost to finish a bachelor's degree at the University of Pennsylvania in total?
  要念完宾州大学学士学位，总共需要多少钱？
  ★ 短语 in total 总共，一共

- Most universities care about a student's accomplishments in and out of the classroom.
  大部分的大学都很关心学生校内和校外的成就。
  ★ 短语 care about... 关心～，在乎～

- Brown University asked for my transcript and letter of recommendation.
  布朗大学向我要成绩单和推荐信。
  ★ 短语 ask for... 要～，要求～

- Getting into an Ivy League University is not easy. You have to be one of the top students.
  要进入一所常春藤大学并不容易，你必须是前几名的学生。
  ★ 短语 "Ivy League" 的意思是 "常春藤联盟"，这一词是指美国东部8所历史悠久、高名望、高学术水平的大学。

- You will get extra points for participating in extracurricular activities.
  参加课外活动会有额外的加分。
  ★ 短语 extracurricular activity 课外活动

- Orientation is compulsory because it is the time for you to get to know the campus and all the facilities.
  新生训练是一定要参加的，因为你要趁这个时间多了解校园和学校设施。
  ★ 短语 get to know 了解

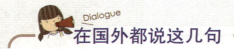

在国外都说这几句

- My brother took some time to get to know the university's course curriculum.
  我哥哥花了一些时间了解大学课程大纲。
  ★ 短语 take some time to... 花时间～

- How many credits do I need to take per semester?
  我每个学期需要修多少学分？
  ★ 短语 per semester 每一个学期

- Figuring out how to study at university is a very important task.
  想好如何在大学念书是很重大的任务。
  ★ 短语 figure out... 想出～；算出～

- I want to learn something practical; it's more useful for my future.
  我想学一些实用的东西，这样对我的未来比较有帮助。

- In my opinion, college is the time to take risks and make mistakes.
  我认为，大学正是冒险和犯错的时候。
  ★ 短语 take risks 冒险

- The online add/drop system is done on a first come, first served basis.
  线上加选/退选依照先抢先赢（先到就可先报名）的准则。
  ★ 语法 first come, first served 先到先得、先抢先赢

- Students may make adjustments to their schedules via the Internet.
  学生可以通过网络做课表的调整。
  ★ 短语 make an adjustment 调整

- Login details will be given to you during orientation.
  登录信息会在新生训练的时候提供给你们。
  ★ 短语 login details 登入信息

- You cannot withdraw core subjects, because they are compulsory.
  你不可以退选核心课程，因为它们是必修课目。
  ★ 短语 core subject 核心课程

在国外都说这几句

- Students are not permitted to take for more than four subjects each semester.
  学生每个学期都不可以注册超过 4 门课程。
  ★ 短语 more than　超过

- A registration consent form must be signed and dated in order to add extra course.
  注册同意表一定要签上名字和日期后，才可加选课程。
  ★ 短语 registration consent form　注册同意表

- Can I add a minor through web registration?
  我可以通过网络注册增加辅修吗？
  ★ 短语 add a minor　辅修

- You must attend classes regularly to maintain your attendance.
  你一定要正常上课，才能维持你的出席率。
  ★ 短语 attend classes　上课

- If you have questions about a particular course, please contact your advisor.
  如果关于某一课程你有问题，请与你的导师联系。

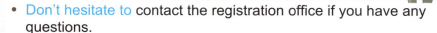

- Don't hesitate to contact the registration office if you have any questions.
  你如果有任何问题，请不要犹豫与注册办公室联系。
  ★ 短语 don't hesitate to...　不要犹豫～

- College orientation sessions provide a college overview to freshmen and their families.
  大学新生入学指导让大学新生和他们的家长能够了解大学生活概况。
  ★ 短语 provide A to B　将 A 提供给 B

- If you're nervous about how to approach people on campus, keep in mind that everyone feels the same.
  如果你对于如何在大学校园接近人群感到紧张，记住，每个人都跟你一样。
  ★ 短语 on campus　在（大学）校区

- Generally speaking, orientation programs include tours of the campus and meetings with school staff.
  一般来说，新生训练包含参观校园和与学校人员见面。
  ★ 短语 generally speaking　一般来说

在国外都说这几句

- Your student advisor will soon explain the importance of your attendance. Please pay attention to it.
  你们的导员很快会向各位解释出席率的重要性。请仔细听。
  ★ 短语 pay attention to　注意，关心

- For me, orientation is a great chance to socialize with new people.
  对我来说，新生训练是认识新朋友的好机会。
  ★ 短语 socialize with...　与～交朋友；与～交际

- Do I look okay? I'm going to student services and have my student ID card done.
  我看起来还好吗？我现在要去学生服务中心请他们帮我做学生证。
  ★ 短语 student ID (card)　学生证

- I should search for student hangouts such as cafés and cinemas.
  我应该寻找学生常去的地方，像是咖啡厅和电影院。
  ★ 短语 search for　寻找

- If you are a senior, you don't have to sign up for on-campus accommodations.
  若你是大四生，就不须登记校园住宿了。
  ★ 短语 on-campus accommodation　校园住宿

- College orientation programs can ease your tensions.
  大学新生入学指导课程可以舒缓你的紧张。

- The student cafeteria provides all sorts of meals that can accommodate students from all over the world.
  学生餐厅为来自世界各地的学生提供各种不同的食物。
  ★ 短语 student cafeteria　学生餐厅

- My brother is nervous about being on his own for the very first time.
  由于即将开始自己的第一次独立生活，我哥哥感到很紧张。
  ★ 短语 be nervous about...　对～感到紧张，对～感到不安

- The whole point of orientation is to help you get more familiar with the university.
  新生入学指导的重点就是帮助你更加熟悉大学。
  ★ 短语 get familiar + 事物　通晓某事物，熟悉某事物

- Students will also be introduced to the library system.
  将会给学生们介绍图书馆系统。
  ★ 短语 be introduced to... 被介绍～；被引见给～

- I will be staying in shared accommodations, so I'm looking forward to meeting my new roommate.
  我会跟别人合租房子，所以我很期待见到我的新室友。
  ★ 短语 look forward to... 期待～

- You should buy books from a second-hand bookstore, they're cheaper there.
  你应该到二手书店买书，那边比较便宜。
  ★ 短语 second-hand 二手的

- Do you feel stressed to make a hasty decision about a major?
  你对于仓促决定专业感到有压力吗？
  ★ 短语 make a decision 做决定

- Don't be passive; you should face the problem and deal with it.
  别太被动，你应该面对问题并想办法解决它。
  ★ 短语 face the problem 面对问题

- I should be prepared and think about my questions before I join the open day.
  参加学校开放日之前，我应该准备好，想想要问哪些问题。
  ★ 短语 think about... 彻底想清楚～，好好想想～

- Some of the freshman courses are taught by teaching assistants.
  有一些大一的课程会由助教授课。
  ★ 短语 be taught by... 由～教，由～上课

- What are the deadlines for financial aid applications?
  申请助学金或助学贷款的截止日期是什么时候？
  ★ 短语 financial aid 助学金；助学贷款

- How can I borrow a book or a magazine from the school library?
  我要怎么从学校的图书馆借书或杂志？
  ★ 短语 borrow A from B 从 B 那里借出 A

在国外都说这几句

- You can take the book to the information desk and present your student ID to the staff.
  你可以将书拿到服务柜台，并出示你的学生证给工作人员。
  ★ 短语 information desk　服务台

- The cost for having a library card reissued is $5.
  补办借书证的费用是 5 美元。
  ★ 短语 library card　图书馆借书证

- How long can I borrow this book for?
  这本书我可以借多久？
  ★ 短语 how long　时间多久

- It depends. If no one else reserves the book, then you can have it for as long as you want.
  要看情况。如果之后没有人预约这本书，那你想借多久都可以。
  ★ 语法 it depends　看情况

- If we don't have the book you need, you can make a request through the Internet library reserve service.
  如果我们没有你要的书，你可以通过线上图书预订服务申请。
  ★ 短语 make a request　（提出）要求，请求

- The library is open 7 days a week, even on Sunday.
  图书馆一个星期 7 天都开门，星期日也不例外。

- Reference books cannot be taken out of the library, as others might need them.
  参考文献的书籍不可带出图书馆，因为其他人可能也会需要。
  ★ 短语 be taken out of...　被带出～

- Unpaid library fines can result in a hold on your diploma.
  不付图书馆罚款将导致你的证件被扣留。
  ★ 短语 result in...　导致～；结果是～

- The lost book fee is a flat rate of $500 per book.
  若遗失书本，每本将统一收费 500 美元。
  ★ 短语 flat rate　统一收费率，单一费率

在国外都说这几句

- All students should return library books on time.
  每个学生都该准时归还图书馆的书。
  ★ 短语 on time　准时

- Food and drinks are not allowed in the library.
  食品和饮料不可带进图书馆。

- Do not make any marks on any library materials.
  不可以在图书馆的任何书籍上做记号。
  ★ 短语 make marks　做记号

- Students are not permitted to go topless in the library.
  学生不可光着上身在图书馆走动。
  ★ 短语 be not permitted　不被允许

- Students are expected to follow the guidelines while in the library.
  在图书馆内，学生应该遵守守则。
  ★ 短语 be expected to...　被要求～；被指望～

- Please switch your mobile phones to mute.
  请将手机调成静音模式。
  ★ 短语 switch... to mute　转成静音模式

- This library is a mobile phone free zone. Please take your calls outside.
  本图书馆禁止使用手机。请到外面接听电话。
  ★ 短语 take (a) call　接（一通）电话

- By law, smoking in the library is strictly prohibited.
  图书馆依法严格禁止吸烟。
  ★ 短语 by law　依法

- The library is not responsible for any lost or stolen items, so keep your eye on your personal belongings.
  遗失或被偷窃的物品，本图书馆概不负责，所以请看管好自己的私人物品。
  ★ 短语 be responsible for...　对～负责

- Overdue fees are two dollars per day after the two-day grace period.
  两天宽限期到期后，图书馆的逾期费用是每天 2 元。
  ★ 短语 grace period　宽限期

跟任何人都可以用英语聊聊天

Unit 18 校园与房屋租赁

[生活便利贴]

大学生活多彩多姿，除了上课之外，课外活动也相当重要。交友、派对、逛街及旅游样样不能少。另外，体验当地的文化特色也非常重要，可以试着参加当地的文化庆典或是一些节日的游行，每种活动都可为你的人生增添不同的色彩，为日后留下美好深刻的回忆。不过，玩虽然很重要，但还是要记得自己的本分，好好读书！

Vocabulary 在国外都用这些词

MP3 04-11

senior student
ph 大四学生

exchange
[ɪks'tʃeɪndʒ]
v / n 交换，互换

skip class
ph 逃课

homesick
['həʊmsɪk]
n 思乡，想家

dormitory
['dɔːmətri]
n 学生宿舍

official
[ə'fɪʃl]
a 正式的

supermarket
['suːpəmɑːkɪt]
n 超市

welcoming
['welkəmɪŋ]
a 欢迎的

alone
[ə'ləʊn]
ad 单独地，独自地

settle
['setl]
v 安顿

mentor
['mentɔː]
n 指导者

out of the question
ph 不可能的

coin
[kɔɪn]
n 硬币

together
[tə'geðə]
ad 一起地

take turns
ph 轮流

lease
[liːs]
n 租约

toothpaste
['tuːθpeɪst]
n 牙膏

curfew
['kɜːfjuː]
n 宵禁

Dialogue 在国外都说这几句

- I'd like to learn more about campus lifestyle.
  我想多认识有关校园的生活方式。
  ★ 短语 learn about... 获得；得知

- Are campus tours led by senior students?
  参观校园之旅是由大四的学生带领的吗？
  ★ 短语 be led by... 由～领路；由～引导

- Will I have the chance to learn some information about overseas exchange students during the trip?
  校园之旅中，我会有机会获得有关出国当交换学生的信息吗？
  ★ 短语 have the chance to... 有～的机会；有～可能性

- Sleeping in and skipping my early morning class is very tempting at times.
  偶尔晚起并逃掉一大早的课听起来很诱人。
  ★ 短语 sleep in 睡得很晚才起床

- We should take advantage of the study resources on campus.
  我们应该善用学校的学习资源。
  ★ 短语 take advantage of... 利用～；善用～

- My dad told me to take responsibility for my own actions.
  我爸爸告诉我要为自己的行为负责。
  ★ 短语 take responsibility for... 对～负责

- Being away from home, most people will become homesick.
  远离家乡，大部分的人都会受思乡之苦。

- I am nervous about going to college this coming September.
  对于在今年9月要开始上大学，我感到很紧张。
  ★ 短语 be nervous about... 对～感到紧张；对～不安

- What is the distance between the dormitory and the classrooms?
  宿舍和上课教室的距离有多远？
  ★ 短语 distance between A and B A和B的距离，A和B的路程

- It is important for college students to keep a record of their spending.
  对大学生来说，将自己的花费清楚地记录下来是很重要的。
  ★ 短语 keep a record of... 记录～

跟任何人都可以用英语聊聊天

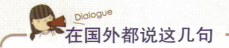
在国外都说这几句

- I now understand why there is a saying called "freshman fifteen". You can't say no to all the good food here.
  我现在理解了为什么会有"大学新人发胖十五磅"的说法了，因为你无法拒绝这里的美食。
  ★ 短语 freshman fifteen　大学新人发胖的十五磅。美国大学中，曾有调查显示，在大学的第一年，平均每个新人都会胖十五磅。

- I'm a bit overwhelmed by the new environment and all these new people.
  对于这些新环境和要认识的新朋友，我有一点不知所措。
  ★ 短语 be overwhelmed by...　因～而受不了，因～不知所措

- You should take a few minutes to read the notice boards when you visit the academic buildings. They contain some important information.
  参观教学大楼时，你应该花几分钟阅读一下布告栏。上面有一些重要信息。
  ★ 短语 notice board　布告栏

- Eating in the student cafeteria is the best way to get a good feel for social life on campus.
  在学生餐厅用餐是能体验校园社交生活的最好方式。
  ★ 短语 a good feel for...　体验～的感觉

- A group of new students are having a campus tour.
  一群新生正在参观校园。
  ★ 短语 a group of...　一群～，一组～

- During the campus visit, you should make the most out of it by asking questions.
  你应该充分利用校园之旅，多多提问。
  ★ 短语 make the most out of...　充分利用～

- We can not only learn about culture on campus by joining a campus tour, but also the facilities offered by the college.
  参加校园之旅，我们不但可以了解校园文化，还可以看到学校提供的相关设备。
  ★ 短语 not only... but also　不但～还可以～

- The more time you spend on getting to know the campus, the less likely you will get lost and miss your classes.
  你花越多时间认识校园，你就越不可能会因为迷路而没去上课。
  ★ 短语 spend on + n.　花（时间/金钱）在 n.

在国外都说这几句

- Should I sign up for the official campus tour, or just poke around by myself?
  我应该报名参加正式的校园之旅，还是自己随便逛一下就好？
  ★ 短语 poke around... 闲逛～

- Are there supermarkets for grocery shopping within walking distance?
  这附近有步行就可到达并供应生活用品的超市吗？
  ★ 短语 within walking distance 步行范围内，走路就可抵达

- Do you like the atmosphere of the campus?
  你喜欢校园里的气氛吗？
  ★ 短语 atmosphere of... ～的气氛

- Do you feel safe and sound off campus?
  你在校园外感到安全吗？
  ★ 短语 safe and sound 安全无恙

- People in this city are very welcoming toward international students.
  这个城市的人非常欢迎国际学生。
  ★ 短语 international student 国际学生

- I scheduled an appointment with a director of studies.
  我与教务长预约会面。
  ★ 短语 schedule an appointment with... 与～会面；与～有约定

- Is the campus safe enough for students to go out alone at night?
  学生晚上自己在校园走动安全吗？
  ★ 短语 at night 在夜里，在夜间

- You should avoid asking personal questions of people your've just met.
  对于才认识不久的人，你应该避免问他们私人问题。
  ★ 短语 avoid + v-ing / n. 避免～

- What are the services that the school provides to help freshmen settle in?
  学校提供哪些服务可以帮助新生安顿下来？
  ★ 短语 settle in 安顿下来

- All freshmen will be assigned to a senior student as their mentor.
  所有新生将被指派一位大四学生来指导他们。
  ★ 短语 be assigned to... 指定给～；分配给～

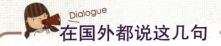

在国外都说这几句

- Being a college student means you need to deal with all your own problems and be independent.
  成为大学生意味着你要会处理自己的问题并且要独立。
  ★ 短语 deal with 处理

- For students with financial issues, tuition fees can be paid in installments.
  学生若财务上有问题的话，可以以分期付款的方式支付学费。
  ★ 短语 in installments 以分期付款方式付费

- The student residence is full at this stage. I can put you on the waiting list.
  现阶段学生宿舍是满的。我可以把你放入候补名单。
  ★ 短语 waiting list 候补名单

- All freshmen are required to stay in the on-campus accommodations.
  所有的大一新生都必须住在学生宿舍。
  ★ 短语 on-campus 在校内

- What types of security measures are in place in the student residence?
  住宿大楼都有哪些安全措施正在使用？
  ★ 短语 in place 适当的；在正确的地方

- The cost for room and board goes up every year.
  食宿的费用每年都会调涨。
  ★ 短语 go up 上升，攀升～

- How many roommates will be allocated to a dorm room?
  每间宿舍房间会安排几个室友？
  ★ 短语 be allocated to... 分配～

- I'm a college student on a tight budget. Renting an apartment is out of the question.
  我是经济拮据的大学生。租一间公寓对我来说是不可能的。
  ★ 短语 on a budget 缺钱，拮据

- A security deposit is usually equal to two months rent, which will be refunded to you at the end of your contract.
  押金通常等于两个月的房租。合约到期之后会退给你。
  ★ 短语 be equal to... 等于～，与～相等

在国外都说这几句

- **My resident assistant is always there to help me get used to dorm life.**
  我的宿舍管理员总是帮助我适应宿舍生活。
  ★ 短语 resident assistant　宿舍管理员

- **Make sure you have plenty of coins before you go to the laundry room.**
  去洗衣房之前，要确认你有很多硬币。
  ★ 短语 plenty of　大量的

- **There are a lot of apartments near campus with a "For Lease" sign on them. You should find a new place to stay easily.**
  学校附近有很多公寓正在出租。你应该可以很快就找到新的地方住了。
  ★ 短语 for lease　供租用的，出租的

- **My classmate and I decided to move into this house together.**
  我同学跟我决定要一起搬进这间房子。
  ★ 短语 move into　搬进去

- **If you want to move in together, it's better to set out the rules first.**
  如果你们打算一起住，那最好先把合住规则讲清楚。
  ★ 短语 set out　说明；阐述

- **We should take turns to being in charge of household chores every week.**
  我们应该每个星期轮流负责家务。
  ★ 短语 in charge of...　负责～；照料～

- **A one-bedroom apartment may be ideal for me because I don't want to share with anyone else.**
  因为我不想跟别人一起共享空间，单间公寓对我来说很理想。
  ★ 短语 be ideal for...　对～来说是完美的；对～来说很理想

- **My parents suggested that I figure out what I can afford, stick to my budget and not buy things I don't need.**
  我爸妈建议我想好自己能负担的范围，坚持自己的预算并且不要买不需要的东西。
  ★ 短语 stick to...　坚持～；忠于～

- **My friend got carried away and signed up for an apartment she can't afford at all.**
  我朋友太冲动，她登记了一间完全负担不起的公寓。
  ★ 短语 carry away　忘乎所以，因过于激动而失去自制力

跟任何人都可以用英语聊聊天

在国外都说这几句

- **Be sure to** read the lease thoroughly before you sign it.
  签租约时，一定要从头到尾详读完合约。
  ★ 短语 be sure to...　务必~，一定要~

- Utility bills usually **are excluded from** the monthly rent.
  水电气等费用通常不包含在每个月的房租之内。
  ★ 短语 be excluded from...　不包含~，不包括~

- A lease must **be signed by** both the tenant and the landlord.
  租约一定要由房客和房东双方签约。
  ★ 短语 be signed by...　由~签名，由~签署

- Rent should be paid **in advance** by the first day of every month.
  房租要在每个月第一天之前缴清。
  ★ 短语 in advance　事先，预先

- Wanted to have a **mini-TV** in our room, so I split the cost with my roommate.
  我想要在房间放一台迷你电视，所以费用我和室友共同分摊。
  ★ 短语 mini-TV　迷你电视

- We are **running out of** food in the fridge. Would you like to go food shopping later?
  我们的冰箱快没有食物了。你一会儿要不要跟我一起去买些食物？
  ★ 短语 run out of　用完、耗尽

- The space gets smaller when you have to **share with a roommate**.
  当你需要和室友共用宿舍时，空间似乎变得更小了。
  ★ 短语 share... with A　与A分享~，与A共用~

- My roommate is **driving me crazy**. She is unreasonable.
  我的室友快把我搞疯了。她简直不可理喻。
  ★ 短语 drive A crazy　把A逼疯，使A发狂

- I **forgot to** buy some more toothpaste. Can I borrow yours?
  我忘了买新牙膏。可以借用你的吗？
  ★ 短语 forget to...　忘记去~

- I **got along** with my roommates very well after I moved into the college dorm.
  我一搬进大学宿舍，就和室友处得非常融洽。
  ★ 短语 get along　和睦相处，相处融洽

在国外都说这几句

- One of the advantages of being a college student is that you have no curfew.
  当大学生的其中一个好处就是没有宵禁。

- My roommate and I are both international students. Sometimes we will talk to each other about the culture shock.
  我的室友和我都是国际学生。有时候我们会跟彼此说我们遇到的文化冲击。
  ★ 短语 culture shock　文化冲击

- My roommate is such a neat freak. Living with her gives me so much pressure.
  我的室友有很严重的洁癖。跟她住在一起有很大的压力。
  ★ 短语 neat freak　有洁癖的人

- We should come to some agreements about how to keep our room clean and livable.
  对于如何保持房间干净并适合居住，我们应该达成一个协议。
  ★ 短语 come to (an) agreement(s)　达成协议，达成协定

- My roommate and I take turns doing the laundry.
  我的室友和我轮流洗衣服。
  ★ 短语 take turns + v-ing　轮流做～

- My roommate is such a slob. He never cleans up the kitchen after cooking.
  我室友真是个不修边幅的脏鬼。他煮完饭后，从不清洁厨房。
  ★ 短语 clean up...　打扫～，清理～

- Calm down. I'm sure your roommate is not that bad. Just talk to him.
  放轻松。我确定你的室友没有那么糟。去跟他谈谈吧。
  ★ 短语 calm down　放轻松，冷静

> **常识补给站**
>
> 　　与外国同学合租房子时，要特别注意，一般西方国家的人非常注重个人隐私，如果要使用他人的物品，要事先询问，对方同意后才可以使用。另外，想进出他人的房间时，记得敲门后要等到对方回应，才可以开门进入，不然会被认为非常没有礼貌。

在国外都说这几句

- Do not give your roommate the **silent treatment**. It will make things worse.
  不要以沉默来表达你对室友的不满。这样只会让事情愈来愈糟。
  ★ 短语 silent treatment　沉默相待（持续冷漠的态度表达生气或不赞同）

- My annoying roommate is **out of his mind**. I don't agree with most of the things he says.
  我讨人厌的室友一定是疯了。他讲的很多事情我都不同意。
  ★ 短语 out of A's mind　A疯了

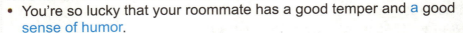

- You're so lucky that your roommate has a good temper and **a good sense of humor**.
  你有个脾气好又有幽默感的室友真是幸运。
  ★ 短语 a sense of humor　幽默感

- My roommate never **takes out** the trash and that leaves the room with a disgusting smell.
  我的室友从不倒垃圾，这让房间有一股恶心的味道。
  ★ 短语 take out...　把～拿出去，带～出去

- The food in the refrigerator is not **for sharing**.
  冰箱内的食物不是共享的。
  ★ 短语 for sharing　共享的，共有的

- I have to jump over **a pile of** dirty laundry every time I want to use the toilet.
  每次我想用厕所的时候，我就必须要跳过一堆脏衣服。
  ★ 短语 a pile of...　一堆～，大量的～

- Can you please **turn down** the TV? I'm trying to study here.
  你可以把电视（声音）关小一点吗？我正想在这儿学习呢。
  ★ 短语 turn down...　将～关小声，将～调小声

- You should **decorate your room** in your own personal style.
  你应该将房间装饰得有个人风格。
  ★ 短语 decorate A...　装饰A

- **I'm aware of** the fact that I cannot punch any holes in the wall.
  我知道我们不能在墙壁上凿洞。
  ★ 短语 be aware of...　知道～

在国外都说这几句

- Will this mattress **fit into** my room?
  这张床垫放得进我房间吗？
  ★ 短语 fit into　适合；相合

- How long does it take for the **shipping company** to deliver the closet?
  货运公司要多久才会把衣橱送来？
  ★ 短语 shipping company　货运公司

- Can you please **write down** your e-mail address and your phone number?
  请问你可以写下你的电子邮箱地址和电话号码吗？
  ★ 短语 write down...　记下～，写下～

- In my opinion, buying furniture online is like being set up on a **blind date**. It's very risky.
  对我来说，上网买家具就像被安排去相亲一样。风险很大。
  ★ 短语 blind date　盲目约会，相亲

- You should know your needs before purchasing any furniture.
  购买任何家具前，你应该了解你自己的需求。

- A futon is a mattress that could be **rolled up** and stored away during the day. It can save a lot of space.
  日式床垫是可以在白天卷起来并收纳起来的床垫。它可以节省很多空间。
  ★ 短语 roll up　滚动、卷起来

- A comfortable bed is the most essential piece of furniture for your apartment.
  一张舒适的床是你公寓中最重要的一件家具。
  ★ 语法 因为"furniture"是不可数名词，因此，在形容"一件家具"时，一定要使用量词"a piece of"，若是两件以上的家具，则在"piece"后加"s"，变成"two/many pieces of furniture"。

- I would like to buy a **table lamp** so that it can provide me a better study environment.
  我想买一盏台灯，让我有更好的学习环境。
  ★ 短语 table lamp　台灯

跟任何人都可以用英语聊聊天

Unit 19 面试就像是一台舞台剧

[生活便利贴]

面试有很多事情是不可忽视的，比如准时抵达面试地点、合宜的穿着、大方的谈吐……事前要针对面试公司做一些研究，才不会在面试官问你有关公司的问题时，一问三不知。另外，不知道的问题绝对不可以乱猜，大方地承认自己对这个方面的认知不够多，未来希望可以有进一步的接触，让对方知道你有心学习。

Vocabulary 在国外都用这些词 04-21

nervous ['nɜːvəs]
a 紧张的

review [rɪ'vjuː]
v 复习

professionally [prə'feʃənəli]
ad 专业地

assessment [ə'sesmənt]
n 评估

skill [skɪl]
n 技术；技能

potential [pə'tenʃl]
n 可能性；潜力

résumé ['rezjumeɪ]
n 履历表

multi-national
a 跨国的；多国的

corporation [ˌkɔːpə'reɪʃn]
n 公司

introduce [ˌɪntrə'djuːs]
v 介绍

tricky ['trɪkɪ]
a 微妙的；难处理的

briefly ['briːflɪ]
ad 简短地

cost of living
ph 生活花费

literature ['lɪtrətʃə]
n 文学

editor ['edɪtə]
n 编辑

task [tɑːsk]
n 工作；任务

challenge ['tʃælɪndʒ]
n 挑战

satisfaction [ˌsætɪs'fækʃn]
n 满意

在国外都说这几句

- The HR department called me in for an interview.
  人力资源部门打电话叫我参加面试。
  ★ 短语 call A in 请 A 来

- I am prepared for that job interview. Wish me luck.
  我已经为面试准备齐全了。祝我好运吧。
  ★ 短语 be prepared for + n. 为～准备好，准备好做～

- My brother is getting ready for an important job interview. He is quite nervous.
  我哥哥正在为重要工作的面试做准备。他非常紧张。

- It's important to make a good impression on my future employer.
  让未来雇主对我有好印象是非常重要的。
  ★ 短语 make an impression on... 让～有印象

- I was told that the best way to answer interview questions is to be honest.
  我被告知，回答面试问题最好的方法就是诚实。
  ★ 短语 the best way to... ～最好的方法，～最棒的方式

- I should take the time to review some common questions for a job interview.
  我应该花些时间复习工作面试时常会问的问题。
  ★ 短语 take the time to... 花时间～，花费心思～

- I asked my mom to practice interviewing with me.
  我请妈妈跟我一起练习面试。

常识补给站

面试的时候，请尽量避免带朋友或家人一起到面试的场所，这样会让该公司的人觉得你的自理能力很差或是完全没有独立性，这样只会造成负面效果，留下非常差的第一印象。如果真的需要别人的陪同，面试时请他在附近逛逛，不要跟着一起进入面试地点。否则，录取的机会真的是微乎其微。

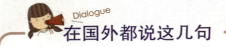

在国外都说这几句

- You have to dress up professionally for a job interview.
  面试时你一定要穿得正式、专业。
  ★ 短语 ▶ dress up　盛装打扮

- Before going to a job interview, you should visit the company's website and find out about what it is doing.
  参加面试前，你应该到这家公司的网站上看看，了解他们是做什么的。
  ★ 短语 ▶ find out...　找出关于～的，查明与～有关的

- You will be requested to talk about your previous work experience during the job interview.
  面试的过程中，你会被要求谈谈你过去的工作经验。
  ★ 短语 ▶ work experience　工作经验

- Please remember to give us full and detailed answers during the assessment.
  请记得给我们完整并详尽的答案，以便于评估。
  ★ 短语 ▶ remember to...　记得要～；记得做～

- I hope the employer will be impressed by my professional skills.
  我希望雇主会对我的专业技能印象深刻。
  ★ 短语 ▶ be impressed by...　因为～印象深刻，对～留下印象

- A good résumé is very important. It can show an employer that you have potential for the job.
  一份好的履历表是非常重要的，它可以让雇主知道对于这份工作你是有潜力的。
  ★ 短语 ▶ have potential for...　对～是有潜力的

- The employer was concerned about the fact that English is not my first language.
  这位雇主担心英语不是我的母语。
  ★ 短语 ▶ be concerned about...　对～感到担心；关心～

- You need to continue to improve your English skills because we are a multi-national corporation.
  因为我们是一家跨国公司，所以你需要继续加强英语能力。
  ★ 短语 ▶ continue to...　继续～；持续～

在国外都说这几句

- Our district manager would like to schedule a **telephone interview** with you for 3:00 p.m.
  我们的区域经理想跟你约下午 3 点进行电话面试。
  ★ 短语 telephone interview　电话面试

- Being on time for an interview is basic good manners.
  面试准时是基本的礼貌。

- I will send a **thank-you note** to the interviewer for taking the time to interview me.
  我将寄感谢函给面试人，感谢他花时间对我进行面试。
  ★ 短语 thank-you note　感谢函

- Shall I call and **follow up** after each interview?
  我应该打电话追踪每个面试（结果／进度）吗？
  ★ 短语 follow up...　在～之后，采取后续行动；监督／追踪～

- Just be yourself. Don't **show off**.
  做你自己就好。不要炫耀。
  ★ 短语 show off...　卖弄～，炫耀～

- I **introduced myself to the interviewers**.
  我对面试官们做了自我介绍。
  ★ 短语 introduce A to B　将 A 介绍给 B 认识

- **Breaking the ice** can be tricky. You don't want to give the wrong first impression.
  打破僵局是很难拿捏的，因为你不想给对方一个不好的第一印象。
  ★ 短语 break the ice　打破沉默，打开话题

- I **was surprised by** how friendly the interviewer was.
  我很惊讶面试官居然这么友善。
  ★ 短语 be surprised by...　对～感到惊讶，对～感到意外

- The interviewers smiled and tried to **put me at ease**.
  面试官们面带着微笑，试着要让我自在一些。
  ★ 短语 put A at ease　让 A 感到自在，使 A 感到安心

- I briefly **talked about** my educational background and work experience.
  我简单地描述了一下我的教育背景跟工作经验。
  ★ 短语 talk about...　谈论～，谈到～

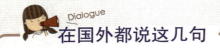

在国外都说这几句

- I studied at Harvard University from 2002 to 2006.
  我于 2002 年到 2006 年在哈佛大学读书。
  ★ 短语 from... to ... （时间／地点）从～到～

- I graduated with a degree in commerce.
  我毕业并得到商学学位。
  ★ 短语 a degree in... ～的学位，～的学历

- During the summers, I worked as a receptionist for a small company to cover my living costs.
  暑期时，为了贴补生活费，我在一家小型企业担任前台接待员。
  ★ 短语 work as... 担任～、做～工作

- I finished my studies at the University of Pennsylvania where I majored in English Literature.
  我之前在宾州大学读书，主修英国文学。
  ★ 短语 English Literature 英国文学

- At present, I am looking for a job as a teacher. I hope I can be part of your team.
  目前，我正在寻找教职工作。希望我可以加入你们的团队。
  ★ 短语 look for 寻找

- Johnson Corp. employed me in the PR department three years ago.
  强生股份有限公司 3 年前雇用我担任公关。
  ★ 短语 PR 是 Public Relations 的缩写，意为"公共关系；公关"。

- I enjoy working with different people. I can learn different things from them.
  我真的很喜欢跟不同的人一起工作。我可以从他们的身上学到不同的东西。
  ★ 短语 enjoy + v-ing 喜欢做～、享受做～

- I worked for I'm Publishing from 2010 to 2012 as an editor.
  我在 2010 年到 2012 年在我识出版集团担任编辑。
  ★ 短语 work for... 为～工作，帮～做事

- I work as a front desk clerk at a Four Seasons Hotel.
  我在四季饭店担任前台接待员。
  ★ 短语 front desk 前台

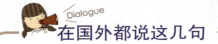

在国外都说这几句

- I hope I won't **be late for** the interview because of the traffic.
  我希望我不会因为交通的关系而面试迟到。
  ★ 短语 be late for... ～迟到；赶不上～

- I **was born and raised** in Beijing, so I speak fluent Mandarin.
  我在北京出生长大，所以我普通话讲得很流利。
  ★ 短语 be born / raised in... 在～出生／长大

- I received my **Master's degree** in science in 2010.
  我在 2010 年获得理学硕士学位。
  ★ 短语 Master's degree 硕士学位

- I worked for various companies as a **salesperson** in Beijing for three years.
  我在北京几家不同公司担任业务员有三年之久。
  ★ 短语 salesperson 业务员，这个单词没有性别之分，可同时指男／女业务员。

- I just **graduated from** Brown University with a degree in Journalism.
  我刚从布朗大学毕业，并获得新闻学学位。
  ★ 短语 graduate from... 从～毕业，毕业于～

- I usually fulfill the tasks **ahead of schedule**.
  我总是提前完成工作项目。
  ★ 短语 ahead of schedule 提前，提早

- I **was responsible for** several projects at the same time.
  我同时负责许多不同的企划。
  ★ 短语 be responsible for... 对～负责任，负责～

- I quit my job because I'm ready to **move on to** a new environment and a new challenge.
  我辞职是因为我准备好继续前进并面对新的环境以及新的挑战。
  ★ 短语 move on to... 前进～；往前走～

常识补给站

　　国外的英语履历表和国内的有些差别。一般履历表会尽量限制在 1～2 页，好让一开始做初步审核的人方便作业。至于内容上面也会比较专注在教育背景、工作经验以及专业知识，这样一来就可以马上看得到你个人过去的学习经历以及是否有特殊技能，来判断出你是否符合该职位。

Dialogue 在国外都说这几句

- That sounds like a very exciting and challenging job. It would be an honor to be offered a job here.
  这听起来像是很刺激又有挑战的工作。若得到这份工作，我将会觉得非常荣幸。
  ★ 短语 ▶ A sound like... A 听起来像～

- I combat stress by working out at the gym three times a week.
  我抗压的方法就是每个星期到健身房健身 3 次。
  ★ 短语 ▶ work out 健身、运动

- When I work on a project, I always do my best to meet everyone's satisfaction.
  当我忙于一项企划案时，我总是尽力让每个人满意。
  ★ 短语 ▶ meet A's satisfaction 让 A 感到满意

- People normally act a bit different when they under pressure.
  当人们处在压力下时，通常表现也会跟平常不一样。
  ★ 短语 ▶ under pressure 处于压力之下，承受压力的

- I am impressed by your rich work experience.
  我对你丰富的工作经验印象深刻。
  ★ 短语 ▶ be impressed by... 对～有印象

- Did you have any trouble finding a job?
  你找工作碰到过困难吗？ / 工作好找吗？
  ★ 短语 ▶ have trouble + v-ing 做～有困难

- Is there anything in particular you have in mind when looking for a job?
  找工作的时候，你有什么特别的要求吗？
  ★ 短语 ▶ in particular 特别地

- Please tell us in detail what visions you have in yourself in 5 years.
  请详细地告诉我们，5 年内你对自己有什么愿景？
  ★ 短语 ▶ in detail 详细地

- What makes you think that you are qualified for this job?
  你为什么认为自己能胜任这份工作？
  ★ 短语 ▶ be qualified for... 对～有资格

- Please tell me why you think you are capable of doing this job.
  请告诉我你为什么认为自己有能力胜任这个工作？
  ★ 短语 ▶ be capable of v-ing / n. 有能力做～

在国外都说这几句

- What do you like to do in your spare time?
  你空闲时间喜欢做些什么？
  ★ 短语 in A's spare time　A 的空闲时间

- What type of position are you looking for?
  你在寻找哪种职务？
  ★ 短语 look for...　寻找～；搜寻～

- Are you interested in a full-time position or a part-time job?
  你对全职工作有兴趣还是想要找一份兼职的工作？
  ★ 短语 be interested in...　对～感兴趣，有兴趣～

- Please tell me about your duties at your previous job.
  请告诉我你上一份工作的职责。
  ★ 短语 tell A about...　告诉 A 有关～，与 A 谈论关于～

- I'm motivated by this challenging work. I'm sure I can do it very well.
  我被这个富有挑战性的工作所激发了。我相信我一定可以做得很好。
  ★ 短语 be motivated by...　被～激发，被～激励

- What are you passionate about?
  你对哪些事情有激情？
  ★ 短语 be passionate about...　对～有热情，对～有热忱

- What will your previous boss say about you?
  你之前的上司会怎样评价你？

- Do you think you learned from your mistakes in the past?
  你觉得你有从过去你犯的错误中学到什么教训吗？
  ★ 短语 learn from...　由～中学习，从～吸取教训

- What did you dislike about your last job?
  关于上一份工作，你不喜欢什么？
  ★ 短语 dislike about...　不喜欢～，厌恶～

- What do you expect from our company?
  你对于我们这家公司有什么期待？
  ★ 短语 expect from...　对～有期待

- What can you bring to this company?
  你会为公司带来些什么？
  ★ 短语 bring to　带来～

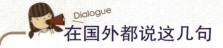

在国外都说这几句

- In our company, we do not want our employees to **take** their work **home with them**.
  我们公司不希望员工把工作带回家做。
  ★ 短语 take... home with A　A 把～带回家、A 带～回家

- May I ask if you **make any contributions to** your previous company?
  我可以问一下，你对之前的公司有什么样的贡献吗？
  ★ 短语 make a contribution to...　对～有所贡献

- What is your biggest failure, and what did you **learn from** it?
  你最大的失误是什么？你从中学到什么？
  ★ 短语 learn from...　从～学到教训

- What would you do if your supervisor asked you to do something you **disagreed with**?
  如果你的上司要求你做某件你不认同的事，你会怎么做？
  ★ 短语 disagree with...　与～争执；与～意见不合

- What do you pursue **in terms of** career development?
  就职场发展来说，你追求的是什么？
  ★ 短语 in terms of...　就～而论，在～方面

- Are you the kind of person who **takes no for an answer**?
  你是那种会接受拒绝的人吗？
  ★ 短语 take no for an answer　接受否定的答复

- Do you **subscribe to** any magazines or newspapers?
  你订阅任何杂志或报纸吗？
  ★ 短语 subscribe to...　订购～；订阅～

- What do you know about our corporation **so far**?
  你目前对于本公司有什么样的认识？
  ★ 短语 so far　到目前为止

- What salary range do you **hope for**?
  你期待的薪水范围是多少？
  ★ 短语 hope for...　期待～，希望～

- This job requires you to **pay attention to** all the details.
  这份工作你需要非常注意细节。
  ★ 短语 pay attention to...　注意～；关心～

在国外都说这几句

- **Do you have the ability to do multi-tasking?**
  你有能力一心多用吗？
  ★ 短语 multi-tasking 一心多用

- **Are you easily distracted from work?**
  你工作中容易分心吗？
  ★ 短语 distract from... 从～分心；转移～注意力

- **Are you capable of keeping everything on track under great stress?**
  你有能力在巨大的压力下将所有事情都依照计划进行吗？
  ★ 短语 keep A on track 让 A 上轨道

- **Do you perform worse under pressure?**
  你在压力之下会表现得比较差吗？
  ★ 短语 under pressure 在压力之下；被逼迫的

- **My ideal salary is ￥40,000. However, it's negotiable.**
  我的理想薪水是 4 万元，但还是有讨论的空间。

- **This is the end of the interview. Thanks for your time. We will contact you in a week.**
  面试结束了。谢谢你的宝贵时间。我们会在一个星期内通知你。
  ★ 短语 thanks for your time 谢谢你的宝贵时间

- **Thank you very much. Please don't hesitate to contact me if you have any further questions.**
  非常感谢您。如果你还有任何问题的话，请不要犹豫，马上跟我联系。
  ★ 短语 hesitate to... 犹豫～

Tell me about yourself.

My name is Shelby. I graduated from Soochow University.

跟任何人都可以用英语聊聊天

Unit 20 做个有活力的职场人

[生活便利贴]

第一天上班，迎接新环境、新气象。要注意：不管是面对上司还是同事，都要笑脸迎人，给大家留下好的第一印象。遇到不清楚的问题，一定要开口询问，绝对不可以有"反正是第一天，不知道是正常的"这种心态，否则只会让大家对你产生反感。最重要的是要保持积极的态度，努力地学习。

Vocabulary 在国外都用这些词

MP3 04-31

publishing
['pʌblɪʃɪŋ]
n 出版业

executive
[ɪɡ'zekjətɪv]
a 行政上的；行政部门的

conference
['kɒnfərəns]
n 会议

personal assistant
ph 个人助理

professor
[prə'fesə]
n 教授

order
['ɔːdə]
n 订单

assign
[ə'saɪn]
v 分配；指定；分派

campaign
[kæm'peɪn]
n 活动；运动

inconvenience
[ˌɪnkən'viːnɪəns]
n 不便，麻烦

sample
['sɑːmpl]
n 样品

annual
['ænjuəl]
a 一年的；一年一次的

punch
[pʌntʃ]
v 用力按；打孔

colleague
['kɒliːɡ]
n 同事

agent
['eɪdʒənt]
n 代理人；中介；专员

overtime
['əʊvətaɪm]
ad 超过地；加班地

accountant
[ə'kaʊntənt]
n 会计师

agreement
[ə'ɡriːmənt]
n 协议；同意

delegate
['delɪɡət]
v 授权

198

在国外都说这几句

- **Welcome to** I'm Publishing Group. I will introduce you to everyone.
  欢迎进入我识出版集团。我给你介绍一下大家。
  ★ 短语 welcome to 欢迎（来）到～

- Let's walk around the office and **say hello to** everyone.
  我们绕一圈办公室，然后跟每个人打声招呼吧。
  ★ 短语 say hello to... 跟～打招呼；问候～

- Let's **go over** what we usually do in the office.
  我们来看看上班时都要做些什么。
  ★ 短语 go over... 查看～；重温～

- Are there any company policies I should **be aware of** on my first day?
  第一天上班，有什么公司规定是我需要知道的吗？
  ★ 短语 be aware of... 意识到～，知道～

- The manager assigned his personal assistant to **show** me **around**.
  经理指派他的个人助理带我到处参观。
  ★ 短语 show... around 带～到处参观；带～逛逛 / 到处看看

- Please **fill in** these forms that are requested by HR. Here are the samples you can follow.
  人力资源部门请你填写这些表格。你可以参考这些范例来填写。
  ★ 短语 fill in... 填写～，填入～

- The working hours are from 9 to 6 with a ninety-minute lunch break from 12 to 1:30 p.m.
  上班时间9点到6点，12点到1点半有90分钟的午休时间。
  ★ 短语 lunch break 午休时间

- We are **going for lunch**. Would you like to join us?
  我们要去吃午餐了。你要跟我们一起吗？
  ★ 短语 go for lunch 吃午餐

- You should not **leave a new employee alone** during lunch on the first day.
  你不应该第一天就让新员工在午餐时间落单。
  ★ 短语 leave A alone 让A落单；避免打扰A

在国外都说这几句

- **Your salary will be transferred directly into your bank account.**
  薪水会直接转入你的银行账户。
  ★ 短语 bank account 银行账户

- **I'm sure I will get along with my colleagues.**
  我跟我的同事们一定可以相处得很好。
  ★ 短语 get along with... 与～和睦相处；与～相处得很好

- **My name is Chris. I am in charge of this department. Let me know if you have any questions.**
  我的名字是克里斯。我是这个部门的负责人。你有任何问题都可以问我。
  ★ 短语 in charge of... 负责～，主管～

- **I had butterflies in my stomach before I stepped into the office.**
  我在走进办公室之前，觉得非常紧张。
  ★ 短语 butterfly in one's stomach 神经紧张，怕得发抖

- **It is important to make the right impression on the first day at a new job.**
  新工作的第一天就创造好印象是很重要的。
  ★ 短语 the first day at... 在～的第一天

- **I'd like to introduce you to our accountant, Mr. Chris Fluellen.**
  我想向你介绍我们公司的会计师，克里斯·弗艾伦。
  ★ 短语 introduce A to B 向 A 介绍 B

- **Ms. Summers, please allow me to introduce myself.**
  桑默斯女士，请容许我进行自我介绍。
  ★ 短语 allow A to... 允许 A ～，容许 A ～

- **Mr. Fluellen, this is Kevin Silvers, the company's CEO.**
  弗艾伦先生，这位是凯文·西尔维斯，他是这个公司的总裁。
  ★ 短语 CEO (Chief Executive Officer) 总裁

常识补给站

办公室政治（workplace politics）是出现于办公室、学校及职场内的人事及利益的竞争。办公室政治的成因通常是由于人的野心无限但是资源有限。文化差异、组织内部之间的利益不平衡和利益冲突也可能导致办公室政治。办公室政治是无法避免的，它可能会内耗生产力，也可能会激发竞争力。

 是不是渐渐地敢开口说英文了呢？   Finish!!

 在国外都说这几句

- It's all about making a good first impression, so dress properly.
  第一印象非常重要，所以你要穿着正式一点。
  ★ 短语 first impression 第一印象，最初的印象

- Relax. Just follow the instructions and do your best.
  放轻松，只要遵照指示并且尽力就好。
  ★ 短语 do one's best 尽力

- Look before you leap. Do not make a rushed decision.
  三思而后行。不要匆匆忙忙做决定。
  ★ 短语 look before you leap 三思而后行

- Thank you for calling I'm Publishing Group. What can I do for you?
  谢谢您致电我识出版集团。有什么可以帮你的吗？
  ★ 短语 Thank A for n. / v-ing 谢谢A～

- Hello, this is Jessica, John's assistant, calling.
  你好，我是杰西卡，约翰的助理。
  ★ 语法 当表达是某人来电时，需要使用"This is A（身份／职称／姓名）calling"。

- This is Dean Samuels calling. May I speak to the executive manager?
  我是狄恩·塞缪尔斯，可以请行政经理接电话吗？
  ★ 短语 speak to... 和～谈话

- This is she / he speaking. = Speaking.
  我（本人）就是。
  ★ 语法 接电话时，若你就是对方要找的人，就必须使用"This is she（女生）／he（男生）"的句型，也可直接简略地讲"Speaking"。

- May I ask what this is regarding?
  我可以请问你找他有什么事吗？

- Just a second, please.
  请稍等片刻。
  ★ 短语 just a second 等一下，等等

- I'm going to put you on hold for a second.
  我要麻烦请你等一下。
  ★ 短语 put A on hold 请A稍等一下

在国外都说这几句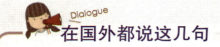

- I'll put you through to Dr. Greens' office.
  我将帮你转接到格林医生的办公室。
  ★ 短语 put through... 转接到~

- Bear with me, please.
  请稍等我一下。
  ★ 短语 bear with... 耐心地忍受某人、某事物

- Would you mind spelling your last name for me?
  请问你介意拼出姓氏吗？

- I can't hear you very clearly. Could you speak up a little please?
  我听得不是很清楚。你说话可以大声一点吗？
  ★ 短语 speak up 讲大声一点，大声说

- Mr. Black is not available at the moment. Would you like to leave a message?
  布莱克先生目前没空。你想要留言吗？
  ★ 短语 leave a message 留言

- Could you please hold for a minute? I have another call.
  你可以稍等一分钟吗？我接个电话。
  ★ 短语 hold for a minute / second / moment 等一下，稍待片刻

- I'm afraid that Mr. Fluellen just stepped out of the office.
  弗艾伦先生恐怕刚刚离开他的办公室。
  ★ 短语 step out （暂时）外出

- Would you like him to call you back later?
  待会他再回你电话，可以吗？
  ★ 短语 call back 回电

- Could you ask Miss Evans to call Brian when she gets in?
  埃文斯小姐抵达时，你可以请她打电话给布莱恩吗？
  ★ 短语 get in 到达，抵达

- Let me confirm your phone number by repeating it to you.
  让我重复你的电话号码，以作确认。
  ★ 短语 phone number 电话号码

在国外都说这几句

- Please leave him a message and he will get back to you as soon as possible.
  请留言给他，他会尽快回复。
  ★ 短语 leave A a message 留言给 A

- Professor Dickinson is not available to take your call right now.
  狄更生教授目前无法接听你的电话。
  ★ 短语 take A's call 接 A 的电话

- The number you dialed is busy now. Please try again later.
  您拨叫的用户正在通话中，请稍候再拨。

- Well, I'd better get going. See you there.
  好，我最好现在出发。不见不散。
  ★ 短语 get going 出发，开始

- I have another urgent call coming in. I will call you back later.
  我有另一通紧急电话打进来。我等会再给你回电话。
  ★ 短语 come in 拨通；接通

- I am unable to answer the phone right now. Please leave a message, I will return your call as soon as possible.
  我现在无法接听电话。请留言，我将尽快回电给你。
  ★ 短语 be unable to... 无法～，没有办法～

- Hold on, please. I'll transfer your call to Customer Service.
  请稍等。我会将你转接给客服人员。
  ★ 短语 transfer to... 转接给～

Thanks!

This is a wonderful project!

Dialogue 在国外都说这几句

- Jason is on another line now. Can you please hold on?
  杰森现在正在接听另外一通电话。你可以稍等吗？
  ★ 短语 be on another line 正在接听另一通电话

- I'm calling to discuss the new product campaign with Mr. Sacks.
  我打电话想与萨克斯先生讨论新产品的企划活动。
  ★ 短语 discuss with... 与～讨论，跟～商谈

- Could you give me more information about the renovation to the office?
  你可以提供我更多关于办公室翻修的信息吗？
  ★ 短语 give A information about... 给予 A 有关～的信息

- Hi, it's Jennifer again. We got cut off for no reason.
  你好，又是我，珍妮弗。不知道为什么我们刚刚断线了。
  ★ 短语 cut off 切断；中断

- I'm afraid Mrs. Curtis is on leave today.
  恐怕柯蒂斯太太今天请病假。
  ★ 短语 on leave 休假

- I'm sorry, but the line's engaged at the moment. Is there anything I can help you with?
  我很抱歉，但电话目前忙线中。有什么我可以帮你的吗？
  ★ 短语 be engaged 占线中，忙线中

- The agent is on the other line at the moment.
  专员现在正在另一条线上。
  ★ 短语 at the moment 现在，目前

- This is Matt Damon. Can I have extension 217?
  我是麦特·达蒙。可以帮我接通分机 217 吗？
  ★ 短语 extension + 号码 分机号码

- I need to talk to Matt about the annual meeting. It's urgent.
  我需要与麦特讨论有关年度会议的事情，这很紧急。
  ★ 短语 talk to A about... 与 A 谈论～，与 A 讨论～

- I'm sorry. There's nobody here by that name.
  很抱歉，这里没有叫这个名字的人。
  ★ 短语 by the name 叫这个名字

在国外都说这几句

- I'm afraid you have the wrong number.
  恐怕你打错电话了。
  ★ 短语 have the wrong number 打错电话

- All of the lines are currently busy. Please stand by for the next available operator.
  所有的电话目前都忙线中。请等待下一位有空的接线员。
  ★ 短语 stand by 候补；待命

- Mr. Douglas is not there? When is he coming back?
  道格拉斯不在？他什么时候会回来？
  ★ 短语 come back 回来

- I need to reach an agreement with Dr. Jones on a meeting for Tuesday.
  关于星期二的会议，我还需要与琼斯博士达成一致。
  ★ 短语 reach an agreement 达成协议

- I'm calling to talk about the upcoming conference in Melbourne.
  我打这通电话的目的是要讨论即将在墨尔本举行的会议。
  ★ 短语 upcoming conference 即将举办的会议

- This is Samantha calling to follow up on your order with Efficiency Company.
  我是莎曼莎，我打电话是想追踪有关你与效率公司订单的后续发展。
  ★ 短语 follow up 把～贯彻到底；持续追踪～

- I'm sorry if I caused any inconvenience.
  如果造成任何不便，我很抱歉。
  ★ 短语 cause any inconvenience 造成任何不便

- Don't forget we have to punch the time card every day.
  不要忘记我们必须每天上班打卡。
  ★ 短语 time card 工作时间记录卡，工时卡

- Please remember to clock in and clock out.
  上下班都要记得打卡。
  ★ 短语 "clock in"的意思是"打卡上班"，"clock out"的意思是"打卡下班"。

 ## 在国外都说这几句

- Please do not clock in for others.
  请不要帮别人打卡。

- Let's **call it a day**. I'm having dinner with my friends.
  我们结束一天的工作吧，我要跟我的朋友们出去吃饭。
  ★ 短语 ▸ call it a day 结束一天（的工作）；停止进行某件事

- Do we usually work overtime **at the end of** the month?
  我们通常月底要加班吗？
  ★ 短语 ▸ at the end of... ～底；～结束时

- The manager needs to **delegate** some tasks **to** his assistants. They must be done by next Friday.
  经理要分配一些任务给助理们。下星期五以前必须要把它们完成。
  ★ 短语 ▸ delegate... to A 将~委托给 A，将~交付给 A 做

- I collect statisics from all of our branches **on a weekly basis**.
  我每周都会收集我们分公司的资料。
  ★ 短语 ▸ on a weekly basis 每周，每个星期

- The manager **developed** a new in-house database **for** the personnel department. It saves us a lot of time.
  这位经理为人事部开发一套（公司）内部资料库，省了我们不少时间。
  ★ 短语 ▸ develop... for... 为~开发~

- At the moment, we are planning to **expand** our sales **to** South America.
  目前，我们正计划扩充业务部门到南美洲。
  ★ 短语 ▸ expand to... 扩充到~，扩展到~

- In general, I **am responsible for** the pay check.
  通常，我负责全体员工的薪资发放。
  ★ 短语 ▸ be responsible for... 负责~，为~负责

- I am a **sales representative** of a medium-sized retailer.
  我是一家中型零售商的销售代表。
  ★ 短语 ▸ sales representative 销售代表

- Victoria **advises** customers **on** financial matters.
  维多利亚为客户提供理财信息。
  ★ 短语 ▸ advise on... 提供~的忠告

在国外都说这几句

- I **collaborate with** colleagues to prepare the best possible proposal for our clients.
  我与同事共同合作，为客户准备最棒的计划。
  ★ 短语 collaborate with... 与～共同合作

- **At first**, a new employer will be provided an account number and password, then he or she can log into the computer.
  首先，新员工会得到一组账号与密码，然后才可以登入电脑。
  ★ 短语 at first 首先，一开始

- You need to **be familiar with** our products before starting your job.
  你需要在开始工作前，先熟悉一下我们的产品。
  ★ 短语 be / get familiar with... 熟悉～（事物），通晓～（事物）

- You are responsible for **staying in touch with** our key customers.
  你负责与我们的主要客户保持联系。
  ★ 短语 stay in touch with... 与～保持接触，与～保持联络

- Do you think everyone can finish the assignment **on time**?
  你认为每个人都能及时完成任务吗？
  ★ 短语 on time 及时

- **Congratulations on** the huge success of Project A. Well done.
  恭喜你取得 A 计划的大胜利。做得很好。
  ★ 短语 congratulations on... 恭喜～，祝贺～

- I **have faith in you**. I know you will do a great job.
  我对你有信心。我知道你一定可以做得很好。
  ★ 短语 have faith in A 对 A 有信心

常识补给站

企业文化（Corporate Culture）是一个企业或组织由其共有的价值观、仪式、符号、处事方式和信念等组成的其特有的文化形象，包括可以观察到的人员行为规范、工作团队的主要价值、指导组织决策的哲学观念等；是企业主动通过一系列活动来塑造的文化形态。当这种文化被建立起来后，会成为塑造内部员工行为和关系的规范，是企业内部所有人共同遵循的价值观，对维系企业成员的统一性和凝聚力有很大的作用。

跟任何人都可以用英语聊聊天

Unit 21 职场就像社会的缩影

[生活便利贴]

开始上班后，每天相处得最多的就是同事。办公室的环境取决于同事之间的相处，若大家和乐融融，那么公司内部也会有向心力，对公司是有益的。但如果大家搞小团体，甚至对彼此不闻不问，对公司不但没有帮助，而且可能会造成大家矛头都指向对方、互相推卸责任。因此，同事与工作环境可是息息相关的！

Vocabulary 在国外都用这些词

goof-off ['gu:f,ɔ:f] n 逃避工作的人

attitude ['ætɪtjuːd] n 态度

angry ['æŋgrɪ] a 生气的，发怒的

assistant manager ph 副经理

promotion [prə'məʊʃn] n 升职

interrupt [ˌɪntə'rʌpt] v 打断

favor ['feɪvə] n 恩惠

illness ['ɪlnəs] n 疾病

official [ə'fɪʃl] a 正式的

complaint [kəm'pleɪnt] n 抱怨；抗议

gossip ['gɒsɪp] v 闲聊，讲八卦

useless ['juːsləs] a 无用的，无价值的

habit ['hæbɪt] n 习惯

conversation [ˌkɒnvə'seɪʃn] n 对话

underling ['ʌndəlɪŋ] n 下属，部下

bluntly ['blʌntlɪ] ad 不客气地

marry ['mærɪ] v 结婚

recently ['riːsntlɪ] ad 最近

在国外都说这几句

- My colleague is such a goof-off and this is creating extra work for me.
  我同事整天在偷懒，造成我的工作量增加。

- My co-worker bugs me with incessant questions that are not related to work.
  我同事总是没完没了地烦我，问我一堆跟工作没关系的问题。
  ★ 短语 bug A with... 用～烦 A；以～激怒 A

- We can always rely on Jason to show up to work on time.
  我们相信杰森总是会准时上班。
  ★ 短语 rely on... 依赖～，信任～

- Stop acting like you are my boss. I don't like that attitude.
  不要表现得好像你是我老板。我不喜欢你的那种态度。
  ★ 短语 act like... 表现得好像，假装像

- Why are you picking on me all the time?
  你为什么总是要找我的麻烦？
  ★ 短语 pick on A 找 A 的麻烦

- Maybe he is not doing it on purpose.
  也许他不是故意的。
  ★ 短语 on purpose 故意地

- Why did you get so angry with Tom this morning?
  你为什么今天早上对汤姆发那么大的火？
  ★ 短语 be / get angry with A 对 A 生气，对 A 发火

- Can we talk in private for a minute?
  我们可以私下谈一下吗？
  ★ 短语 in private 私底下

- The assistant manager wants to talk to you face to face about what happened yesterday.
  副经理想要和你面对面谈谈昨天发生的事。
  ★ 短语 face to face 面对面，当面

- I expect that all colleagues should treat each other with respect.
  我期望同事们之间相处要互相尊重。
  ★ 短语 with respect 怀着敬意；以慎重的态度

在国外都说这几句

- Everyone knew the conference is at 10 a.m. Why did you make us **wait for** you for at least 10 minutes?
  大家都知道会议上午 10 点开始，为什么你要让大家等了你至少 10 分钟？
  ★ 短语 wait for...　等待～，等候～

- He always **talks on speakerphone** when everyone is trying to have a break.
  他总是在大家正在休息的时候使用免提打电话。
  ★ 短语 talk on speakerphone　使用免提打电话

- She lets everyone else do the work, but is always there to **take the credit**.
  她让其他人工作，但总是自己揽下功劳。
  ★ 短语 take the credit　揽下功劳，抢走荣誉

- He always **sucks up to** the boss in order to get a promotion.
  他总是拍老板马屁，想要借由这样获得升职机会。
  ★ 短语 suck up to...　拍～的马屁；讨好～

- That **brown-noser** tried so hard to impress the boss.
  那个马屁精很努力地想要让老板对他有印象。
  ★ 短语 brown-noser　拍马屁的人

- She always **takes care of** personal matters during working hours.
  她总是拿上班的时间来做自己的事情。
  ★ 短语 take care of　照顾，处理

- Leo just loves to **burst into** my office and interrupt my work.
  利奥总是喜欢闯入我办公室，打扰我工作。
  ★ 短语 burst into...　冲进～，闯进～

常识补给站

玻璃天花板（glass ceiling）是指在公司企业和机关团体中，限制某些人（女性、少数族裔）晋升到高级经理及决策阶层的障碍。正如玻璃一样，这个障碍虽然不是明文规定，却是实实在在存在着的。另外，玻璃地板（glass floor），是指限制某些群体向更低阶层下降的障碍。比如对待女性同事时，在减少相对于男性在公司的升迁机会的同时，也减少她们落到做低下的矿工等处境的机会。

在国外都说这几句 Dialogue

- He thinks that he is doing everyone a favor by coming to work while he is sick.
  他认为自己生病还来上班，是帮大家的忙。
  ★ 短语 do... a favor 帮～的忙；对～施惠

- In fact, he should just stay at home and not pass his illness on to others.
  事实上，他应该待在家中，不要把病菌传给别人。
  ★ 短语 pass on... 把～传递下去，传递～

- My words continue to fall on deaf ears. Maybe I should file an official complaint.
  我说的话一直被当成耳边风。也许我该提出正式的抗议。
  ★ 短语 ...fall on deaf ears ～被当成耳边风，～未被理睬

- Your secretary always drops by to gossip while I'm trying to work.
  你的秘书总是在我工作的时候跑过来和我讲八卦。
  ★ 短语 drop by 顺便拜访，顺便访问

- My assistant is driving me nuts.
  我的助理快把我搞疯了。
  ★ 短语 drive A nuts 让 A 抓狂，让 A 精神错乱

- He has to turn his mobile phone on silent mode when we are having a meeting.
  当我们开会的时候，他必须把手机调成静音模式。
  ★ 短语 turn... on silent (mode) 将～调成静音（模式）

- Please do not forward any junky e-mails to me. They are useless.
  请不要把垃圾信件转寄给我。它们一点用都没有。
  ★ 短语 junky e-mail 垃圾信件，垃圾邮件

- She complains about her supervisor behind his back.
  她总是背地里抱怨她的上司。
  ★ 短语 behind A's back 在背后

- Have you ever worked with someone who really annoyed you?
  你和惹恼你的同事工作过吗？
  ★ 短语 work with... 与～一起工作，与～一起上班

在国外都说这几句

- Is there someone in your office whose habits you cannot stand at all?
  你办公室有没有一些人的习惯是你完全没办法忍受的？
  ★ 短语 cannot stand　无法忍受

- I hate the way my boss clears his throat. Normally that sound means someone is going to be in trouble.
  我讨厌我老板清喉咙的方式。听到那声音通常代表有人要倒霉了。
  ★ 短语 clear A's throat　A 清喉咙

- Jessica did something silly the other day. Now everyone makes fun of her when she is around.
  杰西卡前几天做了一件蠢事。现在只要她在，大家就会取笑她。
  ★ 短语 make fun of...　嘲笑～，取笑～

- Teddy always butts in on my conversations with others and tries to get everyone's attention.
  泰迪总是在我跟别人说话的时候插嘴，想要得到大家的注意。
  ★ 短语 butt in...　插入～

- Please do not talk with your mouth full. I can barely understand what you are saying.
  吃东西的时候不要讲话。我根本听不懂你在讲什么。
  ★ 短语 talk with your mouth full　边吃东西边讲话

- Adam has terrible personal hygiene. I wish someone would tell him about it.
  亚当的个人卫生很糟糕。真希望有人去跟他说这件事。
  ★ 短语 personal hygiene　个人卫生（习惯）

- Stop picking your nose constantly during meetings. Do it in private.
  在会议中不要一直挖鼻孔。这种事情等没有人的时候再做。
  ★ 短语 pick nose　挖鼻孔

- She hummed the same tune over and over again. Now the song is stuck in my head.
  她一直哼相同的音乐。我现在整个脑子都是那首歌。
  ★ 短语 over and over (again)　一而再，再而三；一直

- She never cleans up her mess after having lunch.
  用完午餐后，她从来不会整理。
  ★ 短语 clean up...　打扫～；整理～

在国外都说这几句

- Jenny always **takes up** my space in the kitchen cabinet.
  珍妮总是占用橱柜里属于我的位置。
  ★ 短语 ▶ take up　占用

- Arthur's **body odor** is so strong; I feel like I can't breathe.
  亚瑟的汗臭味实在太重了，我觉得我都快要不能呼吸了。
  ★ 短语 ▶ body odour　汗臭味

- I'm on **lunch break**. Do you want to get something to eat together?
  我在午休。你想要一起去吃点东西吗？
  ★ 短语 ▶ lunch break　午（餐）休息时间

- Nobody likes Tina because she always **looks down upon** others; like she's the queen.
  没人喜欢蒂娜，因为她总是瞧不起别人，好像她是女王一样。
  ★ 短语 ▶ look down upon　瞧不起

- If you finished your lunch, then start **tidying up** the public area; don't expect others to do it for you.
  如果你已经吃完午餐，那就开始整理公共区域，不要指望有人会帮你做。
  ★ 短语 ▶ tidy up　整理

- If you have any problem with Sally, then you should **talk it over** with her.
  如果你对萨利不满，你应该去跟她讲清楚。
  ★ 短语 ▶ talk over　讨论

- Jeremy sometimes comes into my office and starts talking to me even though I'm **in the middle of** something.
  杰里米有时候会进我办公室并开始跟我聊天，即使我当下正在忙别的事情。
  ★ 语法 ▶ in the middle of...　在～的当中；正忙于～

- If he coughs so much, then he should get some **cough syrup**.
  如果他咳嗽咳得很厉害，那么他应该喝些止咳糖浆。
  ★ 短语 ▶ cough syrup　止咳糖浆

- I hate it when my secretary clips her **finger nails** at work. It's like she is getting paid for nothing.
  我讨厌秘书在上班时间剪指甲。这样好像是花钱请她来什么事情都不用做。
  ★ 短语 ▶ finger nail / toenail　手指甲 / 脚趾甲

213

在国外都说这几句

- My supervisor always yells across the office for me. It can be very embarrassing sometimes.
  我的上司总是在办公室大喊要找我。有时候真的让我觉得很尴尬。
  ★ 短语 yell for... 叫喊着找～

- Justin just called in sick, so we need to cover for him today.
  贾斯汀刚刚打电话来请病假，所以今天他的工作我们要帮他完成。
  ★ 短语 call in sick 打电话请病假

- Christine is constantly on a cigarette break. Her supervisor is not happy about it.
  克莉丝汀常常要休息抽烟，她的主管对这点很不满意。
  ★ 短语 on (lunch / cigarette / coffee) break 休息（午休／休息抽烟／休息喝咖啡）

- She should just cut back on her smoking or maybe even quit.
  她应该少抽烟甚至戒掉它。
  ★ 短语 cut back on... 削减～，减少～

- I am so tired of working with Jessica. She thinks she's Ms. know-it-all.
  我受不了跟洁西卡一起工作。她老是认为自己是万事通。
  ★ 短语 know-it-all 自以为是的万事通，自称无所不知的人

- I start to get annoyed with Richard's irresponsible attitude. We lost a few clients because of it.
  我开始受不了理查不负责任的态度了。因为这样我们失去了几个客户。
  ★ 短语 be / get annoyed with... 被～激怒，被～惹恼

- Louise never gossips about other colleagues. She is a fine example.
  露易丝从不讲其他同事的八卦。她真是个好榜样。
  ★ 短语 gossip about... 闲聊～的八卦，说长道短～

- Claire is a good supervisor because she never points fingers when things go wrong.
  克莱儿是位好上司，因为出事情的时候，她从不指责别人。
  ★ 短语 point fingers 指责别人；（未经确认）诬赖别人

- This is clearly not my fault. I will not take the blame for it.
  这件事很明显不是我的错。不要把错误怪到我的头上。
  ★ 短语 take the blame for... 承担～的责任

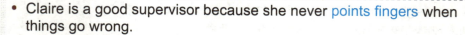

在国外都说这几句

- Louise is never jealous of her colleagues; instead, she is always pleased for them when they do well.
  路易丝从不嫉妒她的同事；反而当同事表现好时，她也为他们感到开心。
  ★ 短语 be / get jealous of... 对～感到嫉妒；对～吃醋

- Terry is a sincere person and always treats his underlings well.
  泰瑞是个真诚的人，而且对下属非常好。
  ★ 短语 treat A well 对 A 很好，善待 A

- My director never glares at me. I guess that means I'm a good employee.
  我的主管从不会怒目瞪我。我想应该是因为我是个好员工。
  ★ 短语 glare at... 怒目注视～，生气地瞪～

- Sam is thoughtful and never bluntly points out other people's mistakes.
  山姆很体贴，他从不会很不客气地指出其他人的错误。
  ★ 短语 point out... 指出～，提出～

- Chloe does not like buttering up her boss or any other authorities.
  克洛伊不喜欢奉承老板或其他有权势的人。
  ★ 短语 butter up... 讨好～；奉承～

- Keeping eye contact when talking with people is very important.
  跟别人讲话时，保持眼神的接触是非常重要的。
  ★ 短语 eye contact 眼神／视线接触

- Chris is always willing to take on additional responsibilities.
  克里斯总是愿意承担额外责任。
  ★ 短语 take on... 承担～；接受～（挑战）

- Mr. Anderson, I'd like to introduce you to Miss Leeds, our client from San Francisco.
  安德森先生，我想帮你介绍利兹小姐，她是我们旧金山的客户。
  ★ 短语 introduce A to B 向 A 介绍 B

- I think that was a really successful meeting. Hope we will hear from our clients soon.
  我认为会议很成功。希望我们会马上听到客户的消息。
  ★ 短语 hear from... 听到～的消息

Dialogue 在国外都说这几句

- Gary can't make it here today, but he sends his regards.
  盖瑞今天没有办法来，但他要我向你致意。
  ★ 短语 send regards 传达敬意

- I really appreciate it. How is Gary? Please tell him I said hello as well.
  我真的很感激。盖瑞他最近好吗？请转告盖瑞我也向他问好。
  ★ 短语 as well 也，同样地

- Did you know that Kirk is going to get married next month?
  你知道柯克下个月要结婚了吗？
  ★ 短语 get married 结婚

- He has been going out with Jessica for 3 years.
  他已经跟杰西卡交往了3年了。
  ★ 短语 go out with... 与～约会；与～外出

- Has anyone heard from Steve lately? It's like he has gone missing.
  有人知道史蒂夫的近况吗？感觉他好像失踪了一样。
  ★ 短语 go missing 失踪

- Come to think of it. I have not seen Steve for ages.
  现在想起来，我很久没看到史蒂夫了。
  ★ 短语 for ages 很长的一段时间

- David just got promoted last week. He is now the Marketing Manager.
  大卫上个星期升职了。他现在是行销部门的经理。
  ★ 短语 get promoted 升官，升职

- I heard about David's promotion and the big raise. I have to say, he deserves it.
  我听说大卫升职和加薪的事了。我必须说这是他应得的。
  ★ 短语 hear about... 听说～，得知～，表示间接获得某人或某事的情况以及消息。

- What have you been up to recently? Is everything okay?
  你最近在忙什么？一切都还好吗？
  ★ 短语 be up to... 忙于～，在做～

- Monica is on maternity leave. She is about to have a baby.
  莫妮卡最近在休产假。她快要生小孩了。
  ★ 短语 maternity leave 产假

Dialogue 在国外都说这几句

- I <u>ran into</u> my previous assistant yesterday. He's got a new job.
  我昨天与上任助理不期而遇。他找到新工作了。
  ★ 短语 ▸ run into... 碰到～，偶遇～

- I try to avoid <u>making small talk</u> with colleagues when I am busy.
  当我在忙的时候，我会尽量避免跟同事闲聊。
  ★ 短语 ▸ make small talk 闲聊，闲话家常

- How long <u>have</u> you worked for I'm Publishing Group? Do you like it?
  你在我识出版集团工作多久了？你还喜欢这边吗？
  ★ 短语 ▸ work for... 为～工作，为～做事

- Let's share one <u>little-known fact</u> about each other. What we talk about today does not leave the room.
  每个人都分享一件有关自己的事情吧！我们今天在这边所讲的，都不可以告诉别人。
  ★ 短语 ▸ little-known fact 几乎没有人／很少人知道的事情

- We are all exhausted but we are having so much fun and no one wants to <u>stand up</u> and say goodbye.
  我们大家都筋疲力尽了，但因为今天实在过得太有趣了，所以大家都不想站起来说再见。
  ★ 短语 ▸ stand up 起立，站起来

- Do you always feel self-conscious about being the first one to <u>take off</u>?
  成为第一个离开的人，你会感到不安吗？
  ★ 短语 ▸ take off 离开；匆忙离去

- <u>Thank you for</u> inviting me to this dinner party. I had a great time.
  谢谢你邀请我来这个晚餐派对。我玩得很愉快。
  ★ 短语 ▸ thank A for... 感谢 A ～，谢谢 A ～

- Okay. It is time to <u>wrap it up</u> and let everyone go home.
  好了。该结束并让大家回家了。
  ★ 短语 ▸ wrap up 完成，结束。

跟任何人都可以用英语聊聊天

Unit 22 沟通是最好的桥梁

[生活便利贴]

进一家公司，对于刚毕业或是之前的工作经验不够多的人来说，通常都会从基层的职位开始做起。所以被分配的工作也属于杂务性的工作，这时候千万不要气馁，趁这个时候多听、多看、多学习。很多专业的技能并不是在学校学习得到的，而是在开始工作之后一项一项地从前人那里传承过来的。因此，要放开心胸，努力学习。

Vocabulary 在国外都用这些词

MP3 04-51

first of all
ph 首先

vice president
ph 副总裁

conclusion
[kənˈkluːʒn]
n 结论

on business trip
ph 出差

boost
[buːst]
v 增加，提高

report
[rɪˈpɔːt]
n 报告；纪录

agenda
[əˈdʒendə]
n 议程

envelope
[ˈenvələʊp]
n 信封

project
[ˈprɒdʒekt]
v 企划、投入

brainstorm
[ˈbreɪnstɔːm]
n 集思广益；发散思维

sight
[saɪt]
n 视觉；见解，看法

post
[pəʊst]
v 邮寄，寄送

scale
[skeɪl]
n 磅秤

postage
[ˈpəʊstɪdʒ]
n 邮资

studio
[ˈstjuːdiəʊ]
n 工作室；录音室

dental
[ˈdentl]
a 牙齿的；牙医的

document
[ˈdɒkjumənt]
n 文件

mailroom
[ˈmeɪluːm]
n 收发室

在国外都说这几句

- Our meeting today is divided into three parts.
  我们今天的会议可以分成三个部分。
  ★ 短语 ▶ divide into... 分成~，划分成~

- Let's get started if everyone is here.
  如果大家都到了，我们就开始吧。
  ★ 短语 ▶ get started 开始

- First of all, I'd like you to join me in welcoming Peter Vincent.
  首先，我想请大家跟我一起欢迎彼得·文森特。
  ★ 短语 ▶ join in... 参加~；参与~

- He is from Boston and he is also our Asia sales vice president.
  他来自波士顿，而且是我们亚洲区的销售副总裁。
  ★ 短语 ▶ A is from... A来自~，A从~来

- Thank you for having me. I'm honored to be here to meet all of you.
  谢谢大家邀请我来。很荣幸可以到这里来跟大家见面。
  ★ 短语 ▶ be honored to... 很荣幸可以~

- I'm looking forward to the meeting today. Hope we will come to a conclusion.
  我很期待今天的会议。希望我们可以得出结论。
  ★ 短语 ▶ look forward to 期待~，盼望~

- May I introduce my assistant, Jerry Murray as well.
  容我一并介绍我的助理，杰瑞·默里。
  ★ 短语 ▶ as well 也，同样地

- It's a pity that our international sales director can't join us today.
  很可惜，我们的全球销售主管今天无法加入我们。
  ★ 短语 ▶ it's a pity that... 遗憾~

- She cannot be here because she is on business trip in Sydney at the moment.
  她今天无法来是因为目前正在悉尼出差。
  ★ 短语 ▶ at the moment 现在，目前

- We should discuss ways of boosting sales in Asia. Anyone has any ideas?
  我们应该讨论增加亚洲业务的方法。有人对这个有想法吗？
  ★ 短语 ▶ way(s) of... ~的方法，~的方式

在国外都说这几句

- Why don't we start by going over the report from the last meeting?
  我们为什么不先温习一下上次开会的报告呢？
  ★ 短语 go over... 查看～；重温～

- The last meeting was held on 18th of May.
  上次会议于5月18日召开。
  ★ 短语 be held on... 在～（日期）举行

- Jerry, would you please tell us the main points of last meeting?
  杰瑞，你愿意告诉我们上次会议的要点吗？
  ★ 短语 main point(s) of... ～的要点

- Mr. Anderson, may I have a word, please?
  安德森先生，我可以说句话吗？
  ★ 短语 have a word 谈谈；（简短）说句话

- Please raise your hand if you want to make a comment.
  如果你想发言的话，请举手。
  ★ 短语 make a comment 发言

- The way I see things, we need to work on our customer service to make improvement.
  以我的看法，我们需要改善我们的客户服务。
  ★ 短语 the way A see things 依照A（的观点）来看，以A的看法

- Sorry for interrupting, but I would like to add a few points to this case.
  很抱歉打断你们。但针对这个案子，我想增加几个重点。
  ★ 短语 add to 增加

- You'll find a copy of the agenda in the envelope in front of you.
  你们将会在面前的信封里看到今天的会议议程。
  ★ 短语 in front of... 在～前面，在～前方

> **常识补给站**
>
> 非正式会议（casual meeting），在国外，除了一般在会议室的正式会议之外，还有所谓的非正式会议。通常这些会议不会选择在公司内部的会议室进行，而是把整个会议放到公司外面的咖啡厅之类的地方来举行。这样的做法是希望员工在会议之余也可以稍微从忙碌的工作中轻松一下。不过，这种类型的会议通常讨论的主题也不会太严肃。

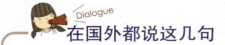

在国外都说这几句

- Could you please share with us how the project B is coming along?
  你可以跟我们分享一下，目前 B 企划进展如何吗？
  ★ 短语 come along　进展；出现

- If there is nothing else to add, let's move on to the next item.
  如果没有什么其他需要讨论的，我们就继续下一个讨论项目。
  ★ 短语 move on to...　继续往～前进；出发前往～

- Let's go around the table and make sure that everyone has a say.
  让我们一一询问会议桌上的人，确保每个人都有机会发言。
  ★ 短语 have a say　有发言权，有理由说话

- What is the main purpose of the conference?
  此次会议的主要目的是什么？
  ★ 短语 purpose of...　～的目的，～的用途

- Am I making myself clear? Any questions?
  大家清楚我（要表达）的意思了吗？有任何问题吗？
  ★ 短语 make oneself clear　让大家了解某人的意思、想法

- Could you please run that by me one more time? I don't quite understand it.
  你可以再跟我解释一次吗？我不是很了解。
  ★ 短语 run... by　解释给～听

- Frankly, I don't actually understand what you are getting at.
  老实说，我不太了解你想表达什么。
  ★ 短语 get at　解释，意指

- Everyone pitched in to complete this proposal. Good job!
  大家对这个企划案都做出了贡献。做得非常好！
  ★ 短语 pitch in　协力，做出贡献

- We are running out of time. Why don't we get back on track?
  我们快没有时间了。我们何不回到正轨？
  ★ 短语 get back　回来；恢复

- In my opinion, we should focus more on marketing stratgies.
  我认为，我们应该将重点更多地集中在市场策略上。
  ★ 短语 focus on...　集中～，使集中于～

在国外都说这几句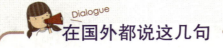

- That's a really good point. However, I'm afraid I don't agree with you.
  你说得很有道理，但是恐怕我无法同意你。
  ★ 短语 agree with A 同意 A，赞同 A

- I'd like to begin this meeting with PowerPoint presentation.
  我想用简报来开始这个会议。
  ★ 短语 begin with... 以～开始；以～着手

- As you can see, our sales number has gone up slightly since last year.
  如你所见，我们的销售数字从去年开始有一些增长。
  ★ 短语 as you can see 如你所见

- It is time for us to break up into groups and do some brainstorming.
  现在是我们分成小组并讨论想法的时候了。
  ★ 短语 break up into... 分解～；拆开～

- Are we short of time? The deadline is tomorrow.
  我们时间快不够了吗？明天就是最后期限了。
  ★ 短语 be short of... 少于～；缺乏～

- Let's get back to the main focus of today's meeting.
  我们回到今天会议的主要焦点。
  ★ 短语 get back to... 返回～

- Are you sure we are not losing sight of this topic?
  你确定我们没有忽略掉这个主题的重点？
  ★ 短语 lose sight of... 看不见～；忽略～

- We are out of time. I'm afraid we'll have to leave that to another time.
  我们没时间了。恐怕我们要下一次再继续了。
  ★ 短语 leave... to A 将 A 留给～，将 A 交给～

- Do our sales teams have enough support from administration teams?
  我们的业务团队得到了行政部门足够的支援吗？
  ★ 短语 sales team 业务团队

- I'm here to inform you that the meeting is expected to finish at 3 p.m.
  我要告知你们，今天的会议预计下午 3 点结束。
  ★ 短语 inform A that... 告知～；通知～

在国外都说这几句

- Please pay attention to both proposals. We will need to choose one later.
  这两个企划案大家都要仔细听。我们将要从其中选出一个来。
  ★ 短语 ▶ pay attention to　注意

- Last but not least, I'd like to thank Jerry for particiating to our meeting.
  最后但同样重要的是，我想谢谢杰瑞来参加我们的会议。
  ★ 短语 ▶ last but not least　最后但同样重要的

- I would like to open a bank account.
  我想开一个银行账户。
  ★ 语法 ▶ bank account　银行账户；活期存款

- Do you offer better interest rates on saving accounts?
  储蓄账户的利率会比较好吗？
  ★ 语法 ▶ interest rate　利率

- Is there any extra service charge for exchanging currency?
  兑换外币时，会收取手续费吗？
  ★ 语法 ▶ exchange currency　兑换货币

- The bank statement will be posted to you every month.
  银行明细每个月将会邮寄给你。
  ★ 语法 ▶ bank statement　银行明细

- You can open a savings account with an initial deposit of 1,000 dollars.
  你可以以1000美元的起存额开立一个储蓄账户。
  ★ 语法 ▶ initial deposit　起存额，开户存款／押金

Absolutely!

The number is increasing!

在国外都说这几句

- I'd like to **set up** a direct debit payment for my gas bill.
  我想要设定煤气费的定期自动转账。
  ★ 短语 ▶ set up　设定

- I would like to rent a **safe deposit box**. How much does it cost a month?
  我想租一个银行保险箱。一个月的费用是多少？
  ★ 短语 ▶ safe deposit box　银行保险柜；安全信托柜

- Who may I **speak to about** a business loan?
  我可以和谁讨论商业贷款？
  ★ 短语 ▶ speak to about...　谈论有关～，讨论与～相关的事

- Do you charge a **managing fee** in this bank?
  你们这家银行收账户管理费吗？
  ★ 短语 ▶ managing fee　（银行）账户管理费

- Please enter your **PIN** number to make confirmation.
  请输入个人密码并确认。
  ★ 语法 ▶ "PIN"是"Personal Identification Number"的缩写，意思是"个人识别密码"。

- Can I please have **a dozen of** 5-dollar stamps?
  我想买一打5美元的邮票。
  ★ 短语 ▶ a dozen of...　一打～；很多个～

- I would like to send a package to London **by airmail**.
  我想要寄航空包裹到伦敦。
  ★ 短语 ▶ by airmail　以航空邮件（信）寄送

- I am **expecting a package from** New Zealand.
  我在等一件来自新西兰的包裹。
  ★ 短语 ▶ expect A from...　等待来自～的 A

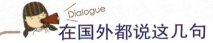

在国外都说这几句

- How long does it take to send this letter to Scotland by ordinary mail?
  把这封信以平邮的方式寄往苏格兰需要多久？
  ★ 短语 by ordinary mail　以平邮方式寄送

- Please fill in the name and address in capital letters. Thank you.
  请用大写字母填写姓名及地址。谢谢。
  ★ 短语 capital letter　大写字母

- How much does it cost to send the parcel to Paris?
  寄这件包裹到巴黎要多少钱？
  ★ 短语 how much　多少钱

- Please put the package on the scale. Thanks.
  请将包裹放到磅秤上，谢谢。
  ★ 短语 put... on the scale　把～放到磅秤上

- How much postage is required to send a letter to London? Can I pay by cash?
  寄一封信到伦敦需要多少邮资？我可以直接用现金付款吗？
  ★ 短语 ... be required to　需要～，要求～

- If you are in a hurry, you can send the letter by registered mail.
  如果你很急的话，你可以寄挂号信。
  ★ 短语 registered mail　挂号邮件，挂号信件

- Would you prefer to send the package C.O.D.?
  你喜欢用货到付款的方式寄包裹吗？
  ★ 短语 C.O.D. 是 cash on delivery 的缩写，意为"货到付款"。

- Ronda, could you please come over here for a moment?
  朗达，我可以请你过来一下吗？
  ★ 短语 come over　过来

- I'd be pleased to look through the proposal your team completed.
  我看过你们团队完成的企划案了，我很满意。
  ★ 短语 look through...　看看～，看过～

- I will pass the result of this survey on to the general manager.
  我会把这份调查报告的结果传给总经理。
  ★ 短语 pass on　传递

在国外都说这几句

- Could you stop by the studio and give me a hand later?
  你晚一点可以来工作室帮我个忙吗？
  ★ 短语 give A a hand　帮 A 一个忙

- I need to reschedule my dental appointment.
  我需要重新预约看牙时间。

- Who is in charge of keeping the minutes this time?
  这次谁负责写会议记录？
  ★ 短语 in charge of　负责

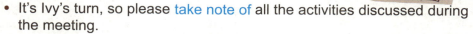

- It's Ivy's turn, so please take note of all the activities discussed during the meeting.
  这次轮到艾薇了，所以请注意开会时讨论的所有事项。
  ★ 短语 take note of　注意～

- I need you to make sure all the important projects are on schedule.
  我需要你确认所有重要项目都是按照预定时间进行。
  ★ 短语 on schedule　准时；按照预定时间

- I need you to set up an emergency meeting with all departments.
  我需要你跟公司所有部门开一个紧急会议。
  ★ 短语 emergency meeting　紧急会议

- Please fax the document to the head quarter right away.
  请立刻将这份文件传真到总部。
  ★ 短语 head quarter　总公司，总部

- I'm sorry. I didn't know you were in a hurry for that documents. I will get them for you right now.
  我很抱歉。我不知道你急着要这份文件。我现在就去拿给你。
  ★ 短语 in a hurry　匆忙地；迅速地

- I finished the report you requested. Do you want to have a look at it now?
  我完成你要求的报告了。你现在要看看吗？
  ★ 短语 have a look at...　看一看～

在国外都说这几句

- I am also responsible for assisting with the president's daily schedule.
  我还负责协助安排总裁每天的行程。
  ★ 短语 assist with... 协助～；帮助～

- Did the mailroom distribute the mails to this floor today yet?
  今天收发室已经把信件分配到这层楼了吗？
  ★ 短语 distribute to... 分发给～，分配给～

- As an office assistant, dealing with customer complaints is one of my duties.
  作为办公室助理，处理客户投诉也是我的工作内容之一。
  ★ 短语 deal with... 处理～；应付～

- I am told to take part in every administrative meeting from now on.
  我被告知从现在开始要参与每场行政会议。
  ★ 短语 take part in... 参加～；出席～

- Please prepare all the necessary documents on request.
  请依照要求，将所有文件准备好。
  ★ 短语 on request 应要求；经请求

- Please make an official announcement, saying that the shareholders meeting will be on next Friday.
  请你做一个正式的通告，说明股东会议将在下星期五举行。
  ★ 短语 official announcement 正式的公告、发表

- One of my duties is to greet and guide clients to the show room.
  我的一项工作内容就是接待访客，并引导他们去样品室。
  ★ 短语 guide to... 带领～；引导～

- I also need to maintain the inventory of stationary supplies.
  我也需要维持办公室文具用品的库存。
  ★ 短语 stationary supply 办公用品，办公文具

- When is the meeting?
  会议在什么时候？

跟任何人都可以用英语聊聊天

Unit 23 增长见识的**贸易博览会**

[生活便利贴]

　　国际级的展览，是一个能够增长见识的好机会。在展览中可以遇到来自世界各地不同领域的精英，若有机会，可以试着与对方交谈，互相切磋切磋。没机会也不要紧，在展览中学习，相信也会受益良多。另外，通过展览也可以看看目前市场走向，借此调整自己的营销手法或是进行商品改良等。

Vocabulary 在国外都用这些词

MP3 04-61

jewelry
['dʒuːəlrɪ]
n 珠宝

topnotch
['tɒpnɒtʃ]
a 最高级的

average
['ævərɪdʒ]
a 平均的，一般的

antique
[ænˈtiːk]
n 古董

definitely
['defɪnətlɪ]
ad 肯定地；当然

president
['prezɪdənt]
n 总裁

guarantee
[ˌgærənˈtiː]
v 保证

washing machine
ph 洗衣机

scam
[skæm]
n 骗局

TV (television)
['telɪvɪʒn]
n 电视

detergent
[dɪˈtɜːdʒənt]
n 洗洁剂

format
['fɔːmæt]
n 格式

durable
['djʊərəbl]
a 耐用的

TV commercial
ph 电视广告

security
[sɪˈkjʊərətɪ]
n 保安

garment
['gɑːmənt]
n 服装，衣服

laptop
['læptɒp]
n 笔记本电脑

inquiry
[ɪnˈkwaɪərɪ]
n 打听；询问；调查

在国外都说这几句

- **The scope of our** business in our company is mainly coffee beans roasting and selling.
  我们公司的经营范围主要是烘焙及贩售咖啡豆。
  ★ 短语 the scope of... ～的领域；～的范围

- We **deal** mainly **in** diamonds and jewelry, occasionally antiques.
  我们主要经营钻石以及珠宝，偶尔也涉及古董。
  ★ 短语 deal in... 经营～；交易～

- We provide **a series of** fashion accessory, which includes necklaces, bracelets, earrings and hats.
  我们提供一系列的流行饰品，包含了项链、手链、耳环以及帽子。
  ★ 短语 a series of... 一连串的～；一系列的～

- Our products **range from** tea leaves, coffee beans to chocolate.
  我们的产品范围包括茶叶、咖啡豆及巧克力。
  ★ 短语 range from A to B 涉及 A 到 B、范围从 A 到 B

- We guarantee that you will get **at least** a 15% increase in production by using this machine.
  我们保证一旦使用这种机器，你们产量至少会增加 15%。
  ★ 短语 at least 至少

- Could you please tell me what the main items that your company deals in are?
  请你告诉我，你们公司经营的主要产品是什么？
  ★ 短语 main item 主要产品，主要品项

- Because of the great quality, this TV is often **out of stock**.
  我们的电视由于品质优良，常常缺货。
  ★ 短语 out of stock 无现货，无库存

- The products are **in** excellent **quality** and reasonable **in price**. You won't regret it.
  我们的产品品质优良，价格合理。你一定不会后悔。
  ★ 短语 in quality / price 就品质 / 价格来说

- This model the of oven is **not only** durable **but also** practical for small business.
  这个型号的烤炉对小型企业来说，既耐用又实用。
  ★ 短语 not only... but also... 不但～，也～

在国外都说这几句

- All of our beautiful garments are made of topnotch materials. You won't find the same thing in other stores.
  我们所有美丽的服装都使用最高级的材质制作。你在别家店找不到一样的。
  ★ 短语 ▸ be made of... 以～（为材料）制成

- Hi, could you please help us by completing this survey? Your comment is valuable to us.
  你好，可以麻烦请你帮我填写这份问卷吗？你的意见对我们来说很重要。
  ★ 短语 ▸ help by 以～（方式）帮助 / 协助

- Have you ever ordered fortune cookies from Kong Fu Panda Company?
  你曾经跟功夫猫熊公司订购过幸运饼干吗？
  ★ 短语 ▸ fortune cookie 幸运饼干

- All in all, on the scale of 1 to 10, what would you rate Wonder Company?
  总而言之，分数从 1 到 10，你会给惊奇公司几分？
  ★ 短语 ▸ all in all 总而言之

- I will definitely recommend your product to all my friends.
  我一定会将你们的产品推荐给我所有的朋友。
  ★ 短语 ▸ recommend to... 推荐给～，介绍给～

- For your next purchase, will you be willing to purchase from Happy Horn Company?
  下次消费时，你是否愿意再一次购买快乐角公司的产品呢？
  ★ 短语 ▸ purchase from... 从～购物

- How did you place your last order for I-8 smartphone? By Internet?
  你上次订购 I-8 智能手机时采用了什么方式？是通过网络吗？
  ★ 短语 ▸ place an order 下订单；订购

- If you could change one thing about Wellington Company, what would it be?
  惠灵顿公司有哪一点是你觉得可以改变的？
  ★ 短语 ▸ change about... ～的改变

- What model of washing machine is usually used for household laundry?
  洗涤家用衣服时，通常使用洗衣机的哪种模式？
  ★ 短语 ▸ be used for... 用于～

在国外都说这几句

- I **used to** use powder detergent for laundry, but now I found out the liquid one is better.
  我之前洗衣服都是用洗衣粉，但我现在发觉洗衣液比较好用。
  ★ 短语 used to　曾经

- Give me a **rough number** on how many online purchases you made last year.
  给我一个去年你网购的大概数字。
  ★ 短语 rough number　概略数量

- Why did you **choose** online shopping **over** visiting actual stores?
  你为什么选网络购物而不是到实体商店去买东西呢？
  ★ 短语 choose... over...　选择～而舍弃～

- Before today, **were** you **familiar with** A.I. Company and its products?
  在今天以前，你对 AI 公司以及它的产品熟悉吗？
  ★ 短语 be familiar with...　熟悉～，通晓～

- I **heard about** your company website by TV commercial.
  我是通过电视广告才知道贵公司网址的。
  ★ 短语 hear about...　得知～，知道～

- Your advice **is beneficial to** our company. We appreciate it.
  你的建议对我们公司有很大的帮助。真的是非常感谢。
  ★ 短语 be beneficial to...　对～有益，对～有利

- I'm fully **satisfied with** your laptop, no complaint at all.
  我对你们的笔记本电脑非常满意，一点怨言都没有。
  ★ 短语 be satisfied with...　对～感到满意，满足于～

- I'm **interested in** purchasing a few items from your company. Can I place my order through telephone?
  我有兴趣购买你们公司的几样产品。我可以通过电话订购吗？
  ★ 短语 be interested in...　对～有兴趣；关心～

- How often do you buy **holiday greeting cards** for the past few years?
  在过去几年里，你多久购买一次节庆贺卡？
  ★ 短语 holiday greeting card　节庆贺卡

跟任何人都可以用英语聊聊天

在国外都说这几句

- Think about the bookstore you go to the most. Is it close to your house?
  想想你最常去的书店。它离你家近吗？
  ★ 短语 be close to...　离～（距离）近的；与～亲密的

- How much money do you spend on books on average a month?
  你一个月平均花多少钱买书？
  ★ 短语 spend (money) on ...　花（多少钱）在～，花（多少钱）买～

- Based on your experience with Super Smartphone, what do you like the most about it?
  根据你购买超级智能手机的经验，你最喜欢它的哪个部分？
  ★ 短语 based on...　根据～，基于～

- As the president of Crystal Company, I want to thank you for choosing our product.
  作为水晶公司的总裁，我想要谢谢你选择本公司的产品。
  ★ 短语 thank for...　谢谢～，感谢～

- Don't miss out such a great deal!
  别错过这么棒的机会！
  ★ 短语 miss out...　失去～的机会，丧失～

- Don't leave without this comfortable mattress. This special offer is only for today.
  不要不买这组舒服的床垫就回家了。只有今天特价哦。
  ★ 短语 leave without...　没有～就～

- We have the best money saving deal in your neighborhood.
  我们所提供的是这附近最优惠的价格。
  ★ 短语 money saving deal　最省钱的交易 / 优惠

- Buy one get one free promotion ends this Friday.
  买一送一的促销于周五结束。
  ★ 短语 buy one (item) get one (item) free　买一送一

- Sign up for our membership and enjoy $50 off your next purchase.
  加入我们的会员，就可享有下次消费抵扣 50 美元的优惠。
  ★ 短语 sign up for...　参加～；登记加入～

在国外都说这几句

- Check out this week's laptop deals and get extra one-year **international warranty**.
  来看看本周笔记本电脑的优惠，另外还可多获得一年的国际保修。
  ★ 短语 international warranty 国际保修

- We offer you the wide **selection of** smartphones, including your favorite brands.
  我们有各种智能手机可供选择，包括你最喜爱的品牌。
  ★ 短语 selection of... ～的选择

- You need to be careful when **shopping for** cheap laptop online, sometimes it might be a scam.
  在网上购买便宜的笔记本电脑要小心，有时候它可能是一场骗局。
  ★ 短语 shop for... 购买～，选购～

- We **sort** notebooks and personal computers **by** brand.
  我们依照品牌来分类笔记本电脑和个人电脑。
  ★ 短语 sort by... 以～区分；以～分类

- How much does it cost to **set up** a booth at a trade show?
  在贸易展上设摊位需要花费多少钱？
  ★ 短语 set up... 建立～；架设～

- **Deciding on** the location and style of the booth is very important.
  选定摊位的地点和风格都非常重要。
  ★ 短语 decide on... 选定～

- We should set up our stand a night before. That will **save** us a lot of **time**.
  我们应该在前一个晚上就把摊位布置好。这样可以省下很多时间。
  ★ 短语 save time 节省时间

- Why don't we **upload** banners **on** our website that contain invitations to this exhibition?
  为什么我们不将展览邀请函架设成横幅广告，并放在我们的网站上呢？
  ★ 短语 upload on... 上传到～，上载到～

- The trade show is so important because it **gives us a chance to** meet our potential customers.
  商展十分重要，因为它让我们有机会认识我们的潜在顾客。
  ★ 短语 give A a chance to... 让 A 有～的机会

在国外都说这几句

- We should give out free samples at the show.
  我们应该在展览上发送免费的样品。
  ★ 短语 give out 发送，分派

- There will be security at the exhibition, so we don't need to worry that someone will walk off with something that doesn't belong to them.
  展场上有安保人员，所以我们不用担心有人会顺手牵羊。
  ★ 短语 walk off with... 拿走～；偷走～

- Right now, we are at the 3C exhibition.
  现在我们位于电子产品展览会的现场。
  ★ 短语 3C（computer, communication, consumer electronics） 电子产品

- Our exhibition stand is spacious. The location is perfect as well. It's very close to the information center.
  我们的摊位很宽敞、位置绝佳。而且离信息中心很近。
  ★ 短语 information center 信息中心

- Shall we offer Mandarin Chinese to English interpreting service at the exhibition booth?
  我们应该在展位上提供中英文口译服务吗？
  ★ 短语 (Mandarin) Chinese to English interpreting 中英文口译

- It's a pleasure to offer you the quotes as follows.
  我们很荣幸向你方进行如下报价。
  ★ 短语 as follows 如下

- In answer to your inquiry for the products, please find the following for the reply.
  就你方对该商品的询价，我方的回复如下。
  ★ 短语 in answer to... 作为对～的回答

- As requested, we are offering you the following price and this offer will only remain open within seven days.
  应你方要求，我方就如下产品报价，此报价 7 日内有效。
  ★ 短语 as requested 应要求

- As a matter of fact, we're willing to make you a firm offer at this price, providing you place a huge order.
  事实上，如果你大量订购的话，我们愿意以此价格为你方报实价。
  ★ 短语 as a matter of fact 事实上，其实

在国外都说这几句

- We can quote you a price of USD $2,200 per refrigerator with a 5% discount on shipping.
  我方可以给你方一台冰箱 2200 美元的报价，运费可以优惠 5%。
  ★ 短语 USD (United States Dollar)　美元，美金

- We will keep in mind your requirement for the batteries and shall contact you once they are available.
  我方会记住你方对此款电池的要求，一旦有货，将立即与你方联系。
  ★ 短语 keep in mind　记住，放在心上

- As you have been our client for a long time, we are pleased to make you a special offer as follows.
  因为你是老客户，我方很高兴就以下商品给予你方优惠价。
  ★ 短语 special offer　优惠报价

- We can offer you 300 jeeps at the price of USD $30,000 each.
  我方可以提供 300 辆吉普车，每辆的价格为 3 万美金。
  ★ 短语 at the price of...　~的价钱，~的价格

- Due to the fact that the goods are in short supply, we won't be able to make you any offer.
  由于货源短缺，所以无法提供任何报价。
  ★ 短语 in short supply　供应不足，缺乏的

- The quotations we offer are all subject to the fluctuations of the market.
  上述报价将随市场变化而有所变动。
  ★ 短语 be subject to...　受~管制；容易遭受~

- We would like to make an inquiry about the product in catalouge in March.
  我们想要对 3 月份的目录产品进行询价。
  ★ 短语 make an inquiry　询价

- We look forward to your quotations for the unicycle that we are interested in.
  我们期待你方能对我们所感兴趣的单轮车报价。
  ★ 短语 look forward to...　期待~，盼望~，后面接名词或动名词。

跟任何人都可以用英语聊聊天

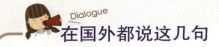

在国外都说这几句

- I would like to know the price for the yacht your company provides. Freight and handling must include.
  我方想知道贵公司生产的游艇价格，须包含运费和手续费。

- Do you offer F.O.B. or C.I.F.?
  你方报价是离岸价还是到岸价？
  ★ 短语 "F.O.B." 是 "Fee On Board" 的缩写，意思是 "离岸价、船上交货价（格）"。"C.I.F." 则是 "Cost Insurance Freight" 的缩写，意思是 "到岸价"。这两个缩写都是报价或询价时常会用到的术语。

- Would you please tell us the price of the fireplaces as soon as possible?
  请问能否尽快告知壁炉的价格？
  ★ 短语 as soon as possible　尽快，越快越好

- We are anxious to get an offer for your products. Can we have it by the end of today?
  我方急于想要你方产品的报价。我们可以在今天之前拿到吗？
  ★ 短语 be anxious to...　渴望的～，急于～

- We can't accept your offer unless the price is 15% off.
  除非你方降价 15%，否则我们无法接受报价。
  ★ 语法 "unless" 在此是 "从属连词"，意思是 "如果不，除非"。

- If you insist on your original price, I'm afraid I'm going to pass this deal.
  如果您坚持原定价格，恐怕我会放弃这笔交易。
  ★ 短语 insist on...　坚决宣告～；强烈要求～

- Wait a minute. There's always room for negotiation.
  等一下。事情总是还有协商的空间。
  ★ 短语 wait a minute　等一下

- This is our final offer. Take it or leave it.
  这是我们最后可提供的价格。接不接受随便。
  ★ 短语 take it or leave it　接不接受随便你

- Your AD on TV caught my eye and I be happy to receive samples with your prices.
  你们在电视上的广告引起了我的注意。若可以寄来样品并附上价格，我将很感激。
  ★ 短语 catch A's eye　引起 A 的注意

在国外都说这几句

- I would find it extremely helpful if you could provide free sample.
  如果你可以提供免费的样品，将对我极有帮助。
  ★ 短语 free sample 免费样品，试用品

- I can send you a few samples for your reference.
  我可以寄一些样品供你们参考。
  ★ 短语 for A's reference 供 A 参考

- I'm sorry, but we are out of samples.
  很抱歉，所有的样品都送完了。

- We no longer provide samples of this product. Sorry for the inconvenience.
  针对这件商品，我们已经不再提供任何的样品了。很抱歉给您带来不便。
  ★ 短语 no longer 不再

- Can I ask for samples of the lotion? I need to see if I am allergic to it.
  我可以要一些乳液的试用品吗？我想看看我用这个会不会过敏。
  ★ 短语 be allergic to... 对～过敏

- Having sensitive skin is hard to find products that are suitable for me. Can you give me some suggestions?
  拥有敏感性肌肤让我很难找到适合的产品。你可以给我一些建议吗？
  ★ 短语 be suitable for... 对～适合，合适～

- Are you giving out sameples of the liquid foundation? Can I please have one?
  你在分发粉底液的试用品吗？可不可以给我一个？
  ★ 短语 give out... 分发～，散发～

- You have asked for samples of the same product over and over. I'm afraid I can't give you any anymore.
  你不断要求相同产品的试用品。恐怕我无法再给你试用品了。
  ★ 短语 over and over 一再，反复

- Unfortunately, free sample is for memebers only.
  抱歉，免费试用品只限提供给会员。
  ★ 短语 for members only 只限会员

跟任何人都可以用英语聊聊天

Unit 24 接待礼仪很重要

[生活便利贴]

因各国文化的不同，所以接待外宾可是一门非常大的学问。代表公司接待外宾之前，最好事先查查贵宾是从哪个国家来的，该国家有哪些文化禁忌，而且要尽量避免。否则的话，自己闹笑话事小，如果因为这样导致生意没谈成功或是让公司失去了客户，那问题可就大了。

Vocabulary 在国外都用这些词

04-71

introduce
[ˌɪntrəˈdjuːs]
v 介绍

chauffeur
[ˈʃəʊfə]
n （私人）汽车司机

status
[ˈsteɪtəs]
n 情况；状况

difficult
[ˈdɪfɪkəlt]
a 困难的

concern
[kənˈsɜːn]
n 关心

market
[ˈmɑːkɪt]
n 市场

GPS (Global Positioning System)
ph 全球定位系统

apologize
[əˈpɒlədʒaɪz]
v 道歉

associate
[əˈsəʊʃɪeɪt]
n 合伙人

turnover
[ˈtɜːnəʊvə]
n 营业额

million
[ˈmɪljən]
n 百万（元）

compromise
[ˈkɒmprəmaɪz]
n 妥协，折衷办法

competitive
[kəmˈpetətɪv]
a 有竞争力的，竞争的

rival
[ˈraɪvl]
n 竞争对手

elaborate
[ɪˈlæbərət]
v 详细说明

frustrating
[frʌˈstreɪtɪŋ]
a 令人泄气的

urgently
[ˈɜːdʒəntli]
ad 紧急地

在国外都说这几句

- Welcome back, Mr. Thomason. How was your flight?
  欢迎回来，托马森先生。旅途还顺利吗？
  ★ 短语 welcome back　欢迎（旅途）回来

- Good morning, sir. I hope you have a good day.
  早安，先生，希望你会有美好的一天。
  ★ 短语 have a good day　祝有美好的一天

- Please allow me to introduce myself. My name is Jessica. I'm your new personal assistant.
  请允许我进行自我介绍。我是杰西卡。我是你的新私人助理。
  ★ 短语 allow A to...　允许 A ～，准许 A ～

- Mr. Wilson, this is Claire Lewis, our new general manager. She will show you around.
  威尔森先生，这位是克莱儿·路易斯，我们新上任的总经理。她会带你到处参观。
  ★ 短语 show around　带某人各处参观一下

- Did the chauffeur pick you up at the airport on time?
  请问司机准时到机场接你了吗？
  ★ 短语 on time　准时

- Mr. Hampton, would you like a cup of coffee?
  汉普顿先生，你想要一杯咖啡吗？
  ★ 短语 a cup of　一杯

- Mrs. Summers, all the files have been backed up as requested.
  萨默斯女士，我已经依照你的要求，将档案全都备份了。
  ★ 短语 back up...　备份～；支持～

- Do you have a minute? I'd like to keep you updated with the status of the new proposal.
  你有时间吗？我想跟你报告新提案的进度。
  ★ 短语 keep A updated with...　更新 A 对～的信息，让 A 知道～的最新情况／状况

- Good morning, Miss Farrell, I picked up a latte for you on my way to the office.
  早安，法雷尔小姐，我来办公室的时候，帮你带了一杯拿铁。
  ★ 短语 pick up...　抓起～；购买～

在国外都说这几句

- Hello, sir. You are supposed to meet Mr. Rocks at 12 p.m. tomorrow.
  你好，先生，你明天中午12点要与洛克斯先生会面。
  ★ 短语 be supposed to...　应该～；可以～

- I hope the office is not too difficult for you to find.
  我希望办公室对你来说不会太难找。
  ★ 语法 too... to...　太～，以至于无法～

- Don't worry! I have GPS system in my car. Thank you for your concern.
  别担心！我的车上配有导航系统。谢谢你的关心。
  ★ 短语 thank A for...　谢谢 A ～，感激 A ～

- I shook hands with everyone I met in the office. Everyone seems to be very friendly.
  我与我在办公室见到的每个人握手。大家看起来都很友善。
  ★ 短语 shake hands with...　与～握手

- Miss Peterson apologized for not being able to come here.
  彼特森小姐无法前来，所以感到非常抱歉。
  ★ 短语 apologize for...　为～而道歉

- My name is Ricky Martin. We met at the trade show in Los Angeles.
  我的名字是瑞奇•马汀。我们在洛杉矶的贸易展览上见过面。
  ★ 短语 trade show / exhibition　贸易展览

- Mr. Marcus introduced himself as he handed his business cards to the customers.
  马库斯先生在介绍他自己的同时，也将名片递给客户。
  ★ 短语 business card　名片

- You should make every effort to remember the names of the important associates. It's basic manner.
  你应该尽全力记住重要合伙人的名字。这是基本的礼貌。
  ★ 短语 make every effort to...　竭尽全力

- It's very important to maintain eye contact with people you are talking to. After all, you don't want others to think you are rude.
  跟别人说话的时候要看对方的眼睛，这很重要。毕竟，你不想让别人觉得你很没礼貌吧。
  ★ 短语 maintain eye contact with...　与～保持眼神接触

在国外都说这几句

- The manager is showing me how to greet a CEO in person with proper manners.
  经理正告诉我要怎么用适当的方式来迎接首席执行官。
  ★ 短语 in person 亲自；本人

- Hi, my name is Will Johnson. I have an appointment with Ian McAdams at 3:00 this afternoon.
  你好，我的名字是威尔·强森。我今天下午3点与伊恩·麦克亚当斯有约。
  ★ 短语 have an appointment with... 与～有约，与～会面

- I exchanged business cards with everyone on the spot at the exhibition.
  我跟所有在展览会现场的人交换了名片。
  ★ 短语 on the spot 现场

- Hello, everyone. May I have your attention, please. I'd like to present you a product that I'm sure you'll find interesting.
  大家好。请注意一下这边，我想向你们展示一样产品，我相信你们会感兴趣。
  ★ 短语 May I have your attention, please. 请注意。

- My name is Will. It is my pleasure to demonstrate our new product.
  我叫威尔，我很荣幸能为你们示范我们的新产品。
  ★ 短语 it is A's pleasure to... ～是A的荣幸，A很荣幸能～

- Our company's turnover for last year was six million dollars.
  我们公司的去年的营业额为六百万美金。

- When you contacted customer service, did our service reach your satisfaction?
  当你联系客服时，你对我们的服务感到满意吗？
  ★ 短语 reach A's satisfaction 让A满意，符合A的要求

- Your first task is to be in charge of doing a market survey. Please have it ready by the end of this month.
  你们的第一项任务是负责一项市场调查。请在这个月月底前完成。
  ★ 短语 be in charge of... 负责～、由～监督

- Thanks to everyone's efforts, the project was completed on schedule.
  由于每个人的努力，我们按计划完成了这项任务。
  ★ 短语 on schedule 按照预定时间

在国外都说这几句

- If you can provide a really competitive offer, we will **place a** large **order**.
  如果你能提供真正有竞争力的报价，我们会大量订货。
  ★ 短语 place an order 下订单，订购 / 货

- Please kindly send us **a copy of** catalogue, with details of the price and terms of shipment.
  请寄给我一份商品目录，并注明价格和装运条件。
  ★ 短语 a copy of... （相同书本 / 杂志 / 报纸的）一份～、一本～

- All the paper documents must be stored **for future reference**.
  所有的纸质文件都必须妥善保存，以作为将来参考之用。
  ★ 短语 for future reference 作为未来参考之用

- We are **sitting at the same table with** our biggest rival and it's a bit awkward.
  我们现在同公司最大的竞争者坐在同一张桌子上，感觉有一点尴尬。
  ★ 短语 sit at a table with... 与～同桌，与～坐在同一桌

- I'm interested in knowing more about the kind of business you do. **Care to** elaborate?
  我对于你是做哪种工作很感兴趣。愿意向我解释一下吗？
  ★ 短语 care to 愿意；想要

- I am **trying my best** to make everyone at my table feel comfortable.
  我尽力让我同桌的每个人都感到轻松。
  ★ 短语 try A's best to... A 尽力～

- Do you know the guy who is sitting **next to** our boss?
  你知道坐在老板旁边那个家伙是谁吗？
  ★ 短语 be next to... 在～旁边；紧邻～

- We should **wait until** everyone's meal is served.
  我们应该要等到大家的餐点都送来了才可以开始。
  ★ 短语 wait until... 等到～再

- Don't **speak with your mouth full**.
  嘴巴塞满食物时，不要讲话。
  ★ 短语 speak with your mouth full 边吃东西、边讲话

在国外都说这几句

- You should not put your napkin on the table until you are ready to leave the dinning table.
  除非你准备离开餐桌，否则你不该将餐巾放在桌上。
  ★ 短语 ▶ be ready to... 准备好～，快要～

- Try not to blow your nose at the dinning table; if you must, please go to the restroom.
  尽量不要在餐桌上擤鼻涕。如果真是避免不了的话，请赶快去厕所。
  ★ 短语 ▶ blow A's nose A擤鼻涕，A擤鼻子

- Please do not leave your personal belongings unattended at all times.
  请随时注意自己的个人物品是否在身边。
  ★ 短语 ▶ at all times 无时无刻，时时

- Quit staring at your phone, get in there and socialize with people.
  不要一直盯着你的手机看，赶快去跟大家交流一下。
  ★ 短语 ▶ stare at 盯着看

- I got a phone call from an angry customer who made a complaint and shouted at me.
  一个愤怒的客户今天打电话跟我投诉，并对我大吼。
  ★ 短语 ▶ shout at... 对～喊，对～喊叫

- As your client, I demand to talk to the person in charge of the company.
  作为你的客户，我要求跟公司的负责人谈话。
  ★ 语法 ▶ "as" 在此当介词使用，"as + n." 的意思是"作为 / 身为 n.，以 n. 的身份"。

- I understand this must be frustrating. However, taking your anger out on me won't get you anywhere.
  我理解这有多么令人感到沮丧。然而，把气出在我身上不会改变任何事。
  ★ 短语 ▶ take A's anger out on... A将气出在～，A将～当成出气筒

- I apologize for not sending your order on time.
  对于我们没有准时发出你的订货，我向你道歉。
  ★ 短语 ▶ apologize for... 为了～道歉

- I'm sorry that you are not happy with our customer service.
  你对我们的客服不满意，我对此感到抱歉。
  ★ 短语 ▶ customer service 客户服务

在国外都说这几句

- Is there anything I can do to turn the situation around?
  有没有什么事情是我可以做，好让你对我们改观的？
  ★ 短语 turn... around 改变～；转动/旋转～

- What would be considered as the most reasonable solution to you?
  你认为最合理的处理方式是什么？

- I certainly hope you are content with the solution we provided.
  我当然希望你对我们提供的解决方式感到满意。
  ★ 短语 be content with... 对～满足，对～感到满意

- I will report your problem to my supervisor and hopefully come up with the best solution for you.
  我会向我的主管提出你的问题，并且希望可以尽快为你找出最好的解决方式。
  ★ 短语 report to... 向～提出

- I'm sorry that you are not pleased with our after-sales service. Could you please tell me what's wrong?
  你不满意我们的售后服务，对此我很抱歉。你可以告诉我出了什么问题吗？
  ★ 短语 after-sales service 售后服务

- It took our corporation months of negotiating to finalize the new sales contract.
  我们公司花了好几个月的时间协商，终于决定新的销售合约。

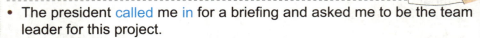

- The president called me in for a briefing and asked me to be the team leader for this project.
  总裁把我叫来做简报，并要我担任这个专案的小组领导人。
  ★ 短语 call in... 请来～；叫～进来

- It's my turn to be the company's sale representative this year.
  今年轮到我作为公司的销售代表。
  ★ 短语 it's A's turn to... 轮到A（去做）～

- The manager walked over to the guests and introduced himself.
  经理走了过来并向宾客们做了自我介绍。
  ★ 短语 walk over to... 走向～，走去～

- Before we sign the contract, there are a few things that I need to reconfirm.
  我们签订合同前，有几件事情我需要再次确认。
  ★ 短语 sign a contract 签约

在国外都说这几句

- We want to discuss the new contract with you urgently.
  我们很紧急地想和你讨论新合约。
  ★ 短语 discuss... with A 与 A 讨论～，与 A 商谈～

- Do you have any questions in regard to the contract? Please let me know if you have any.
  关于合约你还有什么问题吗？如果有的话请告诉我。
  ★ 短语 in regard to... 关于～

- In general, we make a rough draft and then talk it over face to face at a formal meeting.
  通常情况，我们会先拟一份草案，等正式会议时再面对面讨论细节。
  ★ 短语 talk over... 商讨～，讨论～

- To make it worth my time, I would need you to knock off another 10% of the original price. I believe it's reasonable.
  为了让我所花费的时间值得，我需要你照原价再打九折。我相信这非常合理。
  ★ 短语 knock off... （价钱）减去～；除去～

- Since we both attempt to sign the contract, making compromises is necessary.
  既然我们双方都想签合约，那就必须要作出妥协。
  ★ 短语 make compromises 妥协，和解

- After carefully studying your contract, I would like to make a few changes if possible.
  在仔细研究你方的合约后，如果可以的话，我想要修改几个地方。
  ★ 短语 make changes 做变动，做更改

- If you have no problem with the contract, then let's seal the deal.
  如果你对合约没有其他的问题，那就让我们达成协议吧。
  ★ 短语 seal the deal 达成协议

- From my point of view, your terms of payment are far from reasonable.
  从我方的角度来看，你们的付款条件一点也不合理。
  ★ 短语 far from... 完全不～；与～还差得远

在国外都说这几句

- Once a contract is signed, it is legal. Any violation is not allowed.
  合约一旦签署，即具有法律效力。任何的违约行为都是不允许的。

- The buyer does not have the option of canceling the contract.
  买主没有权力撤销合约。
  ★ 短语 option of... （买卖/交易）～的特权、～的选择权

- Once the contract is signed, both parties are obligated to carry out the contract.
  合约一旦签订，双方就有义务履行合约。
  ★ 短语 carry out... 实现～；执行～

- Mr. Willison will sign the contract on behalf of our company.
  威尔森先生将代表我们公司进行签约。
  ★ 短语 on behalf of... 代表～；为了～的利益

- The contract will come into effect immediately, it's for both our sakes.
  此份合约立即生效。这是为了双方着想。
  ★ 短语 come into effect （法律/合约）生效；实施

- I will mail the signed contract to you right away and proceed with your order in no time.
  我会马上将签好的合约邮寄给你，并立刻处理你的订单。
  ★ 短语 proceed with... 着手～；继续进行～

- Let's celebrate the new business partnership with West Company.
  让我们来庆祝跟韦斯特公司的商业合伙关系吧。

- I am still tied up with my work. I probably have to work this Saturday.
  我工作忙得不可开交。我这个周六可能要来上班。
  ★ 短语 be tied up with... 忙于～，忙着～不可开交

- I do not want to work overtime because having personal time is very important to me.
  我不想加班，因为拥有私人时间对我来说很重要。
  ★ 短语 personal time 私人时间

在国外都说这几句

- I'm reluctant to give up my time and energy to do the extra work. I would rather use this time to stay with my family.
  我很不情愿放弃我的时间和精力来做多余的工作。我情愿用这些时间陪伴家人。
  ★ 短语 ▶ give up... 放弃～；让出～

- I'm trying to get a lot of work done before I go on vacation.
  出去度假之前，我试着做完了大量的工作。

- Adam always puts in a few extra hours every day because he tries to get a promotion.
  亚当每天总是加班几个小时，因为他想要升职。
  ★ 短语 ▶ put in... 加进～；花费（时间或精力）

- I've been working ten hours in a row. I can really use a break.
  我已经连续工作 10 个小时了。我真的需要休息一下。
  ★ 短语 ▶ in a row 连续不断地，一个接一个地

- Have you ever worked overtime without getting paid for it?
  你曾经加班却没有加班费吗？
  ★ 短语 ▶ be / get paid for... ～收到付款；～收钱

- You have been working overtime for weeks. You should take a week off to have some quality time with your family.
  你加班加了好几个星期了。你应该请一个星期的假，享受跟家人在一起的时光。
  ★ 短语 ▶ take... off 休假～，请假～

- We are running out of time. That's why everybody is asked to stay late today. The manager will buy us dinner.
  我们现在时间紧迫。因此今天每个人将会被要求加班到晚一些。经理会请我们吃晚餐。
  ★ 短语 ▶ run out of... 用完～，耗尽～

- I believe that one should work to live, not the other way around.
  我相信人应该为生活而工作，而不是为工作而活。
  ★ 短语 ▶ the other way around 相反

247

跟任何人都可以用英语聊聊天

Unit 25 没有一个辞职是真的说再见

[生活便利贴]

有时候，工作到了某个阶段，就会想离职。可能是因为找到待遇更好的工作、在公司和某些同事不合、单纯地想换换新环境，或是老板觉得时候到了该请你走了。不管原因是什么，做一天和尚就要撞一天钟，即使自己将于不久后离职，分内的事情、该交接给同事的工作项目，都要一一地完成，这样才不会造成后人的辛苦。

Vocabulary 在国外都用这些词

trust
[trʌst]
v 相信，信任，信赖

appreciate
[ə'pri:ʃieɪt]
v 欣赏；感激；体会

social life
ph 社交生活

feedback
['fi:dbæk]
n 反馈；意见

incompetent
[ɪn'kɒmpɪtənt]
a 无能的

threaten
['θretn]
v 威胁；恐吓

imply
[ɪm'plaɪ]
v 暗示

at a loss
ph 不知所措

accomplishment
[ə'kʌmplɪʃmənt]
n 成就，成绩，技能

deserve
[dɪ'zɜ:v]
v 应受；该得

challenge
['tʃælɪndʒ]
n 挑战

commute
[kə'mju:t]
v 通勤

long-term
[,lɒŋ 'tɜ:m]
a 长期的

disagreement
[,dɪsə'gri:mənt]
n 意见不一，争论

eliminate
[ɪ'lɪmɪneɪt]
v 淘汰；消除；消灭

transition
[træn'zɪʃn]
n 过渡时期；过渡

nevertheless
[,nevəðə'les]
ad 仍然；不过；然而

government
['gʌvənmənt]
n 政府

在国外都说这几句

- My boss always **picks on** me about everything I do. Nothing I do makes her happy.
  我老板总是对我做的事吹毛求疵。我做的事没有一件会让她开心。
  ★ 短语 pick on... 找～的麻烦

- **It's hard to** work at a place where you can't trust anyone.
  在一个没有任何可以信任的人的地方工作是很辛苦的。
  ★ 短语 it's hard to... ～是很困难的、～是很辛苦的

- I do not appreciate the **pay delay** almost every month.
  对于每个月都延迟发薪，我觉得很不开心。
  ★ 短语 pay delay 延迟发薪

- Unfortunately, the job **messed up** my social life.
  不幸的是，这份工作把我的社交生活弄得一团糟。
  ★ 短语 mess up... 弄脏～；弄糟～

- My supervisor always makes important decisions **on an impulse**.
  我的上司在做重要决策时总是非常冲动。
  ★ 短语 on an impulse 冲动

- I **asked for** more feedback from my boss but never got any reply.
  我向老板询问意见，但从来没有得到任何回复。
  ★ 短语 ask for... 要求～；请求～

- Susan needs a manager that values her education and expertise, not one who always **complains about** how incompetent she is.
  苏珊需要一位可以重视她的学历和专业、而不是整天只会抱怨她到底有多无能的主管。
  ★ 短语 complain about 抱怨

常识补给站

猎头（Headhunting 或 Executive Search），是一种在欧美十分流行的人才招聘方式，指"网罗高级人才"。猎头与一般的企业招聘、人才推荐和职业介绍不同，猎头追逐的目标都盯在高学历、高职位、高价位三位一体的人身上，它搜寻的是那些受教育程度高、实践经验丰富、业绩表现出色的专业人才和管理人才，是一种帮助公司招聘高级人才的方式。

在国外都说这几句

- My manager doesn't introduce me to important contacts. He is worried that I might steal clients from him.
  我的经理从不把我介绍给重要的联系人。他担心我会把客户从他手中偷走。
  ★ 短语 steal from... 从~的手中偷走

- I think the new boss is threatened by my experience and skills. He is trying to get rid of me.
  我认为我的新老板对于我的经验和技能备感威胁。他试着想要挤走我。
  ★ 短语 be threatened by... 被~威胁，被~恐吓

- I imply I'm looking at other jobs. However, my boss doesn't seem to care and simply ignore me.
  我暗示自己正在考虑其他工作。然而，我的老板似乎一点也不在乎，完全忽略我说的话。
  ★ 短语 look at... 考虑~；研究~

- My boss gets mad and yells at me for not being able to do everything perfectly.
  我无法让所有工作完美无缺，老板因此对我生气而且大吼大叫。
  ★ 短语 be / get mad at... 对~生气，对~发怒

- My co-workers always boss me around with terrible attitude.
  我的同事总是用很差的态度指使我做这做那。
  ★ 短语 boss around... 指挥~，指使~

- My supervisor ignores me and discriminates against some employees. Working with him is torture.
  我的上司总是忽视我，并且歧视某些员工。跟他一起工作简直就像是被虐待。
  ★ 短语 discriminate against... 歧视~

- I do not want to work for someone who loves brownnosers. They disgust me.
  我不想为喜欢被别人奉承的人工作。他们令我觉得恶心。
  ★ 短语 work for... 为~工作、为~做事

- My boss turned down my raise request without any explanation.
  我老板没有任何解释，就拒绝了我加薪的请求。
  ★ 短语 turn down... 拒绝~

在国外都说这几句

- My boss wants me to report to her on everything. Some of those things are not even my responsibility.
  我老板要我每天都事无巨细地向她汇报。有些事情甚至不是我负责的。
  ★ 短语 report to... 向～报告；向～报到

- My director changes his mind frequently and often leaves me at a loss.
  我的主管常常改变主意，常让我不知所措。
  ★ 短语 change A's mind A 改变主意

- My boss doesn't seem to trust me to get my work done. He checks up on me many times a day.
  我老板似乎不相信我能完成我的工作。他一天要来检查我的工作好几次。
  ★ 短语 get... done 将～做完，将～完成

- My boss takes credit for the successful accomplishments of every other employee. Everyone hates it when he does that.
  我老板总是抢每个有成就的员工的功劳。大家都很讨厌他这样做。
  ★ 短语 take credit for... 揽下～的功劳

- In my opinion, most of my colleagues are not qualified for their jobs. I wonder how they got into this company.
  我认为，我的大多数同事都无法胜任他们的工作。我想知道他们是怎样进入这家公司的。
  ★ 短语 be qualified for... 对～胜任，合格～

- My boss never lets go of any problems or mistakes, especially if it's someone else's.
  我老板从不对任何麻烦或错误释怀；尤其当这些错误是其他人犯的时候。
  ★ 短语 let go of... 释放～；松开～

- I do not think my boss has the ability to deal with a difficult situation.
  我认为我的老板没有能力处理困难的情况。
  ★ 短语 deal with... 处理～，应付～

- It's frustrating that my boss always asks for my advice and then ignores it.
  我老板总是问了我的意见之后又完全忽略它，真令人感到沮丧。
  ★ 短语 it's frustrating that... ～真令人沮丧，～真令人泄气

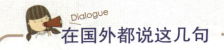
在国外都说这几句

- I have no idea why my boss shows no interest in taking my advice.
  我不知道为什么我老板没兴趣采用我的意见。
  ★ 短语 show no interest...　对～显现不出兴趣，对～不感兴趣

- My manager always thinks she has to clean up my messes even when I do everything right.
  我的经理总是觉得她必须为我善后，就算我根本没搞砸任何事也是如此。
  ★ 短语 clean up...　打扫～；整理～

- My boss is not capable of communicating with his employees. That's why we argue a lot.
  我老板无法与员工沟通，所以我们常常争吵。
  ★ 短语 is capable of...　有～的能力

- My boss never encourages me to work for a raise.
  我的老板从不鼓励我加薪的要求。
  ★ 短语 encourage A to...　鼓励 A～；怂恿 A～

- When it comes to important business decisions, my boss always keeps me away from it.
  每当涉及重要商业决策时，我老板总是不让我知道。
  ★ 短语 keep from...　隐瞒～，不把～告诉

- My boss reduced my hourly wage from $300 per hour to $220 per hour. That is unacceptable.
  我老板将我的时薪从一小时 300 美元压缩到 220 美元。这让人无法接受。
  ★ 短语 from A to B　从 A 到 B

I'm so tired!

在国外都说这几句

- My colleague constantly claims that he is too busy to work on regular tasks and then wants me to do it for him.
  我的同事时常声称他忙得没有时间做日常工作，然后要我帮他处理。
  ★ 短语 too... to ...　太～，以至于不能够～

- I would like the opportunity to discuss a possible future raise with you.
  我希望可以有一个跟你讨论未来可能加薪的机会。
  ★ 短语 discuss with...　与～讨论，与～商谈

- I just told my boss that I should get a raise next year.
  我刚刚跟我的老板说，明年我应该加薪了。
  ★ 短语 get a raise　（获得）加薪

- I have worked for the firm for 5 years and I'm still getting the same amount of salary. It's very frustrating.
  我在这家公司工作5年了。而我现在领的薪资都没有调整过。真是令人沮丧。
  ★ 短语 work for...　为～工作

- After all the accomplishments I achieved, I think I deserve a raise.
  根据我过去所获得的成就，我觉得我应该得到加薪。

- New employees with the same job title as me are being offered more money I'm currently receiving. How is that possible?
  与我职位一样的新同事们却领到比我现在还多的薪水。这样对吗？
  ★ 短语 job title　职称，职务

- I want to have at least 15 percent pay raise.
  我想要至少加薪15%。
  ★ 短语 (pay) raise　加薪

- As you know, I'm more than qualified for this position, so it's not too much to ask for a raise.
  你知道，我完全可以胜任这个工作，所以要求加薪应该不算太过分。
  ★ 短语 be qualified for...　合格～，胜任～

- My boss decided to give me a huge bonus because of my outstanding accomplishment.
  因为我表现优异，所以老板决定给我一笔高额奖金。
  ★ 短语 decide to...　决定～

在国外都说这几句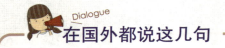

- What are the chances of me getting a promotion this year?
  我今年有可能升职吗？
  ★ 短语 get a promotion （获得）升职 / 升迁 / 升官

- Congratulations on your big raise and promotion. Dinner is on you.
  恭喜你获得大幅加薪和升职。今天你请吃晚餐。
  ★ 短语 congratulations on... 祝贺～

- Turning in my resignation is not always easy. Timing is everything.
  递交辞呈并不总是一件轻松的事。拿捏好递交的时间很重要。
  ★ 短语 turn in... 交上～；归还～

- I quit my job because I think it's about time to move on to a new challenge.
  我辞去工作是因为现在是迎接新挑战的时候了。
  ★ 短语 move on... 前进～、往前走～

- I don't seem to have room to grow with my current company.
  在目前的公司做事，我已没有进步的空间了。
  ★ 短语 grow with... 与～一起成长；与～一起发展

- After several years in this company, I decided to start a business of my own.
  在这家公司服务几年后，我决定开一家自己的公司。
  ★ 短语 start a business 创业

- I want to quit because I am interested in a job with more responsibilities, and I am very ready for a new challenge.
  我想辞职是因为我对有更多职责的工作感兴趣，而且我已准备好面对新的挑战。
  ★ 短语 be ready for... 准备好～

常识补给站

辞职，又称为离职，一个人离开自己原先的工作岗位及组织。离职时，要先与接手之人交接，指导该岗位需交接的事，之后向人事部门归还公司所属的物品，比如职员证、门禁卡、公司钥匙、公务车等。一旦完成离职手续，员工福利会立即停止，薪水则发放最后一次（通常是下个月）后，便不再给付。

- The **reason for** my resignation is that I want to spend more time with my family.

  我辞职的原因是我想多花点时间陪伴家人。

  ★ 短语 ▶ reason for...　～的原因

- I found a new job which is **closer to** home and with better salary.

  我找到一份钱多、离家近的新工作。

  ★ 短语 ▶ closer to...　离～近一点的

- I **am tired of** spending three hours each day on commuting.

  我受够了每天要花 3 小时通勤。

  ★ 短语 ▶ be tired of...　厌烦～，受不了～

- I want to leave the company **owing to** a long-term disagreement with Mr. Robinson.

  基于长期与罗宾逊先生意见不合，我想要离职。

  ★ 短语 ▶ owing to...　由于～，因为～

- I have given my manager **two-week notice** after I got a better job offer.

  我得到更好的工作之后，我向主管递出辞呈并给予两个星期的提前通知。

  ★ 短语 ▶ two-week notice　提前两个星期的辞职通知

- The new position **sounds like** an ideal match for my qualifications and experience. I'm looking forward to it.

  新的职务听起来很适合我的能力和经验。我对这份新工作很期待。

  ★ 语法 ▶ sound like...　听起来像～

- I **am grateful for** everything I had been through with Moonlight Company.

  我很感激在月光公司所经历的一切。

  ★ 短语 ▶ be grateful for...　对～感激，感谢～

- I think it would **make sense** to seek another job before my position is eliminated.

  我认为在我的职务被淘汰前，先行寻找另一份工作是很有道理的。

  ★ 短语 ▶ make sense　有道理

- My manager is formally **announcing my resignation** from Dreamer Company, starting today.

  我的经理现在正式宣布我从梦想家公司辞职，即日起生效。

  ★ 短语 ▶ announce A's resignation...　宣布 A 辞职

在国外都说这几句

- It has been a pleasure to work for East Company. I've learnt a lot from you.
  很荣幸曾为易斯特公司效力。我从你们身上学到了很多东西。
  ★ 短语 work for... 为～工作，为～效力

- Please don't hesitate to let me know how I can assist in making a smooth transition during my remaining time here.
  我还在公司期间，若能做些什么让这段过渡时期更为顺利，请别犹豫告知我。
  ★ 短语 assist in 帮助

- I have already accepted a new position with another company. My decision is final.
  我已经接受另一家公司提供的新职务。我心意已决。
  ★ 短语 accept... with A （求职时）接受 A 的～（邀约／职务）

- I'd like to take this opportunity to thank you for your time and efforts. You will be missed.
  我想借这个机会对你所付出的时间和精力表达感激。我们会想你的。
  ★ 短语 take the opportunity to... 借此机会～

- I'm officially resigning from Sunny Corporation. Here is my resignation letter.
  我正式递交我在阳光有限公司的辞呈。这是我的辞职信。
  ★ 短语 resignation letter 辞职信

- I wish you all the best.
  我祝你一切顺利。
  ★ 短语 all the best 一切顺利

- I was laid off from your current position because of downsizing.
  我是因为公司缩减人事开支而被解雇。
  ★ 短语 lay off 解雇

- Instead of blaming the company, you should admit the industry shrinking.
  不要责怪公司，你应该承认这个行业正在慢慢萎缩。
  ★ 短语 instead of... 代替～

- You have been trying, but I don't think you can make the cut for this high standard job.
  你一直很努力，但我觉得你无法胜任这份高标准的工作。
  ★ 短语 make the cut 合格，符合标准

在国外都说这几句

- You had your chance and I'm sorry that I have to let you go.
  我们已经给过你机会了，我很抱歉我们不得不让你离开。
  ★ 短语 let A go 解雇 A，开除 A

- At least 5 people from sales department are going to be laid off next month.
  公司销售部下个月至少要裁掉 5 位业务人员。
  ★ 短语 at least 至少

- You seem to be working overtime. However, you still failed to meet the requirements.
  你似乎一直加班。然而，你的工作还是达不到我们的要求。
  ★ 短语 fail to... 失败～；无法～

- We have to reduce some staff because the company is not making enough money for the past few years.
  过去几年公司一直都没怎么赚钱，因此不得不裁减一些员工。
  ★ 短语 make money 赚钱

- You are in charge of the sales department, and our sales number is falling off. What do you think the problem is?
  你是销售部的主管，我们的销售量却还是下滑。你觉得问题出在哪里？
  ★ 短语 in charge of... 负责～，照料～

- I am tired of the constant mistakes in your work. Consider it as a final warning.
  我已经受够了你工作上时常出现的错误。这次是我最后一次给你警告了。
  ★ 短语 consider... as final warning 把～当成最后的警告

- We've settled that we need to make a change and we are going to let you go.
  我们决定要做个改变，所以要请你另谋高就了。
  ★ 短语 make a change 做个改变

- Unfortunately, we feel that you're holding the company back. Please hand in your resignation by the end of today.
  不幸的是，我们觉得你阻碍了公司的发展。请你在今天下班前先行提交辞呈。
  ★ 短语 hold... back 抑制～，阻碍～

在国外都说这几句

- I'm sorry, but you are not cut out for the job.
  我很抱歉，你不适合这份工作。
  ★ 短语 be cut out for... 适合～；起到～作用

- We can talk about this as long as you like. Nevertheless, nothing is going to change the decision.
  你想花多少时间讨论都可以。不过，没有什么可以改变这个决定。
  ★ 短语 as long as... 长达～之久；只要～

- I'm sorry to tell you that we made the decision and this is your last month.
  我很抱歉告诉你，我们已决定这个月是你在公司上班的最后一个月。
  ★ 短语 make a decision 下决定；做决定

- The company is currently going through some difficulties. As a result, your position is being eliminated.
  目前公司正在经历一些困难。因此，你的职位已经被淘汰了。
  ★ 短语 as a result 结果；因此

- You are laid off. That's why you are eligible for government unemployment benefits.
  你是被裁员的，因此你符合政府失业补助的资格。
  ★ 短语 government unemployment benefits 政府失业补助，政府失业给付

- I'm more than happy to be your reference if you need it.
  如果你需要的话，我非常乐意当你的推荐人。
  ★ 短语 more than 超过，比～更多

- I'm giving you a letter of recommendation for your future job application.
  我会给你写一封推荐信，你未来申请工作的时候可以用。
  ★ 短语 letter of recommendation 推荐信

- Please go ahead and pack up your personal belongings. I'll meet you here in 30 minutes.
  请去收拾你的个人物品，30分钟后我们在这里见面。
  ★ 短语 pack up 收拾，整理

- If you have any questions about benefits or final paychecks, give me a call. I will help you in any way I can.
  若你有任何与津贴及离职工资有关的疑问，打电话给我。我会尽全力帮助你。
  ★ 短语 have questions about... 有关～的问题／疑问

Chapter 5 特殊节庆与活动
Holidays & Special Occasions

Unit 26 ｜ 浪漫的约会
Unit 27 ｜ 女孩一生最重要的时刻
Unit 28 ｜ 浪漫的圣诞节
Unit 29 ｜ 一年一次的大日子
Unit 30 ｜ 中国人最重视的新年

跟任何人都可以用英语聊聊天

Unit 26 浪漫的约会

[生活便利贴]

有研究指出，由相亲介绍而步入婚姻的伴侣，维系的时间会比自由恋爱来的长久。其实，相亲也好，自由恋爱也罢，最重要的是自己看上眼，喜欢对方，愿意与对方朝夕相处，甚至考虑一起走过一辈子，这才是最重要的。不然，跟一个你完全没有感觉的人在一起，这样的生活，会不会太过乏味了呢？

Vocabulary 在国外都用这些词

MP3 05-01

nerve-racking
[ˈnɜːvˌrækɪŋ]
ⓐ 使人不安的，伤脑筋的

punctual
[ˈpʌŋktʃuəl]
ⓐ 准时的

anywhere
[ˈenɪweə]
ⓝ 任何地方

conversation
[ˌkɒnvəˈseɪʃn]
ⓝ 对话；谈话；谈吐

stain
[steɪn]
ⓝ 污渍；污垢；瑕疵

originally
[əˈrɪdʒənəlɪ]
ⓐⓓ 起初，原来

dislike
[dɪsˈlaɪk]
ⓥ 不喜欢，讨厌

waiter
[ˈweɪtə]
ⓝ 服务生

politics
[ˈpɒlətɪks]
ⓝ 政治

appropriately
[əˈprəʊprɪətlɪ]
ⓐⓓ 适当地；合适地；相称地

tricky
[ˈtrɪkɪ]
ⓐ 微妙的；难处理的

clumsy
[ˈklʌmzɪ]
ⓐ 笨拙的

ease
[iːz]
ⓝ 容易；舒适；自在

sparkle
[ˈspɑːkl]
ⓝ 火花

nominate
[ˈnɒmɪneɪt]
ⓥ 提名，任命，指定

crowded
[ˈkraʊdɪd]
ⓐ 人多的，拥挤的

matchmaker
[ˈmætʃmeɪkə]
ⓝ 媒人

stalker
[ˈstɔːkə]
ⓝ 跟踪者

在国外都说这几句

- Blind dates can be exciting and nerve-racking no matter if it's set up by friends or an online social network.
  不管是朋友撮合还是通过社交网站，相亲都是既刺激又令人紧张不安的。
  ★ 短语 no matter 不论

- I get really worried if my date doesn't show up.
  我很担心如果我的约会对象没有出现怎么办。
  ★ 短语 show up 出现；暴露；露面

- Some friends of mine think their friend, Jessica, is perfect for me.
  我的一些朋友认为他们的朋友杰西卡会非常适合我。
  ★ 语法 "some" 是表示数量的名词，用来表达"（某个团体／群体）之中的一部分"

- They decided to hook me up with her.
  他们决定要介绍我们两个认识。
  ★ 短语 hook A up with B　替 A、B 两个人牵线

- What's wrong with you? Man up. Go and talk to the girl.
  你怎么了？勇敢一点。去跟那个女孩聊聊啊。
  ★ 短语 man up　勇敢一点，拿出你的勇气

- I don't know how to make conversation with my date.
  我不知道要怎么和我的约会对象讲话。
  ★ 短语 make conversation　开启对话，开始讲话

- I hope she will like the restaurant I picked.
  我希望她会喜欢我选的餐厅。
  ★ 短语 pick / choose　挑选

- I have already made a reservation at a fancy restaurant. I want it to be a perfect.
  我已经在一家很高级的餐厅订了位。我希望这个约会可以很完美。
  ★ 短语 make a reservation　预定（餐厅、饭店、～），预约（餐厅、饭店、～）

- It is said that the first impression is everything, so I'd better make a good one.
  有人说第一印象最重要，所以我要给对方留下好印象。
  ★ 语法 It is said...　据说，有人说

在国外都说这几句

- **Don't know what to wear for a date? Casual smart will be perfect for it.**
  约会时不知道该穿什么吗？正式的休闲穿着就一定没问题。
  ★ 短语 ▶ be perfect for ... 对～来说很完美

- **Most girls think that dressing up appropriately for a date shows them you care enough to look good for them.**
  大多数女孩认为，约会时你穿着得体显示出你在意为女孩留下良好的印象。
  ★ 短语 ▶ dress up   装扮

- **The girl will feel at ease if you choose a crowded public location.**
  如果你选择人多一点的公众场合，女生会觉得比较自在。
  ★ 短语 ▶ at ease   安心，自在

- **Are you sure it is time for you to wear your favourite band T-shirt? It's not very appropriate.**
  你确定这是你穿着最爱乐团T恤的好时机吗？好像不是非常恰当。
  ★ 短语 ▶ Are you sure...   你确定～吗？

- **Being punctual for the first date is very important.**
  守时对第一次约会是非常重要的。
  ★ 短语 ▶ be punctual for...   为～准时

- **Do you think we should meet up at a place we are both familiar with?**
  你觉得我们应该约在两个人都熟悉的地方见面吗？
  ★ 短语 ▶ meet up   遇到；不期而遇

- **Before you meet your date, look into the mirror and make sure you don't have a stain on your shirt.**
  在你与约会对象见面前，先找个镜子照照自己，而且确保你的衬衫上没有污渍。
  ★ 短语 ▶ look into the mirror   照镜子

- **Trust me! You should take the lead when introducing yourself.**
  相信我！你应该要先主动自我介绍。
  ★ 短语 ▶ take the lead   主动，领先

- **You should greet your date in a friendly, open manner and with a smile.**
  你应该以友善又大方的态度向约会对象打招呼，并面带微笑。
  ★ 短语 ▶ in a + a. + manner / way   以～的方式

在国外都说这几句

- If you meet at the restaurant, don't order anything before she arrives.
  如果你们约在餐厅见面，要等到她到了餐厅才可以开始点菜。

- If your date has a hard time deciding what to order, give her some suggestions.
  如果你的约会对象无法决定要点什么餐，你可以提供建议。
  ★ 短语 have a hard time + v-ing ～很困难，有困难～

- Do you think I should order for her or let her do it on her own?
  你觉得我应该帮她点餐，还是让她自己点餐？
  ★ 语法 let 后面若接动词，一定要接原形动词，"let +（人）+ 原形动词"的意思是"让人（做）～"。

- At times, blind dates can be tricky and need to be handled carefully.
  有时候，相亲是很棘手的，必须小心处理。
  ★ 短语 at times 有时，不时，偶尔

- Do not make too much body contact if you are not sure whether it is appropriate.
  如果你不确定是否合适，不要有太多的肢体接触。
  ★ 语法 whether 作连接词引导宾语从句时，意思与"if"相近；whether 后可接不定式。

- Always have a backup plan just in case your date doesn't go well.
  一定要有备用计划，以防你的约会进行得不顺利。
  ★ 短语 in case 假使，免得，以防万一

- For instance, I will get a friend to call me after half an hour. If my date sucks, I can use my friend as an excuse and leave.
  例如，我会请朋友半个小时后打电话给我。如果约会很糟，我可以把朋友当成借口，借机离开。
  ★ 短语 for instance 例如

- If there is a sparkle between two of you, that would be great. If there isn't, just let it go.
  如果两个人之间有火花的话，那就太棒了。如果没有，那就算了。
  ★ 短语 let it go 就算了，那就这样吧

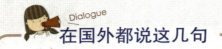

在国外都说这几句

- **My friend loves to play matchmaker and** *set me up with his friends*.
  我的朋友很爱当媒人，喜欢撮合我和他朋友。
  ★ 短语 set A up with B　介绍 B 给 A，撮合 A、B

- **It is important to use your** *body language* **and make eye contact.**
  使用肢体语言和保持眼神接触是很重要的。
  ★ 短语 body language　肢体语言

- **Do not ask** *yes or no questions*, **otherwise there will be in awkward silence.**
  不要问是非问答题，不然的话，你会处于尴尬的沉默。
  ★ 短语 yes or no question　只需回答是/否的问题

- **Guys need to listen and** *pay attention to* **what the girls say.**
  男生必须注意听女生说些什么。
  ★ 短语 pay attention to...　注意~，留意~

- **Do you travel** *a lot*? **Where have you been so far?**
  你常旅游吗？你到目前为止去过哪些地方？
  ★ 短语 a lot　很多，非常

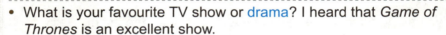

- **What is your favourite TV show or** *drama*? **I heard that** *Game of Thrones* **is an excellent show.**
  你最喜欢的电视节目或是肥皂剧是什么？我听说《权力游戏》很好看。

- **I like reality shows. My favourite one is** *America's Next Top Model*.
  我喜欢真人秀节目。我最喜欢的是《美国名模生死斗》。

- **It is extremely important to find a topic that you** *are* **both** *interested in*.
  找到你们共同有兴趣的话题是非常重要的。
  ★ 短语 be interested in　有兴趣

- **Are you going to travel to anywhere else** *in the future*?
  你计划未来要去其他的地方旅游吗？
  ★ 短语 in the future　将来，未来

- **My favourite hobby is collecting** *vintage cars*. **What's yours?**
  我最大的爱好是搜集古董车。你的嗜好是什么？
  ★ 短语 vintage car　古董车

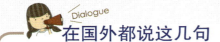

在国外都说这几句

- What do you do for a living?
  你的职业是什么？
  ★ 短语 for a living 谋生

- You have a very interesting accent. Where are you from originally?
  你的口音很特别。你是从哪里来的？
  ★ 语法 问人从哪里来有两种方式，一个是"Where are you from?"，另一个是"Where do you come from?"。

- I'm an only child. Do you have any brothers or sisters?
  我是独生子/女。你有兄弟姐妹吗？
  ★ 短语 only child 独生子/女

- Are you a dog person or a cat person?
  你喜欢狗还是猫？
  ★ 短语 "dog person"的意思是"爱狗的人"，"cat person"的意思是"爱猫的人"。

- We should steer clear of some subjects, such as religion and politics.
  我们应该避开一些话题，比如宗教和政治。
  ★ 短语 steer clear of 避开

- I don't think past relationships are a good topic for a first date. Can we save it for later?
  我觉得第一次约会不要谈到过去的恋情比较好。我们可以留着以后再谈吗？
  ★ 短语 save... for later 先保留～

- My date stood me up last night.
  我的约会对象昨天爽约了。
  ★ 短语 stand A up 未依约与A见面

- Things are going so well tonight. I hope to see you again soon.
  今天晚上一切都很美好，我希望可以很快再见到你。
  ★ 短语 go well 进行得很成功

- If I really don't like my date, then I wouldn't lead her on to feel like there might be a future.
  如果我真的不喜欢约会对象的话，我不会让对方认为我们之间有发展的可能。
  ★ 短语 lead A on to 诱使A相信

在国外都说这几句

- I had so much fun with my date tonight. I lost track of time **at the end of** the date.
  今天晚上我和我的约会对象玩得很开心,到最后我都忘记时间了。
  ★ 短语 at the end of... ~结束时

- I said goodbye to my date and gave her a clumsy kiss **on the cheek** in front of her house.
  我与我的约会对象在她家门口道别,并笨拙地在她脸上亲了一下。
  ★ 短语 on the cheek 在脸颊上

- I found myself in situations when things got quiet and I didn't know what to talk about **on a date**.
  我发现自己常处于不知道该跟约会对象谈论什么的安静状况。
  ★ 短语 on a date 约会的时候

- Are you **into** any kinds of sports?
  你有喜欢的运动吗?
  ★ 短语 be into... 喜欢~

- I'm not **a big fan of** baseball, but I do love tennis.
  我不是棒球球迷,但我非常喜欢网球。
  ★ 短语 a fan of... ~的迷

- You like musicals? So do I. It seems that we have a lot **in common**.
  你喜欢音乐剧?我也是。看来我们有许多共同点。
  ★ 短语 in common 共同的,共有的

- I really enjoyed your company tonight. I hope we can **get to** know each other more.
  我真的很喜欢你今晚的陪伴,希望我们可以进一步认识对方。
  ★ 短语 get to 达到(某一阶段或某一部分);开始

- **No kidding.** *True Blood* is also my favourite TV show. I'm crazy about it.
  真的。《真爱如血》也是我最爱的电视剧。我为之疯狂。
  ★ 短语 no kidding 没有骗人,不骗你,认真的

- Since we are both basketball supporters, we should watch a game together some time.
  既然我们都喜欢篮球,我们应该找个时间一起看场球赛。
  ★ 语法 "看比赛"的动词要用"watch"。

在国外都说这几句

- **Tell me** more **about** your family.
  多告诉我一些你家里的事。
  ★ 短语 tell A about...　告诉 A 有关～的事

- I have always wanted to visit somewhere historic, **such as** London, Beijing and so on.
  我一直都想造访有历史感的地方，例如伦敦、北京等。
  ★ 短语 such as　如此的，像是～，例如

- You've got to read that book. It is nominated as the book **of the year** in 2015.
  你一定要读读那本书。它被提名为 2015 年年度最佳图书。
  ★ 短语 ... of the year　年度最佳

- The actor totally deserved the **best actor award**. He is very talented.
  那位演员得到最佳男主角奖实在是实至名归。他非常有才华。
  ★ 短语 best actor award　最佳男演员奖

- I cannot believe how rude my date was. He **kept checking** me out.
  我不敢相信我的约会对象那么无礼。他一直上下打量我。
  ★ 短语 keep + v-ing　一直～，不断地～

- My date kept **telling** inappropriate dirty **jokes**. It made me uncomfortable.
  我的约会对象一直讲一些不合时宜的黄色笑话，这让我觉得不舒服。
  ★ 短语 tell jokes　讲笑话

- There's nothing worse than **finding out** that my date was a huge liar.
  没有比发现约会对象是个大骗子更糟糕的事了。
  ★ 短语 find out　发现

- If he **is late for** your first date, he's probably not that into you.
  如果他在第一次约会就迟到，他可能根本就没那么喜欢你。
  ★ 短语 be late for...　迟到

- My date told me that he just won a Nobel Prize. **He is so full of it.**
  我的约会对象告诉我他刚获得了诺贝尔奖。他真是满口胡言。
  ★ 短语 A is full of it　A 满口谎言，A 胡说八道

在国外都说这几句

- Do not lie about your occupation. People will find out the truth sooner or later.
  不要谎报你的职业。人们迟早会发现真相。
  ★ 短语 sooner or later 迟早

- I had the most terrible date. My date wouldn't shut up about her ex-boyfriends.
  真是最糟糕的约会。我的约会对象一直不停地讲她前男友。
  ★ 短语 shut up 闭嘴

- I hate blind dates. I have no idea what type of person it's going to be.
  我讨厌相亲。我总是不知道我的相亲对象会是怎样的人。
  ★ 短语 have no idea 不知道

- For all I know, the man I had dinner with could be a stalker or murderer.
  据我所知,跟我共进晚餐的男人可能是个跟踪狂或是个杀人犯。
  ★ 短语 for all A know(s) 就A所知

- I think my date was creepy because he touched me too soon. It was only the first date.
  我认为我的约会对象令人不寒而栗。我们才第一次约会,他就摸我。
  ★ 短语 too soon 太快,太过猴急

- My date said that he would call me. But guess what? He never did.
  我的约会对象说他会打电话给我,但你猜怎么着?他根本没打。
  ★ 短语 guess what 猜猜看,猜猜发生什么事

- My date never showed up. Should I call him and find out what's going on?
  我的约会对象没有出现。我应该打电话给他,问清楚发生了什么事吗?
  ★ 语法 what's going on 发生了什么事

- Things are going well with him. I should order something that we can share.
  一切都进行得很顺利。我应该点些我们可以一起分享的东西。
  ★ 短语 go well with... 跟~进行得很顺利

- Expecting men to pay on the first date is so old-fashioned. Now most girls would like to go dutch.
  期望男生在第一次约会的时候要付钱这种想法太落伍了。现在大部分的女生都想要各付各的。
  ★ 短语 go dutch　买单时各付各的

- I'd like to go out with you again. Are you free tomorrow night? We can go to a movie.
  我很想再跟你出去约会。你明天晚上有空吗？我们可以去看电影。
  ★ 短语 go out with A　与A出去

- The girl gave me a hug and gave me a quick peck on the cheek.
  那个女孩拥抱了我，并在我的脸颊上轻吻了一下。

- I'd like to walk you home and kiss you goodnight if you are okay with it.
  如果你不介意的话，我想陪你走回家，并给你一个晚安吻。
  ★ 短语 walk A home　陪A走回家

- If the date isn't going well, I can make up something after the first drink and leave.
  如果约会不顺利，我可以在喝一杯开胃酒之后就找好借口离开。
  ★ 短语 make up　编造

- Excuse me. There's something stuck in your teeth..
  不好意思，你的牙齿上面有东西。
  ★ 短语 excuse me　不好意思

- I'm sorry. I don't think you and I hit it off. Let's just be friends.
  对不起。我觉得咱俩合不来。我们当朋友就好了。
  ★ 短语 hit off　相处融洽，合得来

- My date hasn't showed up. I will wait for another 20 minutes and leave.
  我的约会对象没出现。20分钟内他若还不来，我就离开。
  ★ 短语 show up　出现

- It was the best date ever. Thank you so much for tonight.
  这是我有过的最好的约会了。谢谢你今天晚上所做的一切。
  ★ 短语 thank you　谢谢你

跟任何人都可以用英语聊聊天

Unit 27 女孩一生最重要的时刻

[生活便利贴]

结婚是每个人人生中相当重要的一个里程碑，它代表了人生即将进入一个崭新的阶段。婚礼当天所要准备、注意的事情会让人忙得不可开交。要遵循的婚礼流程也非常烦琐，再加上新娘还会为化妆、发型等烦恼，所以每个小细节都不能马虎。不过，人一辈子可能就只结一次婚，所以要让它尽善尽美，为以后留下美好的回忆。

Vocabulary 在国外都用这些词

MP3 05-11

bridesmaid ['braɪdzmeɪd]
n 伴娘

flaw [flɔː]
n 裂缝；缺点；瑕疵

rehearsal [rɪ'hɜːsl]
n 排演，预演

foremost ['fɔːməʊst]
a 最重要的

tailor ['teɪlə]
n 裁缝师

informal [ɪn'fɔːml]
a 非正式的；不拘礼节的

bachelorette [ˌbætʃələ'ret]
n 单身女郎，未婚女子

privilege ['prɪvəlɪdʒ]
a 特权；恩典；殊荣

relative ['relətɪv]
n 亲戚

ceremony ['serəmənɪ]
n 典礼，仪式

stylish ['staɪlɪʃ]
a 时髦的，流行的，漂亮的

foundation [faʊn'deɪʃn]
n 粉底（液）

moral ['mɒrəl]
a 精神上的，道德（上的）

expert ['ekspɜːt]
n 专家；能手；熟练者

blend [blend]
v 使混合；使交融

theme [θiːm]
n 主题；论题；题目

get-away
n 逃走；放松的旅游行程

waterproof ['wɔːtəpruːf]
a 防水的

在国外都说这几句

- A bridesmaid is one of the most important persons in the wedding.
  伴娘是婚礼中最重要的人之一。

- I'm going to be my best friend's bridesmaid. I will be there to support her in any way I can.
  我将要担任挚友的伴娘，不管她需要什么帮忙，我都会支持她。
  ★ 语法 am going to... 即将做～，马上要～

- A bride should have a maid-of-honor to help her take care of wedding details.
  新娘应该有一位首席伴娘，帮助她处理婚礼上的细节。

- One of the main responsibilities of being a bridesmaid is to shop for a wedding dress with the bride.
  当伴娘的主要责任之一就是要跟新娘去选购婚纱。
  ★ 短语 shop for... 购买～，选购～

- The maid-of-honor has planned a bridal shower tomorrow night; please be there on time.
  伴娘在明天晚上筹备了新娘送礼会，请记得要准时出席。
  ★ 短语 bridal shower 新娘送礼派对

- The bride's sisters and best friends will chip in for the costs of food, decorations, and venue.
  新娘的姐妹跟好朋友们会帮忙支付食物、装饰跟场地的费用。
  ★ 短语 chip in 捐助，出钱，共同出钱

- The bride's bachelorette party is coming up soon as well.
  新娘的单身派对也快要来临了。
  ★ 短语 as wel 也，同样地

- Normally, the bride will panic easily, so I have to help her stay calm before the ceremony.
  通常婚礼仪式前，新娘很容易会恐慌，我必须帮助她保持镇定。
  ★ 短语 stay calm 保持沉着，冷静

在国外都说这几句

- It is important for a bridesmaid to provide moral support at any time.
  伴娘随时随地为新娘提供精神上的支持是非常重要的。
  ★ 短语 at any time 随时，任何时候

- The couple asked me to inform all the friends where they registered for wedding gifts.
  新人要我帮忙告诉朋友们他们在哪里注册结婚礼物。
  ★ 语法 "register"的意思是"注册"。中国人在婚礼当天包红包给新人。但在西方文化中，即将结婚的新人会到商店注册他们婚后需要的用品，参加婚礼的宾客则可以到这些商店中买下任何新人注册的商品，当作结婚礼物送给新人。

- As a bridesmaid, I will be more and more occupied as the wedding approaches.
  当婚期逼近时，作为伴娘，我会变得越来越忙。
  ★ 语法 more and more 越来越~

- It can be very helpful to figure out ways to save money during the wedding planning.
  筹办婚礼期间，若能想出省钱的方法可能会很有帮助。
  ★ 短语 figure out 算出；想出；搞清楚

- Have you come up with a theme for the wedding? I can't wait to hear your idea.
  你想到婚礼的主题了吗？我等不及要听你的想法了。
  ★ 短语 come up with... 想到~；提供~；想出~

- Make sure the bride picks up the dress, tries it on and inspects it for any flaws. We don't want anything wrong to happen.
  确保新娘选好礼服、试穿礼服并且检查是否有瑕疵。我们不希望发生任何的问题。
  ★ 短语 make sure 确定，设法确保

- I plan to go with the bride to pick out the perfect dress. They serve champagne at the dress shop.
  我计划跟新娘一起挑选完美的礼服。礼服店提供香槟。
  ★ 短语 plan to... 计划去做~

- Maybe we should have bridesmaid's dresses custom-made at a tailor's.
  也许我们应该到裁缝那订制伴娘服。
  ★ 短语 custom-made 订制化的，为顾客量身修改的

在国外都说这几句

- **It is the bride's privilege to** select the color and style of the bridesmaid's dresses.
  挑选伴娘礼服的颜色和款式是新娘的特权。
  ★ 短语 It is A's privilege to...　～是 A 的特权

- The couple is **looking for** stylish wedding invitations. They want to impress everybody.
  新人正在寻找时髦的婚礼请帖。他们想给大家留下深刻的印象。
  ★ 短语 look for...　寻找～，找寻～

- I am helping the bride to choose a classic, elegant wedding invitation. There are so many different choices.
  我正在帮忙新娘挑选经典又优雅的婚礼请帖。有好多种类可以选择。

- A good bridesmaid **has to** attend all the brides' fittings to give her feedback. No matter how long it will take.
  一个好的伴娘应该陪新娘试穿礼服，并提供意见，无论要花多少时间。
  ★ 短语 has to...　必须（做）～，后面接原形动词。

- The bridesmaid's dresses should compliment the bride's wedding gown. And they should also **be attractive** for the guests.
  伴娘礼服应该要能衬托新娘的礼服，也应该能够吸引宾客。
  ★ 短语 be attractive　看起来迷人

- The wedding planner recommends us to **flip through** the popular wedding magazines to see what kind of dress is ideal.
  婚礼筹办人建议我们翻阅流行的婚礼杂志，看看哪个款式的礼服是最理想的。
  ★ 短语 flip through　（草草）翻阅

- It **is recommended by** experts that the bride go shopping with the bridesmaids.
  专家建议新娘应该跟伴娘一起购物。
  ★ 短语 be recommended by　被～所推荐

- The hottest styles **right now** are sleeveless two-piece floor length styles. I think you will love it.
  现在最热门的款式是，无袖两件式及地长礼服。我想你一定会爱上它的。
  ★ 短语 right now　目前，现在

在国外都说这几句

- The color platinum is very in style this season.
  这一季白金色非常流行。
  ★ 短语 in style 盛大，时髦

- Don't know what color to choose when picking out the dresses for brides and bridesmaids? White can never go wrong.
  不知道新娘跟伴娘的礼服应该选什么颜色吗？选白色绝对不会错。
  ★ 短语 go wrong 走错路；失败

- It is crucial to have all of the bridesmaids professionally measured. We might not have enough time to alter the dresses.
  专业地为所有伴娘量好尺寸是最重要的一件事。我们可能没有时间再去修改它们。
  ★ 语法 professionally 是指"专业地"的意思，在此修饰 measure 这个动词。

- You should have the dresses ready at least 2 or 3 months in advance.
  你应该至少要在两三个月以前就把礼服准备好。
  ★ 短语 in advance 预先

- It is important that the bride orders the dresses as soon as she makes a decision.
  一旦做好决定，就该尽快订礼服，这是很重要的。
  ★ 短语 make a decision 做决定，下决定

- As a matter of fact, a custom-made dress will be a good idea. But it's way much more expensive, not everyone can afford it.
  事实上，订制礼服是个好主意。但因为花费太昂贵，不是每个人都可以负担的。
  ★ 短语 as a matter of fact 事实上，实际上

- A bachelorette party often has games. They can get girls in the mood for some fun.
  单身派对通常会有一些游戏。这些游戏可以让女生们玩得很开心。

- Look at those candy rings in the gift bag! They are my favourite gift from the party.
  你看那些礼物袋里面的糖果戒指！它们是派对中我最喜欢的礼物了。
  ★ 短语 look at 看看；仔细检查

- It might be considerate to get the bride sexy lingerie for her honeymoon.
  帮新娘买一些蜜月可以用到的性感内衣是很体贴的。
  ★ 语法 it is considerate to... ～是很体贴的

 在国外都说这几句

- We need to send bridal shower invitations as soon as possible, so that everyone can make time for it.
  我们必须尽早寄出新娘送礼派对的邀请函,大家才可以把时间空出来。
  ★ 短语 as soon as possible 尽快,越快越好,也可简写为 ASAP。

- The bride and groom are planning a great trip to Las Vegas for a get-away.
  新娘和新郎正计划一次到拉斯维加斯的放松旅行。
  ★ 短语 plan for 计划,打算

- I am thinking about buying sexy garters for the bride for her wedding night. But I'm worried that she might not even want to put them on.
  我正在考虑为新娘的新婚之夜买一些性感的吊带袜。但我有点担心她可能连穿都不会穿。
  ★ 短语 put on 穿上

- The bride's opinion always comes first; keep this in mind when you plan the party.
  新娘的意见永远优先;你在计划派对的时候要牢记这件事。
  ★ 短语 keep ... in mind 考虑〜,记得〜

- Most of all, a bachelorette party should be a unique and amazing experience. We want everyone to have a good time.
  最重要的是,单身派对应该是个独特又美好的体验。我们要让每个人都玩得很开心。
  ★ 短语 most of all 最重要的是

- I hired a famous DJ to host the party and play some music.
  我请了一个有名的音乐播放员来主持派对、播放音乐。
  ★ 短语 hire A to... 请 A 做〜

- We will be serving cocktails and shots tonight. It's time for everyone to get out of control tonight.
  今晚我们会提供鸡尾酒以及烈酒,今天晚上就让大家一起狂欢吧。
  ★ 短语 out of control 失控

- The bride needs help in planning the rehearsal dinner.
  新娘需要有人帮忙筹备彩排晚餐。
  ★ 短语 rehearsal dinner 彩排晚餐

- At the rehearsal dinner, the maid-of-honor will give an informal toast to the newly wedded couple.
  彩排晚餐时,首席伴娘会先非正式地向新人致词。
  ★ 短语 give a toast 致词

在国外都说这几句

- A maid-of-honor should try and make sure that everything is in order.
  首席伴娘应该尽量确保每一件事情都依序进行。
  ★ 短语 in order　按顺序；状况良好

- I'm going to help out at the rehearsal dinner. Hope nothing will go wrong.
  我要去帮忙彩排晚餐。希望一切都很顺利。
  ★ 短语 help out　帮忙，帮助

- As one of the bridesmaids, I don't want to miss out on all the bridal affairs, especially the cake tasting.
  身为伴娘中的一员，我不想错过任何跟新娘有关的事情，尤其是试吃蛋糕。
  ★ 短语 miss out　错过

- Later, I will visit the reception lobby to make sure everything is on the right track.
  等一下我要看看宴会大厅，确保每件事情都很顺利。
  ★ 短语 reception lobby　接待大厅

- Do I have to invite distant relatives to the rehearsal dinner?
  我应该邀请远亲参加彩排晚餐吗？
  ★ 短语 distant relatives　远亲

- A rehearsal dinner is an informal meal to thank everybody which comes all the way to join the wedding.
  彩排晚餐是答谢所有大老远跑来参加婚礼的人的非正式餐会。
  ★ 短语 informal meal　非正式的餐会、聚会

- The rehearsal dinner is a chance for the bride and groom to show gratitude to all the people who helped them out with the wedding planning.
  彩排晚餐是新娘和新郎对所有帮助筹备婚礼的相关人士表现感激之意的机会。
  ★ 短语 help out with...　帮忙～，帮～的忙

- A rehearsal dinner doesn't have to be a formal ceremony at a fancy restaurant. A small place with the ones you care about will be enough.
  彩排晚餐不一定是在高级餐厅举行的正式典礼。只邀请一些你在乎的人去个小地方庆祝就够了。
  ★ 短语 at + 的地方　在～（地方）

在国外都说这几句

- If you're doing your own makeup, it is a good idea to schedule a makeup lesson with a professional beforehead.
  如果你要自己化妆，最好事先跟专业化妆师学习化妆课程。
  ★ 短语 it is a good idea to　～是个好主意

- The bride decided to take care of her eyebrows on her own.
  新娘决定自己画眉毛。
  ★ 短语 on A's own　A 自己做，A 自己来

- Never make a decision on foundation unless you apply it first and look at it in the daylight.
  除非上好粉底，并在日光下看了看，否则不要做决定涂那种粉底。
  ★ 短语 in the daylight　日光下

- The shade of a good foundation should blend in and look like you are not wearing anything.
  好的粉底色调应该与肤色融合，并看起来像没有涂粉底一样。
  ★ 短语 look like　好像～，看起来像～

- We suggest the bride wear waterproof makeup in case she cries.
  我们应该建议新娘上防水妆，以防发生她哭的状况。
  ★ 短语 waterproof makeup　防水的化妆品

- Look at that! The bride's makeup is running down her face from her tears. We should re-do it as soon as possible.
  看！新娘的妆被流下的泪水弄糊了，我们应该马上补妆。
  ★ 短语 run down　耗损；用坏

- There are so many choices when it comes to wedding hairstyles. Which one should I choose?
  有好多款式的新娘发型可供选择。我应该选哪一个呢？
  ★ 短语 when it comes to...　当涉及～时，谈到～时

- The bride is determined to find the perfect wedding day look on bridal styles. She wants the best in everything.
  这位新娘决心要找到完美的婚礼造型，每样东西她都要最好的。
  ★ 短语 be determined to...　决心要～，下定决心～

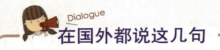

在国外都说这几句

- The classic updo styles work well with a wide variety of headpieces.
  经典的发髻造型与许多款式的发饰都很搭配。
  ★ 语法 ▶ A work well with B A 与 B 很搭配；A 与 B 配合得很好

- How should I wear my hair on my best friend's wedding day? It's going to take me a while to make a decision.
  我最好朋友的婚礼当天，我该梳什么样的发型呢？我可能要花一点时间才能做出决定。
  ★ 短语 ▶ wear A's hair... 将 A 的头发梳成～的样子

- A maid-of-honor has to be useful during the wedding reception. She can't just sit around and do nothing.
  首席伴娘在婚礼上必须很能干。她不能只是坐在那边，什么事情都不帮忙。
  ★ 短语 ▶ be useful... 对～很在行，很熟练

- As a bridesmaid, I have to ensure that everyone is being taken care of, and to make him or her feel welcomed.
  我作为伴娘，必须确保每个人都被照顾到，并让他们觉得宾至如归。
  ★ 短语 ▶ take care of 照顾

- Today is my best friend's special day and I want her to be happy forever and ever.
  今天是我好朋友的特别日子，我希望她永远都开心幸福。
  ★ 短语 ▶ forever and ever 永远

- There's a dance floor! Let's get the party going.
  舞池在那边！让我们一起让这个派对热闹起来。
  ★ 短语 ▶ dance floor 舞池

- At the wedding ceremony, the maid-of-honor has the honor of walking down the aisle before the bride.
  婚礼上，首席伴娘享有能够在新娘之前走上红毯的殊荣。
  ★ 短语 ▶ walk down 沿着走；走向；走上

- The bridesmaid stands next to the bride with the wedding ring during the ceremony.
  伴娘在婚礼仪式中要拿着结婚戒指站在新娘身边。
  ★ 短语 ▶ next to A 在 A 的旁边，在 A 的身旁

- I have to remember to hold the bouquet during the ceremony. It's part of the maid-of-honor's job.
  我必须记得在婚礼仪式时握着捧花。这是首席伴娘的工作之一。
  ★ 语法 ▶ remember + to v. 记得要做

在国外都说这几句

- The bride reminded me to make sure the dress stays clean and wrinkle free on the big day. It's a great responsibility.
  新娘提醒我在婚礼当天，要确保礼服保持干净，不可以有皱褶。真是责任重大。
  ★ 短语 remind A to... 提醒 A 做~

- Maybe I should arrive early to take pictures so that we can remember this big day in the future.
  也许我应该早一点到，拍一些照片为日后留下美好的回忆。
  ★ 短语 take a picture 照相

- The bride freaks out because the bridesmaid cannot find the veil.
  因为伴娘找不到头纱，所以新娘慌了。
  ★ 短语 freak out 暂时对自己失去控制；发疯；行为异常

- The bridesmaid is giving a meaningful toast during the reception. It made everyone cry a little bit.
  伴娘在宴客时，发表了一篇非常有意义的敬酒感言。让每个人都哭了一下。
  ★ 短语 give a toast 发表感言，致词

- I have to make sure the bride and groom get some snacks during the wedding. They barely have time to eat.
  我必须确保新娘新郎在婚礼时吃点点心。因为他们几乎没有时间吃东西。
  ★ 短语 during... 在~的整个期间

- The bride was given away by her father.
  在婚礼上，新娘由父亲交给新郎。
  ★ 短语 give away 在婚礼上把新娘交给新郎

- One moment, please. I have to assist the bride in getting into her dress.
  请等一下。我必须帮助新娘穿上礼服。
  ★ 短语 get into 穿进（衣服）

- It is my task to make sure the groom's ring is in my possession at all times.
  我的任务是随时帮新郎保管戒指。

跟任何人都可以用英语聊聊天

Unit 28 浪漫的圣诞节

[生活便利贴]

一年一度的圣诞节又要到了，你今年在乖孩子的名单上吗？街上、商家又开始出现了浓浓的圣诞节气氛。圣诞老人的玩偶，大大小小的圣诞装饰，自然是少不了的。如果想要多感受圣诞节的氛围，那就一定要在屋内摆上一棵美美的圣诞树，再用五颜六色的灯泡加以装饰，接着，就是等着跟大家一起享受圣诞节的美好时光啦！

Vocabulary 在国外都用这些词

05-21

Christmas ['krɪsməs]
n 圣诞节

holiday ['hɒlədeɪ]
n 假日；节日；休息日

bulb [bʌlb]
n 灯泡

celebration [ˌselɪ'breɪʃn]
n 庆祝

religion [rɪ'lɪdʒən]
n 宗教

peace [piːs]
n 和平

generous ['dʒenərəs]
a 慷慨的，大方的

practice ['præktɪs]
v 实践；实行；练习

exchange [ɪks'tʃeɪndʒ]
v 交换

children ['tʃɪldrən]
n 孩子（复数）

income ['ɪnkʌm]
n 薪水；收益；所得

official [ə'fɪʃl]
a 官方的

North Pole
ph 北极

meaning ['miːnɪŋ]
n 意义

spirit ['spɪrɪt]
n 精神；灵魂；心情

Christmas stocking
ph 圣诞袜

generation [ˌdʒenə'reɪʃn]
n 世代

cuisine [kwɪ'ziːn]
n 美食

 在国外都说这几句

- Christmas originated from christianity, but even people without religion celebrate it nowadays.
  圣诞节源自于基督教，但现今即使没有宗教信仰的人也会庆祝圣诞节。
  ★ 短语 originate from... 源自～、来自～

- Most people's thoughts will turn to Christmas after Thanksgiving every year.
  每年过完感恩节后，大部分人的心思就转到了圣诞节。
  ★ 短语 turn to... 转向～

- A decorated tree in the house has played an important role in Christmas celebrations.
  在家中放一棵装饰过的常青树扮演着庆祝圣诞节中很重要的一部分。
  ★ 语法 A play an important role... A 扮演重要的角色

- Christmas is the day that has a huge effect on the entire world.
  圣诞节在全世界都有很大的影响力。
  ★ 短语 have an effect on... 对～有影响（力）

- Santa Claus can be traced back to the 4th century in a story about Saint Nicholas.
  圣诞老人可以追溯至公元 4 世纪时一个有关圣·尼古拉斯的故事。
  ★ 短语 trace back... 追溯至～

- St. Nicholas was by all accounts a generous man, especially to children.
  圣·尼古拉斯据说是个慷慨的人，尤其对待小朋友。
  ★ 短语 by all accounts 根据各种流传的说法，据说

- It is said that Santa Claus lives at the North Pole with a lot of elves.
  据说圣诞老人跟很多小精灵一起住在北极。
  ★ 短语 a lot of 很多、许多

- For many Christians, Christmas is the day to remember the birth of Jesus.
  对大多数的基督徒来说，圣诞节是为了纪念耶稣诞辰。
  ★ 短语 the birth of... ～的出生、～的诞生

- It is believed that Jesus was born on the 25th, although the exact month is unknown.
  据说耶稣是 25 日出生，但无法确定月份。
  ★ 语法 it is believed that... 据说～，传说～，也常用"it is said that..."。

在国外都说这几句

- Christmas is the time for families to gather together and spend time with each other.
  圣诞节是家人相聚、一起度过美好时光的节日。
  ★ 短语 gather together 集合，集聚

- The spirit of Christmas causes people to decorate their homes and front yards.
  圣诞节氛围是许多人装饰家中及前院的原因。
  ★ 短语 cause A to... 导致 A～，引起 A～

- Children hope that Santa Claus will visit their home via the chimney and fill the Christmas stocking with gifts and sweets.
  小朋友希望圣诞老人会从烟囱进入他们的房子，并给圣诞袜装满礼物和糖果。
  ★ 短语 fill with... 装满～、填满～

- It is common to cook a special meal for your family on Christmas Day.
  在圣诞节当天为家人准备一顿丰富的大餐是很常见的。
  ★ 短语 it is common to... 很常见的，很普及的

- Rudolph the Red-nosed Reindeer, decorated trees and Santa Claus are all associated with this special holiday.
  红鼻子麋鹿鲁道夫、装饰过的圣诞树和圣诞老人都跟这个特别的节日紧密相连。
  ★ 短语 be associated with... 把～联想在一起；使～结合

- One of the Christmas traditions is going home to celebrate it with family, no matter where you are.
  圣诞节的其中一个传统就是，无论你在哪里，都要赶回家跟家人一起庆祝。
  ★ 短语 no matter 无论

- Christmas is now a holiday celebrated by almost everybody, not just people with religions.
  现在，圣诞节几乎是每个人都会庆祝的节日，不仅限于有宗教信仰的人。
  ★ 短语 is celebrated by... 被～所庆祝

- There are lots of Christmas traditions that are practiced by a number of countries all over the world.
  全球有许多国家都沿袭了圣诞节的很多传统。
  ★ 短语 a number of + 可数名词复数形式 大量～

在国外都说这几句

- The kids decorate the tree and top it with a star to welcome this special festival.
  小朋友们装饰圣诞树，并在顶端放一颗星星，来迎接这个特别的节日。
  ★ 短语 ▶ top A with... 把～加盖在 A 上，把～放在 A 顶端

- A lot of families spend a huge part of their income on gifts and food.
  许多家庭都将一大部分薪水花在礼物和食物上。
  ★ 短语 ▶ part of... 一部分～

- In England, Boxing Day is celebrated the day after Christmas. On that day, most stores will provide very good discounts.
  在英格兰，节礼日在圣诞节过后的一天。在这一天，大部分的商家都会提供很好的折扣。
  ★ 短语 ▶ Boxing Day 节礼日

- Boxing Day is one of the most important public holidays in the UK.
  节礼日是英国重要的国家法定假日之一。
  ★ 短语 ▶ public holiday 公定假日，国家法定假期

- Unfortunately, most people tend to forget the true meaning of Christmas.
  不幸的是，大多数的人们似乎忘记了圣诞节的真正意义。
  ★ 短语 ▶ tend to... 有～的倾向；易于～

- I grew up in a family where Christmas was treated as a big event in our house.
  我生长在一个将圣诞节视为年度大事的家庭。
  ★ 短语 ▶ grow up in... 在～长大，成长于～

- On every December 24th, excitement grows with every passing minute.
  在每年的 12 月 24 日，时间每流逝一分，人们的激动情绪就会增长一分。
  ★ 短语 ▶ grow with... 跟～一起变大、随着～而成 / 生长

- In most western countries, nearly all the shops play Christmas songs during this season.
  在大多数的西方国家，几乎所有商家都会在这段时间播放圣诞歌曲。

- Today, decorations for Christmas trees vary from family to family. Everyone has his or her own style.
  现今，每个家庭都有不同的圣诞树的布置方法。每个人都有自己的风格。
  ★ 短语 ▶ from family to family 从一个家庭到另一个家庭，每个家庭

在国外都说这几句

- In many countries, Santa Claus figure is frequently used as decorations. You can see them everywhere.
  在许多国家，圣诞老人常被用来当作装饰。在很多地方都可以看得到这些装饰。
  ★ 短语 be used as...　作为～，当作～使用

- In many families, Christmas decorating has passed on from generation to generation, it becomes a family tradition.
  在许多家庭中，圣诞装饰都是一代一代传承的，现在已经变成一种家族传统。
  ★ 短语 pass on　继续下去；传递

- Christmas is also a time when houses and shopping malls are decorated with all kinds of light bulbs.
  圣诞节期间，房子和购物中心都用各种圣诞灯泡装饰。
  ★ 短语 A is a time when...　A是～的期间、A是～的时候

- The kids will leave some cookies and milk on the dining table for the Santa before going to bed.
  小朋友在睡前会在餐桌上放些饼干和牛奶给圣诞老人。
  ★ 短语 go to bed　上床睡觉

- Rumor has it that Santa arrives on Christmas Eve in a sled carried by reindeers.
  据说圣诞老人在圣诞前夜会搭乘由麋鹿拉的雪橇抵达。
  ★ 短语 rumor has it that...　谣传～，据说～，据传～

- I cannot wait to get up in the morning on Christmas Day to see what Santa has brought me.
  我等不及在圣诞节当天早上起来看看圣诞老人给我带了些什么。
  ★ 短语 get up　起床

- Why do people kiss under the mistletoe, even when they don't know each other?
  为什么即使人们不认识对方，也会在圣诞幸运枝下亲吻呢？
  ★ 短语 under...　在～下方，在～下面

- People who kiss under the mistletoe have the promise of happiness and good luck in the following year, so it becomes a famous Christmas tradition.
  在圣诞幸运枝下亲吻的人们来年会得到快乐和好运，所以它演变成非常有名的圣诞节传统。
  ★ 短语 the promise of...　～的承诺；承诺被给予～

在国外都说这几句

- **Mistletoe is also seen as a symbol of peace.**
  圣诞幸运枝也被视为和平的象征。
  ★ 短语 be seen as... 被视为～，被看做是～

- **You can try and get someone you have a crush on to stand right under the mistletoe. That gives a reason to give him / her a kiss.**
  你可以试着想办法让你喜欢的人跟你一起站在圣诞幸运枝下面，这样你就有机会可以亲吻他（她）了。
  ★ 短语 have a crush on A 喜欢A，对A有意思

- **It is said that enemies who met under mistletoe would disarm and embrace each other.**
  据说站在圣诞幸运枝下的敌人会放下他们的武器，并相互拥抱。

- **The mistletoe was believed to have magical healing powers by the ancient Celtics.**
  对古代的凯尔特人来说，槲寄生（圣诞幸运枝）被认为有神奇的疗效。
  ★ 短语 A be believed to... A被认为～，A被相信为～

- **Christmas stockings are hung on the fireplace for Santa Claus to fill them with gifts.**
  圣诞袜挂在壁炉上，等着圣诞老人装满礼物。
  ★ 短语 fill A with... 把A装满～，把A充满～

- **I always exchange Christmas gifts and cards with my friends.**
  我总是跟朋友交换圣诞礼物和卡片。
  ★ 短语 exchange with... 与～交换

- **My mom and I baked Christmas cookies and gave them away to our neighbors.**
  我和妈妈一起烤圣诞饼干，然后送给邻居们。
  ★ 短语 give away 赠送～；分发～

- **Sometimes the neighbors will give us some pumpkin pie in return.**
  有时候邻居也会送我们南瓜派作为回礼。
  ★ 短语 in return 作为回报

- **During Christmas, you can see people perform Christmas carols on the street.**
  在圣诞节的时候，你会在街上看到有人在表演圣诞歌颂。
  ★ 短语 Christmas carol 圣诞歌颂

在国外都说这几句

- I am neither religious nor a regular churchgoer, although I still have fond childhood memories after hearing Christmas carols.
  我不虔诚，也不上教堂，我依然对圣诞颂歌有着有趣的儿时回忆。
  ★ 语法 neither... nor...　既不～，也不～

- Many organizations will open as usual on Christmas Eve.
  在平安夜，许多公司照常营业。
  ★ 短语 as usual　照常，照例，与平常一样

- Every year, my father sets up a Christmas tree in the living room and we decorate it together.
  每年我爸爸都会在客厅里竖起圣诞树，然后我们会一起装饰它。
  ★ 短语 set up...　竖立～；建造～

- I will hang mistletoe on the doorway. It is traditional for people to kiss when they stand underneath it.
  我会在门口挂槲寄生。人们站在槲寄生下亲吻是个传统。
  ★ 语法 underneath　在～下面，在～底下

- If you need to use public transportation on Christmas Eve, you'd better check the timetable in advance.
  如果你需要在平安夜搭乘公共交通工具，你最好先查一下时刻表。
  ★ 短语 public transportation　公共交通工具

- Since Christmas Eve is not an official holiday, most people still have to work, but they can't seem to focus on their jobs.
  既然平安夜并不是法定假日，大部分人还是要上班，但他们可能已无法专心于工作。
  ★ 语法 since 在此是从属连词，意思是"既然"。

- Many people in the United States decorate their houses and front yards with seasonal ornaments.
  在美国，许多人使用季节性装饰品装饰家里和前院。
  ★ 短语 decorate with　用～装饰

- It's a white Christmas. We can build a snowman outside of our house.
  今年是白色圣诞节。我们可以在房子外面堆个雪人。
  ★ 短语 outside of...　在～的外面

在国外都说这几句

- Reindeer and snowmen may be placed on driveways, roofs or in gardens, depending on where you want them.
  麋鹿和雪人可以放在车道、屋顶或花园中，这就要看你想要把它们放在哪里了。
  ★ 短语 be placed on... 被放置在～，放在～

- In the evening, many kids will hang up stockings on the fireplace or the end of their bed.
  傍晚，许多小孩会将圣诞袜挂在壁炉上或是床尾。
  ★ 短语 hang up... 悬挂～、挂起～

- In general, Christmas stockings are red with a white fluffy trim.
  通常，圣诞袜是红色的，并有白色的茸边。
  ★ 短语 in general 通常，一般地

- It will be my first time to attend a midnight Mass at church.
  这将是我第一次在教堂参加午夜弥撒。
  ★ 短语 attend a mass 参加弥撒

- Don't wait until the last minute to shop for Christmas presents, because all the good ones are sold out.
  不要等到最后一刻才去买圣诞礼物，因为好东西都卖光了。
  ★ 短语 shop for... （购）买～，选购～

- You don't have to engage in religious traditions to have fun on Christmas.
  在圣诞节，你不一定非要参与宗教传统仪式才能玩得开心。
  ★ 短语 engage in... 从事于～，忙于～，埋头致力于～

- The children are writing down wish lists of the gifts they would like to receive from Santa.
  小朋友们正在写下希望圣诞老人可以送给他们的礼物清单。
  ★ 短语 wish list 愿望清单、礼物清单

- The store always provides the best gift ideas and promotions for all occasions.
  这家店总是提供适合各种场合的最佳礼物以及折扣。
  ★ 短语 provide for... 供给～，为～做准备

- My mother and I have fun making a ginger bread house.
  我妈妈和我一起做姜饼屋，玩得很开心。
  ★ 短语 ginger bread house 姜饼屋

在国外都说这几句

- I have no idea about how to brighten the Christmas tree up. Can you help me?
  我完全不知道要怎样点亮圣诞树。你可以帮我吗?
  ★ 短语 brighten up...　照亮～, 点亮～

- I am out of ideas for Christmas. Do you have anything in mind?
  我没有圣诞节的点子了。你们有什么想法吗?
  ★ 短语 have in mind　想要; 想到

- Instead of paper cards, why not send out an electronic Christmas card? It costs you nothing.
  与其寄纸卡片, 为什么不寄电子圣诞贺卡呢? 它不用花费你一毛钱。
  ★ 短语 send out...　寄出～; 放出～

- My sister played Christmas songs in the house to get in the holiday spirit.
  我姐姐在家里播放圣诞歌曲, 营造节日气氛。
  ★ 短语 get in...　到达～, 进入～

- There are some cuisines that only be served during the Christmas holidays.
  有些特定的美食只在圣诞假期供应。
  ★ 短语 during...　在～特定的期间, ～期间

- My company is going to hold a Christmas costume party.
  我的公司将举办圣诞化装舞会。
  ★ 短语 costume party　化装舞会

- I'm not sure if I want to go shopping today. The stores and malls are likely to be packed.
  我不确定今天想不想去购物。商店和购物中心可能人潮涌动。
  ★ 短语 be likely to...　有～的可能, 做～的可能

- My family is going to stock up on food for the festive season, because most restaurants will be closed.
  我的家人准备囤积一些过节食物, 因为大部分的餐厅都会停止营业。
  ★ 短语 stock up...　储备～、囤积～

- My mother prepared a huge Christmas feast with foods such as turkey, ham, vegetables and pies. We are going to gain so much weight.
  我妈妈准备了圣诞大餐，有火鸡、火腿、蔬菜和派。我们一定会吃胖的。
  ★ 短语 prepare with...　准备～，用～

- You should visit family members or friends on Christmas.
  圣诞节，你应该回去拜访家人和朋友。
  ★ 短语 family member　家庭成员

- Apart from festive dinners and expensive gifts, there are other ways to celebrate the holiday.
  除了节日大餐和昂贵的礼物，还有其他庆祝节日的方法。
  ★ 短语 apart from...　除了～以外

- The local church always prepares food for the homeless, to make sure they have a happy Christmas.
  当地的教堂总是为无家可归的人准备食物，确保他们也可以过一个开心的圣诞节。
  ★ 短语 prepare for...　为～准备

- On Christmas, I will stay at home and spend time with my family.
  圣诞节，我要待在家里，和家人一起共度时光。
  ★ 短语 spend time　花时间

- I'm extremely grateful for the gifts my grandpa gave me.
  我很感激爷爷送我的礼物。
  ★ 短语 be grateful for...　感谢～，对～感到感激

- My aunt gave me a shining bike as a Christmas present. I can't wait to have a test ride.
  我阿姨送我一台闪亮的自行车作为圣诞礼物。我等不及要去试骑了。
  ★ 短语 give... as a present　送～礼物，把～当礼物送给

- We should all send Christmas cards to family and friends and wish them a merry Christmas.
  我们大家都该寄圣诞卡给家人和朋友，并祝他们圣诞快乐。
  ★ 短语 send... to A　把～寄给A，寄给A～

- My parents bought gifts for us and piled them up under the tree.
  我父母为我们买了礼物，并把它们堆在圣诞树下。
  ★ 短语 pile up...　堆放～起来；累积～

跟任何人都可以用英语聊聊天

Unit 29 一年一次的大日子

[生活便利贴]

一年一度的生日又到了，又到和三五好友或家人一同庆祝的时候了！但记得狂欢的同时，也要注意自身的安全。若有饮酒的话，千万不要酒后开车，选择搭出租车或是找代驾，这样才不会危及自身跟他人的安全。另外，既然年龄又长了一岁，那么待人处事方面也要更上一层楼！

Vocabulary 在国外都用这些词

MP3 05-31

amazing
[əˈmeɪzɪŋ]
a 令人吃惊的

pretzel
[ˈpretsl]
n 椒盐脆饼

tablecloth
[ˈteɪblklɒθ]
n 桌布

finger food
ph 小餐点

mini
[ˈmɪnɪ]
a 迷你的，袖珍的

atmosphere
[ˈætməsfɪə]
n 气氛

gender
[ˈdʒendə]
n 性别

soft drink
ph 无酒精饮料

tune
[tjuːn]
n 歌曲

tear
[teə]
n 泪水

adorable
[əˈdɔːrəbl]
a 可爱的

background
[ˈbækɡraʊnd]
n 背景

baby
[ˈbeɪbɪ]
a 婴儿（时期）的

cupcake
[ˈkʌpkeɪk]
n 杯子蛋糕

downtown
[ˌdaʊnˈtaʊn]
n 市区

trivia
[ˈtrɪvɪə]
n 琐事

disposable
[dɪˈspəʊzəbl]
a 用完即丢的

dedicate
[ˈdedɪkeɪt]
v 奉献

在国外都说这几句

- I'm going to throw my best friend a birthday party; it's going to be her 30th birthday.
  我要帮我最好的朋友举办生日派对。这是她 30 岁的生日。
  ★ 语法 "throw" 在此的意思是"举行（宴会、派对等）"，是英语口语中常用的表达方式。

- Let me know if you come up with any ideas for an amazing birthday party.
  如果你有任何举办生日派对的好想法，要让我知道。
  ★ 短语 come up with 想出～；提供～

- Feel free to bring some finger food to the party. We can all share them together.
  请随意带一些小餐点参加派对。我们可以一起分享。
  ★ 短语 feel free to... 随意～，自在～

- I'm going to plan a party that will knock my friend's socks off.
  我要办一个让我的朋友惊讶不已的派对。
  ★ 短语 knock A's socks off 让 A 大吃一惊

- It's my sweet 16th birthday, my parents agree to throw me a huge party.
  今年是我 16 岁的生日，我父母同意为我举行一个盛大的派对。
  ★ 短语 agree to... 同意～，赞成～

- We should start off by choosing a theme for the party. Do you have any ideas?
  我们应该一开始先选择派对主题。你有什么想法吗？
  ★ 短语 start off... 开始～；出发～

- I don't want my parents to hover over us at a party. I'm not a baby anymore.
  我不想爸妈在一旁监视我们的派对。我又不是小孩子。
  ★ 短语 hover over... 在～盘旋、徘徊

- A birthday celebration is always fun no matter how old we are.
  不管我们多大，庆祝生日都是很有趣的。
  ★ 短语 no matter... 无论～，不管～

在国外都说这几句

- Let's make this party a success and have a great time together.
  我们办个成功的派对，让大家可以一起玩得很开心。
  ★ 语法 "make" 在此是使役动词。其后的第二个动词需使用动词原形，前面不可再加 "to"。

- Depending on the age and gender, the party theme and activities will be different.
  根据年龄跟性别的不同，派对的主题跟活动也会有所差异。
  ★ 短语 depend on... 取决于～，视～而定

- Remember, age is nothing but a number. Don't be too upset about it.
  记得，年龄不过是个数字。不要为此太过难过。
  ★ 语法 nothing but... 只不过～，仅仅～

- For most people, a birthday is a time for happiness and celebration.
  对大多数的人而言，生日是快乐和庆祝的时刻。
  ★ 短语 a time for... ～的时刻，～的时间

- I hope my birthday wishes will come true.
  我希望我的生日愿望可以成真。
  ★ 短语 come true 实现

- Make some popcorn and get ready for some fun with a movie theme birthday party! We will watch the entire series of *Harry Potter*.
  准备爆米花，并开始庆祝电影主题生日派对！我们要把整个《哈利波特》系列电影看完。
  ★ 短语 get ready for... 准备好～，为～准备好

- We are celebrating the girl's birthday with a chick-flick. It's going to be full of joy and tears.
  我们要看女生爱看的电影来庆祝女孩的生日。一定会充满欢笑和泪水。
  ★ 短语 chick-flick 女生爱看的电影

- We invited our neighbor to come over for our son's 2-year-old birthday party.
  我们邀请了邻居来参加我儿子的两岁生日派对。
  ★ 短语 come over 来访，拜访

在国外都说这几句

- Trust me! A movie party is always full of fun for any age group!
  相信我！不管多少岁，电影派对总是充满欢乐的！
  ★ 短语 age group 年龄层

- Let's have the birthday girl's baby pictures hung on the wall, so everyone can see how cute she used to be.
  我们把寿星小时候的照片挂在墙上，让大家看看她以前是多么可爱。
  ★ 短语 hang on... 挂在～上，悬挂～

- I sent out the invitation letters to all the guests last month.
  我上个月就把邀请函寄给客人了。
  ★ 短语 invitation letter 邀请函

- I want to design the invitations by myself. It will be much more special.
  我想要自己设计邀请函。这样特别多了。
  ★ 语法 by oneslef 某人自己；独自

- Are you sure you have plenty of seating available for everyone?
  你确定你有足够的位置给每个人吗？
  ★ 短语 plenty of... 充足的～，大量的～

- I will rearrange the chairs and couches so that everyone has a good view of the TV.
  我会重新布置椅子和沙发的位置，让每个人都可以看到电视。
  ★ 短语 so that 为的是、以便

- If we are going to host a movie theme party, we should ask everyone to dress up like a super star.
  如果我们要举办电影主题派对，我们应该叫每个人都装扮成超级巨星。
  ★ 短语 dress up 装扮，打扮

- We should come up with some movie trivia questions to ask our guests. Whoever gets the most questions right will win a prize.
  我们应该想一些与电影有关的问题问宾客。答对最多的人可以赢得奖品。
  ★ 短语 movie trivia 跟某部电影有关的信息或讯息、趣事、八卦等

- Let's bring out the popcorn and soft pretzels for this party.
  我们为客人端出爆米花和椒盐脆饼吧。
  ★ 短语 bring out... 拿出～，取出～

在国外都说这几句

- I want to set up a mini bar table and let everyone pour their own soft drinks.
  我想要设立一个迷你吧台，让每个人可以自己倒饮料。
  ★ 短语 set up... 设立～，设置～

- Can you lay out some food on a nice platter? Our guests will be here soon.
  你可以拿个漂亮的盘子把食物摆出来吗？我们的客人马上就要到了。
  ★ 短语 lay out... 放在～，摆放

- Please fill clear glass jars with colorful jellybeans. It will look so pretty.
  请在这些透明的瓶子中装满色彩缤纷的豆豆糖。看起来一定会很漂亮。
  ★ 短语 fill with... 装满～，填满～

- Do not serve soda in that vintage bottle. That's very expensive.
  不要用那个古董瓶子来装苏打水，它很贵。
  ★ 短语 serve in... 用～供应

- We can mix up some salt-water toffees for everyone to enjoy.
  我们可以混合一些盐水太妃糖，然后供应给宾客。
  ★ 短语 mix up... 搅匀～，混合～

- Let's set up the food tables like a food cart for a different feeling.
  我们把这些餐桌布置成像摊车一样，尝试不一样的感觉。
  ★ 短语 food cart 餐车

- Some adorable cupcakes will go well with this party and they taste so good!
  可爱的杯子蛋糕会跟这个派对很搭而且它们非常好吃！
  ★ 短语 go with... 与～相配，配合～

- You don't have to be an Irish by nature to hold an Irish theme party.
  就算你不是爱尔兰人，你还是可以举办爱尔兰主题的生日派对。
  ★ 短语 by nature 天性，生性

- Are you sure we should set up a kissing booth near the entrance of the party? What if somebody doesn't like it?
  你确定我们该在门口设置一个亲吻亭吗？如果有人不喜欢怎么办？
  ★ 短语 what if... 要是～怎么办

 在国外都说这几句

- The party planner encouraged everyone to get creative with a costume. The bolder, the better.
  筹办派对的人鼓励大家创意变装。越大胆，越好。
  ★ 短语 encourage A to...　鼓励 A ～，支持 A ～

- Should we serve our food on disposable plates? It's easier to clean up afterwards.
  我们应该用免洗盘装食物吗？这样之后会比较容易收拾。
  ★ 短语 disposable plate　一次性盘子

- I made up my mind to throw my friend a Super Bowl birthday party. He's crazy about soccer.
  我下定决心要帮朋友举办一个超级杯生日派对。他非常热衷足球。
  ★ 短语 make up A's mind to...　A 下定决心～，A 决定～

- Let's liven up the party by playing some pop music.
  让我们播些音乐，让派对更有活力。
  ★ 短语 liven up...　使～活跃，使～快活

- You should dress up your dining table with a football field tablecloth.
  你应该用足球场图案的桌布布置餐桌。
  ★ 短语 dining table　餐桌

- Choosing the right decorations certainly adds a lot to the atmosphere.
  选择对的装饰品的确可以增添许多气氛。
  ★ 短语 add to　增添～，增加～

- Now let's think about how to decorate this place for your party.
  为了你的生日派对，现在让我们来想想看，要怎么样布置这个场地。
  ★ 短语 think about　考虑，思考

- We should dim the lights and hand out some glow sticks.
  我们应该将灯光调暗，然后发给大家一些荧光棒。
  ★ 短语 dim lights　将灯光调暗一些

- The party planner has this idea to give off romantic lighting by using candles.
  派对筹办者想出了用蜡烛来发出浪漫光线的想法。
  ★ 短语 give off...　发出～，多指液体、气体、雾、烟等

 在国外都说这几句

- I think it's a good idea to sprinkle rose petals around the party area. The girls will feel like they are princesses.
  我觉得在附近洒一些玫瑰花瓣是个好主意。女孩们会觉得她们像公主一样。
  ★ 短语 sprinkle around... 在～附近喷／撒

- You have to set the mood by playing some good tunes in the background.
  你要播放一些优美的音乐当背景以营造气氛。
  ★ 短语 set the mood 营造气氛

- Have a read of this magizine; it is filled with tricks to help you plan an unforgettable party.
  你可以看看这本杂志，它提供许多能够帮助你筹办难忘派对的小技巧。
  ★ 短语 be filled with... 使充满～、填满～

- My party ideas can be used for any occasion; I'm such a genius.
  我的派对想法适用于各种场合；我真是个天才。
  ★ 短语 be used for... 用来做～，当作～

- My friends whipped up some fun invitations in Photoshop. Now we need to print them out.
  我的朋友用 Photoshop 软件做出好玩的邀请函。我们现在只需要把它们打印出来。
  ★ 短语 whip up... 匆匆制成～；激起～

- To help keep costs down, we will ask everyone to bring a 6-pack.
  为了降低花费，我们会请每个人带半打啤酒。
  ★ 短语 6-pack 6 听一组包装的酒水饮料

- The party will be hosted in our living room. My parents' room is off limits.
  派对会在客厅举行，我爸妈的房间是不可以进去的。
  ★ 短语 off limit 禁止入内

- There's nothing better than a birthday gathering full of friends and family members. I feel so loved.
  没有什么比与亲朋好友欢聚一起的生日派对更棒的了。我觉得我备受宠爱。
  ★ 短语 full of... 充满～的，装满～的

- Let's start with some hot soup to get everyone to warm up on a cold winter day.
  我们先喝一些热汤吧，让大家在寒冷的冬天暖和起来吧！
  ★ 短语 warm up... 使～变热，使～渐渐变暖

在国外都说这几句

- Be careful with how many drinks you have at the party, you might get drunk.
  在派对上要注意不要喝太多酒，你可能会喝醉。
  ★ 短语 get drunk　喝醉

- My best friend put some mints on a platter by the door and had everyone take one as they left.
  我最好的朋友将一些薄荷糖放在门口边的盘子上，让每位要离开的人拿一颗。
  ★ 短语 put on...　放在～上面

- What kind of foods and drinks would be a perfect match for this party?
  能够与这个派对完美搭配的食物和饮料是什么呢？
  ★ 短语 match for...　与～相配；～的对手

- Several friends and I were planning on heading downtown to celebrate my birthday.
  我和一些朋友计划到市区庆祝我的生日。

- I bought my friend some inexpensive china on clearance as a birthday gift because I am a bit short on cash.
  我买了一些清仓拍卖的便宜瓷器，当作朋友的生日礼物。因为我最近手头有点紧。
  ★ 短语 on clearance　清仓大拍卖的

- I never cared about presents, so a meal and happy time with my friends would be more than enough.
  我向来不在乎礼物，因此，一顿晚餐以及与朋友在一起的欢乐时光就足够了。
  ★ 短语 care about...　在乎～，关心～

- On my birthday, my friends dropped by and hung out with me at home. It was very sweet of them.
  我的朋友在我生日时到我家拜访并聚一聚。他们真的是非常贴心。
  ★ 短语 drop by　顺便拜访

- I am planning a romantic birthday dinner to sweep my girlfriend off her feet.
  我正在计划一顿浪漫的生日晚餐，要让我的女友神魂颠倒。
  ★ 短语 sweep A off A's feet　使 A 神魂颠倒

在国外都说这几句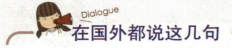

- I do not want my boyfriend to spend a month's paycheck on an expensive dinner or a piece of jewelry. All I need is to have some quality time with him.
  我不想男友将一个月的薪水花在昂贵的晚餐或珠宝上。我只想跟他一起共度珍贵时光。
  ★ 短语 ▶ quality time　珍贵时光

- Friendship is priceless; you just cannot put a price tag on it.
  友情是无价的，你不能为它贴标价。
  ★ 短语 ▶ price tag　价格标签、标价

- I will cook a special dinner for my girlfriend on her birthday.
  我要在女友生日当天为她做一顿特别的晚餐。
  ★ 短语 ▶ cook for...　为～下厨，为～煮菜/做饭

- On my birthday, my wife promised to do whatever I want to do.
  在我生日当天，我老婆答应我想做什么都可以。
  ★ 短语 ▶ promise to...　承诺～，保证～

- I just want to take a trip with the one I love as my birthday present.
  我只想把和我爱的人一起旅游当作我的生日礼物。
  ★ 短语 ▶ take a trip　旅行，旅游

- I am going to celebrate my birthday with my friends at the top of the Empire State Building.
  我要和朋友在帝国大厦的顶楼庆祝我的生日。
  ★ 短语 ▶ Empire State Building　帝国大厦是纽约曼哈顿的地标建筑。

- On my birthday, I want to be surrounded by friends and family. That's all I am asking for.
  我生日时，唯一想要的就是亲友环绕在我身边。
  ★ 短语 ▶ be surrounded by...　被～围绕，围绕在～

- My best friend called in to the radio station and dedicated a song to me.
  我最好的朋友打电话到电台为我点播了一首歌。
  ★ 短语 ▶ dedicate to...　为～点歌；奉献给～

- My neighbor baked a batch of cookies for me on my birthday.
  我的邻居在我生日时，烤了一批饼干送给我。
  ★ 短语 ▶ a batch of...　一批～；一炉～

在国外都说这几句

- I am going to invite my friends over for some cocktails and celebrate his birthday.
  我要邀请朋友过来喝一点鸡尾酒并庆祝他的生日。
  ★ 短语 invite... over 邀请～过来

- My buddy and I decide to take a road trip to Las Vegas.
  我的好朋友和我决定一路开车去拉斯维加斯。
  ★ 短语 road trip 边开车、边玩的旅行

- I just booked a massage appointment at the local spa. I just want to relax.
  我已经在当地的水疗中心预约了按摩疗程。我就是想要轻松一下。
  ★ 短语 book an appointment 预约（约定、会面、设备）

- Come on. Let's dress up nicely and go to the most popular restaurant in town.
  好的。我们打扮一下，然后去城里最热门的餐厅。
  ★ 语法 come on "来呀、好的"，用于祈使句，用来鼓励某人做某事，尤其是指要人加速 / 努力 / 试试看

- My friends had my birthday cake custom made. There's a picture of me on it.
  我朋友特别订制了我的生日蛋糕，上面还有我的照片。
  ★ 短语 custom made 订制的

- Let's bake a birthday cake and give our roommate a big surprise.
  我们烤个生日蛋糕，然后给我们的室友一个大大的惊喜。

- All the tables were covered with purple tablecloths, my favourite color.
  所有的桌子都用紫色桌布覆盖，是我最喜爱的颜色。
  ★ 短语 cover with... 用～遮盖，用～覆盖

- We are planning a surprise party for John. Please don't let him know.
  我们正在为约翰筹备一个惊喜派对。请不要让他知道这件事。
  ★ 短语 surprise party 惊喜派对

- Because of my birthday, I can have 50% off when I go to the restaurant this month.
  因为我生日的关系，我这个月去那家餐厅用餐时，可以享有 5 折优惠。
  ★ 短语 because of 因为

跟任何人都可以用英语聊聊天

Unit 30 中国人最重视的**新年**

[生活便利贴]

"新年到，穿新衣、戴新帽"这可是每个中国小朋友都朗朗上口的一句话。新年就要以新的事物来迎接，除了买新衣服之外，还要围炉吃年夜饭、贴春联及大扫除等，这些都是过年期间会有的传统习俗，有些行为甚至被视为禁忌，如果做了可是会为来年增加霉运。不管如何，既然是过年，大家开开心心、欢欢喜喜地一起度过吧！

Vocabulary 在国外都用这些词

lunar
[ˈluːnə]
a 月亮的；阴历的

country
[ˈkʌntrɪ]
n 国家

furniture
[ˈfɜːnɪtʃə]
n 家具

calendar
[ˈkælɪndə]
n 历法

blessing
[ˈblesɪŋ]
n 祝福

debt
[det]
n 债，借款

prosperity
[prɒˈsperətɪ]
n 兴旺，繁荣

protection
[prəˈtekʃn]
n 保护

reunion
[ˌriːˈjuːnɪən]
n 团聚，重聚

monster
[ˈmɒnstə]
n 怪物

uncle
[ˈʌŋkl]
n 舅舅；叔叔；伯父

resolution
[ˌrezəˈluːʃn]
n 决心

attack
[əˈtæk]
v 攻击

apartment
[əˈpɑːtmənt]
n 公寓

contemplate
[ˈkɒntəmpleɪt]
v 思量

fierce
[fɪəs]
a 凶猛的；残酷的

hide
[haɪd]
v 隐藏

impulse
[ˈɪmpʌls]
n 冲动

在国外都说这几句

- Chinese New Year is one of the most important festivals in Asia, a majority of people celebrate it.
  中国新年是亚洲最重要的节日之一。大部分人都会庆祝这个节日。
  ★ 短语 a majority of　大部分的，大多数的

- Chinese New Year is a time to bring families together.
  中国新年是家人团聚的日子。
  ★ 短语 A is a time to...　A 是～的日子，A 是～的时机

- Chinese New Year begins on the first day of the lunar calendar. That's why it is also known as Lunar New Year.
  中国新年是农历的第一天。因此也被称为农历新年。
  ★ 短语 that's why　这就是为什么

- Chinese New Year not only gives people an opportunity for family to get together, but also allows them to relax from work.
  中国新年不仅让家人有机会相聚在一起，而且也让大家可以从工作中放松一下。
  ★ 短语 not only... but also...　不仅～而且～

- According to the solar calendar, the Chinese New Year never falls on the same date each year.
  根据阳历，中国新年每年的日期都不一样。
  ★ 短语 fall on...　正逢～（日子）；落到～

- Chinese New Year is also known as the Spring Festival.
  中国新年又叫春节。
  ★ 短语 also known as...　又称为～，又叫～

- Businesses often participate in setting off firecrackers in order to bring prosperity and good fortune in the coming year.
  为了祈求来年繁荣及好运，各行各业都会放鞭炮。
  ★ 短语 participate in...　参加～，参与～

常识补给站

　　过年期间不要做打扫的工作，因为这样容易把家中的财气扫掉。过年期间不能扫地，会把家中的金银财宝都扫光光，所以在年三十那一天，就要把所有需要清理的东西都清理干净。在过年时，就不要再打扫了，同时也达到垃圾减量。如果你一定要扫地的话，那就要从外面扫进来。

跟任何人都可以用英语聊聊天

在国外都说这几句

- During Chinese New Year, children will usually get red envelopes that are filled with money.
  中国新年期间，小朋友通常会得到装着钱的红包。
  ★ 短语 be filled with...　充满～、装满～

- The color red is the symbol of good luck in Chinese culture.
  红色在中国文化中是好运的象征。
  ★ 短语 symbol of...　～的象征、～的标志

- In fact, the Chinese word for "eight" rhymes with "getting rich".
  事实上，中文的"八"与发财的"发"押韵。
  ★ 短语 rhyme with...　与～押韵

- The history of the Lunar New Year can be traced back to thousands of years.
  农历新年的历史可追溯至几千年以前。
  ★ 短语 trace back to...　追溯～、找出根源

- Rumor has it that a monster called "Nian" attacked people and animals in the village.
  传说，有一只叫"年"的怪兽攻击了村里的人们和家畜。
  ★ 短语 rumor has it　传说、据传

- The fierce monster, Nian, was afraid of the color red and loud noises.
  这只凶猛的怪兽——年很害怕红色和嘈杂的声音。
  ★ 短语 be afraid of + n.　害怕 n.、惧怕 n.

Me too!

I Love Chinese New Year!

 在国外都说这几句

- It is believed that the sound of firecrackers could **chase** the monster **away**.
  据说鞭炮的声音能赶走怪兽。
  ★ 短语 chase away　驱走，赶走

- Firecrackers were originally used to **drive away** epidemic diseases.
  鞭炮刚开始是用来赶走流行性疾病的。
  ★ 短语 drive away...　把～逼走，把～赶走

- Tangerines are often **given out** to children because they represent good luck.
  小朋友常常会拿到橘子，因为橘子代表吉利。
  ★ 短语 give out...　分发～，分配～

- Is it legal to **set off** firecrackers in your country?
  在你的国家放鞭炮是合法的吗？
  ★ 短语 set off...　使～爆炸；点燃～

- Chinese New Year **is full of** fun activities and celebrations.
  中国新年充满好玩的庆祝活动。
  ★ 短语 be full of...　充满～

- During Chinese New Year, we need to **give offering** to the ancestors for blessing and protection.
  中国新年期间，我们需要祭祖以祈求祝福与保护。
  ★ 短语 give offering　给予祭品，供奉

- The dumplings **look like** ancient Chinese gold or silver ingots, so people eat them for good fortune.
  饺子看起来很像古代中国的金银元宝，所以大家会吃饺子以祈求财富。
  ★ 短语 look like...　看起来像～一样，像是～

- My uncle works far away from home, but every year he still **manages to** come back home on Chinese New year.
  我舅舅工作的地方离家很远，但是他每年都会在中国新年时想办法回家。
  ★ 短语 manage to　设法

在国外都说这几句

- **Staying up** on Chinese New Year's Eve is one of the important traditions.
  在除夕夜守岁是重要的传统之一。
  ★ 短语 stay up 熬夜，不睡觉

- My family is busy **cleaning up** our house to be ready for Chinese New Year's arrival.
  我家人忙着打扫房屋，准备迎接中国新年的到来。
  ★ 短语 clean up... 打扫～，清理～

- My friends and I are going to **shoot off** firecrackers later, and we will have a lot of fun.
  我的朋友和我等一下要去放鞭炮，我们一定会玩得很开心。
  ★ 短语 shoot off... 击发～，发射～

- These delicious dumplings and pot stickers are **made from scratch** by my grandfather.
  这些美味的饺子和锅贴是我外公从头到尾手工做的。
  ★ 短语 make... from scratch 从头到尾做～，从头做～

- You have to make a reservation several months **in advance** if you wish to have dinner at a restaurant on Chinese New Year's Eve.
  如果你想在除夕夜到餐厅用餐，你必须提前好几个月预订。
  ★ 短语 in advance 预先

- It is very important to **sweep away** bad luck before New Year arrives.
  在新年到来之前，借大扫除去除坏运是很重要的。
  ★ 短语 sweep away... 把～扫走，把～扫掉

- Let's clean our apartment to **get rid of** bad luck.
  让我们一起打扫公寓，并借此摆脱坏运气吧。
  ★ 短语 get rid of... 摆脱～，去除～

常识补给站

　　大年初一已经出嫁的女儿不可以回娘家：嫁出去的女儿回娘家，会把娘家吃穷，因此只能在初二或者初三回娘家，但是其中的含义是嫁去的女儿已经是别人家的媳妇了，过年婆家一定有很多人来拜年，媳妇要帮忙奉茶服侍，因此初一不可以回娘家。

在国外都说这几句

- My father painted the door red because red is considered as a lucky color.
  我爸爸将门板漆成红色的,因为红色被认为是幸运的颜色。
  ★ 短语 A be considered as...　A 被认为是〜,A 被视为〜

- My father likes to hang paper couplets on the front door.
  我爸爸喜欢将春联挂在前门上。
  ★ 短语 hang on...　挂在〜上

- Gathering together with family and making dumplings in the evening is my family tradition.
  傍晚跟家人聚在一起包饺子是我家的传统。
  ★ 语法 gather together　聚集在一起

- My grandmother always hides a coin in one of the dumplings; whoever gets the coin will be very lucky in the next year.
  我外婆总是会在饺子里藏一枚硬币,不管是谁吃到硬币,来年都会有很好的运气。
  ★ 短语 hide in...　藏在〜里面

- My grandparents are giving out red envelopes.
  我的祖父母正在发红包。
  ★ 短语 give out...　分发〜,发送〜

- All families are getting ready to celebrate Chinese New Year.
  所有家庭都在准备庆祝中国新年。
  ★ 短语 be / get ready to...　准备好〜

- My cousin decided to start the year off with brand new outfit.
  我表哥决定以一身新衣服迎接一年的开始。
  ★ 短语 start off...　开始〜;出发〜

- Chunlian, paper couplets, are hung around the apartment's doorway to bring in good luck.
  春联(又称为书写在纸上的对联)被挂在公寓的门口以祈求带来好运。
  ★ 短语 bring in...　产生〜;带入〜

- We need to throw away old furniture before Chinese New Year.
  我们需要在过年前丢掉旧的家具。
  ★ 短语 throw away...　扔掉〜,丢掉〜

Chapter 5　特殊节庆与活动

Unit 30

在国外都说这几句

- My father told me not to use dustpans and brooms on New Year's Day so that the good luck won't be swept away.
  我爸爸跟我说大年初一不可以用簸箕和扫把，这样才会把好运扫走。
  ★ 短语 so that 结果，因此

- Today, I'm going to put my feet up and do nothing but relax.
  今天，我要跷起脚来，好好放松一下。
  ★ 短语 put up... 举起~，升起~

- If you're in debt, Lunar New Year is the time for you to pay it off.
  如果你有欠债，农历新年是还债的时间。
  ★ 短语 pay... off 清偿~；还~（债）

- My grandmother will light up incense sticks at the temple.
  我外婆会去寺庙烧香。
  ★ 短语 light up 点燃

- The festive food is one of the hightlights of Chinese New Year.
  中国新年的最重要的一个环节就是充满节日气氛的食物。
  ★ 短语 highlight of... ~的精华，~重点

- Are you going to watch the New Year's Eve special program on TV?
  你要在电视上看新年特别节目吗？
  ★ 语法 on TV 电视上

- My family and I are sitting around the dinner table and enjoying our reunion.
  我家人和我坐在餐桌旁享受相聚的时光。
  ★ 短语 sit around... 坐在~边，围着~坐

- My grandfather went to the temple to pray for good luck during the Chinese New Year.
  我外公在新年期间去寺庙祈求好运。
  ★ 短语 pray for... 祈求~；恳求~

- My favourite Chinese candies are made from dates.
  我最喜欢的中国糖果是由枣子做成的。
  ★ 短语 be made from... 由~做成的，由~制作的

 在国外都说这几句

- My grandmother told me to avoid wearing too much black during the Chinese New Year.

  新年期间，我外婆叫我别穿太多黑色的衣服。

  ★ 短语 avoid + v-ing　避免～，防止～

- My father decided to decorate our home with plastic firecrackers to ward off bad luck.

  我爸爸决定用塑料爆竹装饰室内，借此防止霉运入侵。

  ★ 短语 ward off...　避开～，防止～

- Did you see the people who are disguised as dragons and lions? They are very popular.

  你看到装扮成舞龙舞狮的人了吗？他们非常受欢迎。

  ★ 短语 disguise as...　假扮成～，乔装成～

- The dragon and lion dance plays an important role in the Chinese New Year.

  舞龙舞狮在中国新年中扮演了重要的角色。

  ★ 语法 A plays an important role in...　A 在～中，扮演重要角色

- What is your New Year's resolution this year?

  你今年的新年愿望是什么？

  ★ 短语 New Year's resolution　新年愿望

- New Year is the time to contemplate on my previous mistakes in the past year.

  新年是好好思考我去年过失的好时机。

  ★ 短语 contemplate on...　深思熟虑～，思考～

- New Year's Eve is a perfect time for looking back to the past and seeing how you could have done better.

  新年是回顾过去的好时机，并想想有什么事情是需要改进的。

  ★ 短语 look back...　回顾～

- Do you resolve to make changes at the beginning of a brand-new year?

  你决定在新年开始的时刻，做些改变吗？

  ★ 短语 at the beginning of...　在～的开始，～一开始

在国外都说这几句

- Everybody should reflect on the mistakes he or she made during the Chinese New Year.
  新年期间，每个人都该好好反省犯下的错。
  ★ 短语 reflect on... 深思～，反省～

- I want to make plans to spend more time with my family and friends.
  我计划花时间陪家人和朋友。
  ★ 短语 spend time with A 花时间陪 A，花时间跟 A 相处

- I don't think work should always come first. Peronal life is way more important.
  我认为工作不应该时时优先，相较之下，私生活更为重要。
  ★ 短语 come first 首先考虑到的，优先考虑的

- Remember to work out during New Year; otherwise, you will gain a lot of weight from all the delicious food.
  新年的时候还是要记得运动，不然美食当前，你的体重可是会飙升的。
  ★ 短语 work out 运动

- On New Year's Eve, I chose to spend time helping out at a local orphanage.
  在除夕夜，我选择到当地的孤儿院帮忙。
  ★ 短语 help out 帮忙～，帮助～摆脱困境

- I want to control my budget and spend less than the money I earn each month.
  我想要控制我的预算，将花费控制在月薪之内。
  ★ 短语 less than... 少于～

- We can now look forward to a fresh new chapter in life.
  我们现在可以期待人生中新的阶段。
  ★ 短语 look forward to + n. 期待 n.，盼望 n.

- I am going to try to pay off my credit card debt in installments.
  我要开始分期支付信用卡债。
  ★ 短语 pay off 偿清债务

- You should start setting more realistic goals for yourself. Something that is easier to achieve.
  你应该设定更实际一点的目标。这样会比较好达成。

 在国外都说这几句

★ 短语 ▸ set a goal　设定一个目标

- I will swear off my favourite junk food and go on a healthy diet.
  我发誓要戒掉我最爱的垃圾食品，开始健康的饮食。
  ★ 短语 ▸ swear off...　发誓戒除~

- I do not believe that anyone can actually stick to their New Year's resolutions. Most people are just saying it.
  我不相信有人真的可以将他们的新年愿望坚持到底。大部分的人只是说说而已。
  ★ 短语 ▸ stick to...　坚持

- Starting to eat healthy can have a positive impact on your life.
  开始吃得健康一点对你的生活会有积极影响。
  ★ 短语 ▸ have an impact on...　对~有影响，影响~
  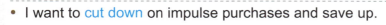

- I want to cut down on impulse purchases and save up.
  我想要减少冲动购物，并开始存钱。
  ★ 短语 ▸ cut down　削减；缩短

- In my opinion, you need to take some risks once in a while to make your life colourful.
  我认为，你应该偶尔冒下险，让你的人生多彩多姿。
  ★ 短语 ▸ take risks　冒险，承担风险

- I made a decision to focus a bit more on the important people in my life.
  我决定将重心放在我生命中重要的人身上。
  ★ 短语 ▸ focus on...　集中在~，集中于~

- I want to be able to finish all my tasks on time at work.
  在工作上，我想要能准时完成交付的任务。
  ★ 短语 ▸ on time　准时

- I booked a hotel where I could invite all my friends to get together.
  我订了一间饭店，在这我可以邀请所有的朋友一起聚一聚。
  ★ 短语 ▸ get together　相聚；聚集

- Let's celebrate New Year's Eve on a luxurious cruise.
  我们一起在奢华的游艇上开个除夕派对吧。
  ★ 短语 ▸ on a cruise　在游艇上，坐船／游艇旅行

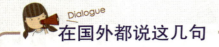

在国外都说这几句

- New Year is coming; we should start thinking of a new theme for our New Year party.
  新年即将来临；我们应该要想个新的新年派对主题。
  ★ 短语 think of... 想出来～，提议～

- We are going to arrange for some karaoke to warm up the party.
  我们要安排卡拉 OK，让这个派对热络起来。
  ★ 短语 warm up... 让～热络起来，使～更活跃

- My friends and I are ready to watch the ball drop in Times Square on New Year's Eve.
  我和我的朋友们在除夕夜准备去时代广场看水晶球落下。
  ★ 短语 每年新年，美国曼哈顿的时代广场都会举办除夕倒数活动。每到这一天，来自全球的观光客都会聚集在时代广场（Times Square），等着广场上著名的水晶球在午夜 12 点时缓缓下降，所有聚集在广场上的游客一同倒数新年的到来，这就是一生一定要体验一次的活动。

- What is the best way to get a good view of the ball drop?
  找到观看水晶球落下最好视野的办法是什么？
  ★ 短语 a good view of... 可以看到～的好视野

- Make certain to arrive as early as possible for the best view of the ball drop.
  确保越早到达越好，才能得到观看水晶球降下的最佳视野。
  ★ 短语 make certain to... 确保～，一定要～

- Ouch, somebody just stomped on my feet.
  哎呀，我刚被人踩了一脚。
  ★ 短语 stomp on... 重踩～，踩脚～

- That guy keeps blocking my view and bumping into me. So annoying.
  那个人一直挡着我的视线，而且还一直撞我。真的是很讨人厌。
  ★ 短语 bump into... 碰撞～，撞到～

- I don't want to lose my spot, so we should be prepared with snacks and drinks and take turns to go to the toilet.
  我不想失去我的位置，所以我们应该准备一些零食和饮料，然后轮流去上厕所。
  ★ 短语 be prepared with... 准备好～，备有～

版权专有　侵权必究

图书在版编目（CIP）数据

跟任何人都可以用英语聊聊天 / 蔡莱蒙德著. —北京：北京理工大学出版社，2019.5

ISBN 978-7-5682-6899-8

Ⅰ.①跟…　Ⅱ.①蔡…　Ⅲ.①英语—口语—自学参考资料　Ⅳ.①H319.9

中国版本图书馆CIP数据核字（2019）第059094号

北京市版权局著作权合同登记号图字：01-2017-2404
简体中文版由我识出版社有限公司授权出版发行
跟任何人都可以用英文聊天，Raymond Tsai著，2015年，初版
ISBN：9789864070183

出版发行 / 北京理工大学出版社有限责任公司
社　　址 / 北京市海淀区中关村南大街5号
邮　　编 / 100081
电　　话 / （010）68914775（总编室）
　　　　　（010）82562903（教材售后服务热线）
　　　　　（010）68948351（其他图书服务热线）
网　　址 / http://www.bitpress.com.cn
经　　销 / 全国各地新华书店
印　　刷 / 天津久佳雅创印刷有限公司
开　　本 / 710毫米×1000毫米　1/16
印　　张 / 20　　　　　　　　　　　　　　　责任编辑 / 龙　微
字　　数 / 421千字　　　　　　　　　　　　 文案编辑 / 龙　微
版　　次 / 2019年5月第1版　2019年5月第1次印刷　责任校对 / 杜　枝
定　　价 / 80.00元　　　　　　　　　　　　　责任印制 / 李志强

图书出现印装质量问题，请拨打售后服务热线，本社负责调换